Mud Island

A history of Ballybough

Produced by The Allen Library FAS Project
Editors: Noelle Dowling and Aran O'Reilly

Contents

Panoramic view of Ballybough, looking towards Dublin Bay

Foreword

Mud Island – a history of Ballybough has been funded under the Publications Grant Scheme 2001 of the Heritage Council. The Heritage Council itself has developed its own plan to the year 2005, a key element of which is the funding of high quality publications on aspects of Irish heritage.

At the core of the ethos of the Council is the premise that local communities are the ultimate custodians of heritage. In order to do this in as effective a manner as possible, sound background information which is readily available to the community, must be available. The Allen Library FAS Project is to be commended in making that information available through the chapters of Mud Island - a history of Ballybough.

The material drawn together in this publication covers many aspects of heritage and will undoubtedly enrich the lives of the community and the wider audience it reaches.

Dr Tom O'Dwyer
Chairperson
The Heritage Council

The Allen Library Project

Project Co-ordinator:
Noelle Dowling

Assistant Co-ordinators:
Joanne Banks, Alison Duck, Richard Kirwan and Aran O'Reilly

Course Particpants:
Lisa Brennan, Jane Carlyle, Lara Byrne, Aisling Kirwan, Alison Lyons, Robert Armstrong, Stephen McCarthy, John Devlin, Elaine Collins, Triona Kenny, Ana Moreno, Aodhin Delaney, Jean Ryan, Tori Lee, Vera Kilshaw, Kevin McSwiggan, Maeve Deeb, Rosamund Brogan, Celine O'Brien, Carol Gilroy, Diane Lee, Meiria Raventos, Vicky Kealy, Brian Crowley, Aoife Hallissey, Margaret Clerkin, Fintan Quinn, Siobhan Dunne, Aoife McSwiney and Marie Dowling.

FÁS Foras Áiseanna Saothair
TRAINING & EMPLOYMENT AUTHORITY

Páirc an Chrócaigh Teo

EUROPEAN UNION
STRUCTURAL FUNDS

An Chomhairle Oidhreachta
The Heritage Council

This is the product of a FAS Training Programme. FAS programmes are funded by the Irish Government and part-funded by the European Union Structural Funds under the National Development Plan, 2000-2006.

Acknowledgements

The Allen Library Project wishes to thank:

Br. Thomas Connolly, Curator & Br. T.C. O'Carroll Chairperson of the Allen Library Committee, Sinead Holland, Elizabeth Barry, Caroline Crowley, Donal O'Connell, Lorna Shields and Sarah Cullinan.

Shay Mulhall, Senior Development Officer, FAS, Mary Carmody, Heritage Consultant and all management and staff of Centre City Training Centre.

The Heritage Council, in particular Fionnuala Lynch.

The staff of Páirc an Chrócaigh Teo, in particular Peter McKenna.

Dr. Colin Stray, Eithne O'Moor, Jimmy Wren, Diarmaid Hiney, Br. P.F. Brogan, Br. Martin Byrne, Shane MacThomais and Fred A. Reilly.

The staffs of:

Dublin City Archives
Dublin Corporation Public Libraries
Fingal County Council Archives
Kilmainham Gaol
Military Archives
National Archives
National Library
UCD Archives

Typeform Repro, in particular Robert Healy, Roy Thewlis, James Farrell, Pat Conneely and Paul O'Neill.

ISBN 0 9526022 2 9

Preface

For the past number of years, participants in the Allen Library FÁS Project have been studying the history of the area surrounding Croke Park. Mud Island – a History of Ballybough is the result of this outstanding and scholarly piece of research. It is an important addition to the list of many fine local histories of age-old neighbourhoods in the greater Dublin area to appear in recent years. It is the first serious attempt to tell the story of Ballybough, which formed a distinctive part of the city from ancient times down to the present day. The research has produced a sizable amount of information which will make this book a very interesting read for the general public and a valuable source for researchers and students alike. The Allen Library FÁS Project participants are to be commended for their contribution to the life of the local community in which they work.

Croke Park is honoured to be associated with this publication. Intimately connected with the area since 1892, the Park today is a most striking landmark but it is not just a physical landmark. It is also a landmark in the history of organised sport in this country and a landmark in the story of the Irish nation.

Croke Park has made a considerable contribution to the history of Ballybough down the years. When the current developments at the site are completed, it will be Ireland's leading sports stadium and as such will continue to make a valuable contribution to the local community in this area.

Beannacht leat, a scríbhinn.

Peter McKenna
Stadium Director
Páirc an Chrócaigh Teo.
Bealtaine 2002

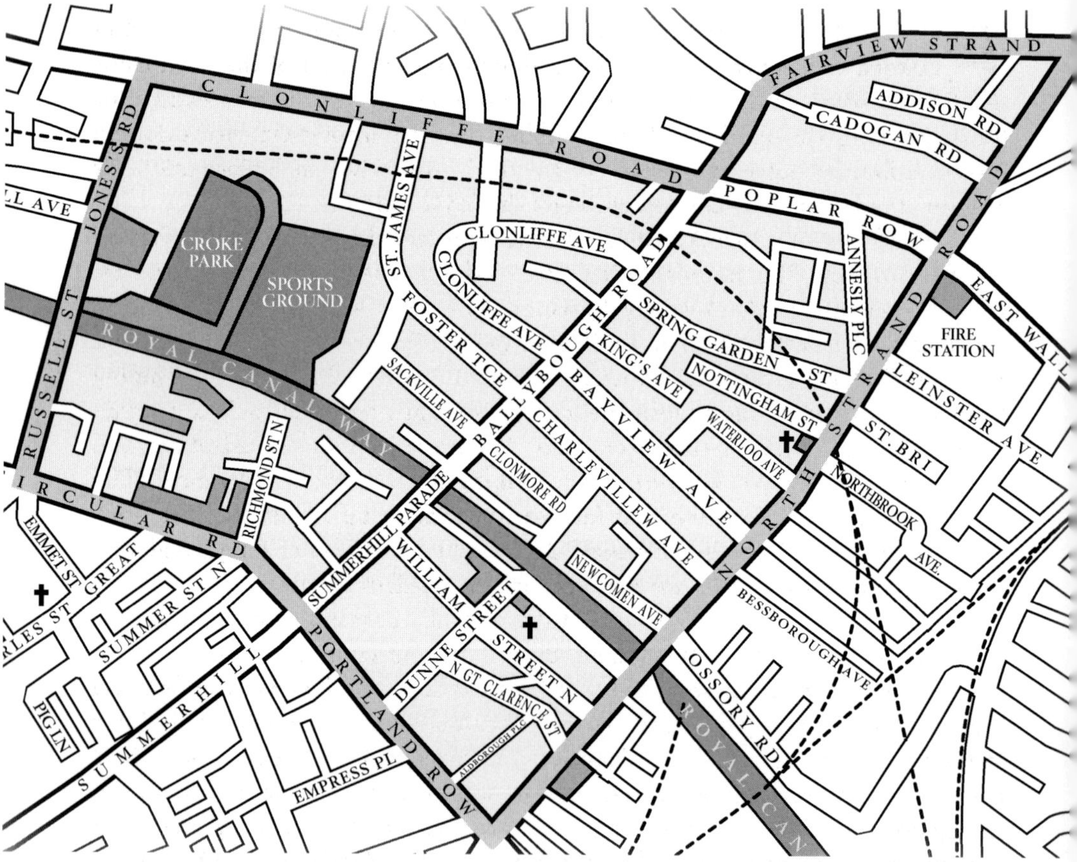

Study Area = shaded area. Base on Ordnance Survey Ireland by permission of the Government. Permit No MP012501. (c) Government of Ireland

Introduction

Ballybough is a district in Dublin which has long roots firmly planted in history. Our journey begins when Ballybough was part of the farm lands of St. Mary's Abbey. Few people would have lived in the area except for those working the land. St. Mary's Abbey was an important institution in medieval Dublin but was not powerful enough to survive the Reformation. As a result, the lands were divided amongst the loyal followers of the King.

Two of the most significant families to arrive in the area were the Bathes and the Coghills. The Bathes built Drumcondra Castle which now houses St. Joseph's School for the Visually Impaired and the Coghills, at a later stage, constructed Drumcondra House. The latter is better known today as All Hallows College. Both families had prominent individual members including William Bathe who was a close friend of Elizabeth I and Marmaduke Coghill who was Chancellor of the Exchequer, Commissioner of the Revenue and Representative of the University of Dublin in the Irish Parliament. The Coghills also established the first known manufacturing industry in the area. Their lands would have encompassed the area known today as Ballybough and their residences are still in use bearing the original family crests.

Other outsiders were attracted to this small borough. The first Jewish community in Ireland settled here during the seventeenth century. Their original cemetery can be seen today at Fairview Strand. However the first real "village" was indirectly founded by the MacDonnell brothers who fled Ulster at the time of the Plantations. They sought refuge in Ballybough as few lived here. During their reign as "Kings" of the area, the locality became home to smugglers, thieves and all other types of wrong-doers. Up until the twentieth century stories were recounted of the antics of the MacDonnells. One of the local streets is named in their honour – King Street.

It is not easy to define the exact boundaries of this place. It was once a coastal district but following some dynamic and innovative reclamation during the eighteenth century, Ballybough is now land-locked. The highway to Howth was originally the Ballybough Road and was superceded by the North Strand Road. With the establishment of a Ballast Board, the subsequent work carried out on the port and the reclamation of the North Lotts, much more land was available for development. One of the biggest property developers in Dublin at that time was the Gardiner family. They were responsible for the creation of the Mall, now O'Connell Street, and many of the fine squares which border it. Their developments shifted the focus of the city centre to the north side of the River Liffey and this had a profound affect on Ballybough.

Industry now located in the area because of its proximity to the port, the Tolka and the Royal Canal. Some of those established included Delamaine pottery works, Chebsey's glass factory, Carrothers & Wilson's iron works, McKenny's Vitriol Works, Dublin Whiskey Distillery, Findlater's brewery and Hutton's coach builders. Many local people would have been employed in these industries and at the port, canal and later the railway. Workers would have had to live close to their employment as costs of commuting would have been prohibitive. This led to the development of associated infrastructure in Ballybough.

Houses were built and others, whose occupants no longer resided in Dublin, were taken over. The latter fell into tenement slums, within a short period, as maintenance would have been too costly. With the advent of these developments, basic facilities such as adequate sewage and water supplies became an ever increasing problem. As Ballybough still remained outside the jurisdiction of the municipality of Dublin city, arguments continuously arose over who was responsible for carrying out such works. Eventually the Drumcondra Commissioners and Clontarf Township (Ballybough over time had been part of one or the other of these) united with the municipal city to furnish the costs of providing water and proper sanitary systems.

Schools and churches were founded to cater for the growing population. The first educational facility to open in Ballybough was the North Strand School in 1786. Later religious congregations such as the Sisters of Charity and the Christian Brothers founded their own establishments. O'Connell Schools were first open for enrolment in 1831. Over 500 pupils attended. In the same year the monastery opened and it was here that Blessed Edmund Rice lived for seven years. The school continues to flourish today. In 1813 Pater Von Feinagle took up residence in Dublin and gave a series of lectures on mnemonics and methodics. His system of education was embraced by several individuals and he founded a school initially in Clonliffe, at the former home of Buck Jones, namely the Red House, and later a larger school at Aldborough House which he renamed "Luxembourg". Other smaller schools could be found in the area, usually run from a parlour in a private house. All these establishments ensured that children of all religious creeds had access to education and would learn to read and write. In both the 1901 and 1911 census material the literacy rate for Ballybough was over 90%.

During the nineteenth century significant events occurred in the realm of religion. Catholic Emancipation allowed for freedom of worship and following the Great Famine, a new era of devotional piety was born. With the growth in the population of Ballybough, it was important that a place of worship be built. In 1855 the Church of the Visitation of the Blessed Virgin Mary was opened at Fairview Strand. It was not until 1908 that the parish church of St. Agatha's was finally completed. Other religious denominations had houses of worship in the locale including the Methodists, Episcopalians and Evangelical Christians. Two missionary colleges were located within a short distance of Ballybough; Holy Cross College, Clonliffe and All Hallow's College.

Many famous people have been born or have lived in Ballybough. These include Edward Smyth, stonemason, whose work can be seen on the Custom House, John O'Donovan who translated the *Annals of the Fours Masters* and the famous playwright Brendan Behan lived on Russell Street. Both Blessed Edmund Rice and Venerable Matt Talbot resided in the area for a period of time and Matt Talbot was a pupil at O'Connell Schools. Many republicans also lived locally including Tom Clarke, one of the signatories of the 1916 Proclamation of Independence, Sean MacDermott who was executed in May 1916, Ned Daly who was Commandant at the Four Courts during the Rising and Peadar Kearney, the composer of the Irish national anthem, *The Soldier's Song*.

In the latter half of the nineteenth century a new sense of nationalism and cultural revival was very much in evidence in all spheres of life. In 1884 the Gaelic Athletic Association was founded in Tipperary. In 1913 the G.A.A. purchased land at Jones's Road and christened the new ground Croke Park. The park had two stands, one at Clonliffe Road end and the other near the canal. Today the development of Croke Park continues with the construction of a state of the art stadium and a recently opened museum which traces the origins of Gaelic Games and highlights their significance in the nationalist movement of the early twentieth century.

From earliest times Ballybough had been a location for many battles and skirmishes. It is believed that the Battle of Clontarf in 1014 was fought in the vicinity of Ballybough Bridge. Later during the rebellion of 1534-35, Silken Thomas and his followers battled with English forces at Ballybough Bridge and many of the English were slaughtered. During the rebellion of 1798 many inhabitants of Ballybough and the surrounding areas were arrested on suspicion of being dissenters. Several individuals from the area were members of secret societies. Watty Cox who was editor of *The Union Star*, a clandestine broadsheet, lived at North Clarence Street. He utilised his publication to play on the hatreds of the suppressed Catholic majority. After his arrest he was given amnesty by the Crown for passing on information concerning the United Irishmen.

The Easter Rising of 1916 did not occur as a spontaneous reaction to some contemporary event. Instead it was a combination of several social and political changes which had been taking place over many generations. There was a growing sense of national identity and the time was ripe for revolution. Social unrest had come to the fore during the Lock-Out of 1913. Many of the residents of Ballybough would have been affected by the strike and at least one local person, James Nolan, died during the struggle. People became unified for one cause, the Irish Citizen Army was formed, people were willing to fight for something they believed in. These people were educated, they had trades and many were devoutly religious, not the usual traits associated with revolutionaries. By 1914 organisations such as the Volunteer movement had gathered momentum. They had a large membership which had managed to secure a number of weapons. It was at this time that guns were landed at Howth giving a morale boost to all involved and also ensuring a supply of weapons for Volunteers to practice with. In April 1914 Cumann na mBan was founded, allowing women to play a vital role in the events which were soon to follow.

Many of the executive members of the Volunteers felt an uprising was imminent. The Irish Citizen Army was also willing to take up arms and fight. On Easter Monday 1916 the Rising began. Ballybough saw many of its residents fight and die in the struggle. Military engagements took place at Newcomen and Annesley Bridges. The Irish Citizen Army eventually took over the factory at Annesley Bridge and remained there until the following day. By this time many of the Volunteers had been summoned to help Pearse at the G.P.O. The Rising only lasted a few days. Irish prisoners were interned in jails throughout Britain and Ireland. Initially little sympathy was felt towards the perpetrators. However the execution of the leaders of the Rising during the following weeks led to an unprecedented change in public opinion. The prisoners returned home to a hero's welcome.

It did not take long for the Volunteers to reorganise. Sinn Fein which had almost ceased to exist soon flourished and by 1917 a new nationwide organisation existed. It drew members from groups such as Conradh na Gaeilge and the G.A.A. When a General Election was called for December 1918 Sinn Fein were determined to win as many seats as possible. Alfie Byrne and Richard Mulcahy were amongst those contesting the seat for the Harbour Constituency which included Ballybough. Richard Mulcahy won the election but it was the only defeat that Alfie Byrne had in his political career, which saw him elected to the position of Lord Mayor of Dublin on ten occasions. Sinn Fein swept the board in the election and all the new representatives were invited to attend the first Dail in the Mansion House on 21 January 1919. Only the Sinn Fein deputies arrived. It was on this day that the War of Independence commenced following an explosion in Soloheadbeg, Co. Tipperary where two policemen were killed.

Again Ballybough saw military activity during the new conflict. The 2nd

Battalion fought against the English at Ballybough Bridge and as a result the area was cordoned off for three days. Frank Flood, a past pupil of O'Connell Schools, was captured after a failed ambush in Clonturk Park and was executed in Mountjoy Jail as a result of his activities. Night after night searches were carried out on homes in Ballybough with no apologies being made after the soldiers had completed their work. It was during this period that the burning of the Custom House took place. Several volunteers died at the Custom House and 80 others were arrested. Sean Doyle, a member of the Active Service Unit, from North Richmond Street was among the dead. One of the darkest episodes in Irish history took place at Croke Park on Sunday 21 November 1920. This day is still referred to as *"Bloody Sunday"*. Fourteen enemy agents had been executed during the early hours of Sunday morning by Michael Collins' hit squad. On the afternoon of the football match Croke Park was surrounded and troops commenced firing into the crowd. Several people were killed and many others were badly injured. A curfew was then put into operation and the streets of the capital had to be cleared by 8 p.m. Cumann na mBan provided both food and shelter for those on the run throughout the conflict. The guerrilla war continued until 1921 and one of the last incidences of the conflict took place at Bayview Avenue when Volunteers engaged in action against British forces.

On 6 December 1921 the Anglo-Irish Treaty was signed, effectively bringing an end to the War of Independence, but this was only the beginning of an even more destructive conflict, the Civil War. Volunteers who had fought together through two previous conflicts were now on opposing sides, some being pro-treaty others being anti-treaty. It was during this time that Cumann na mBan ceased to exist as the split divided once strong and loyal comrades. On 14 April 1922 the occupation of the Four Courts began. Sir Henry Wilson was assassinated in London and his killers were believed to be I.R.A. members. This pushed the Irish situation back into the fore-front of English politics. By the 28 June the last demands for the surrender of the Four Courts were issued. Within an hour the Civil War had begun. It was a bloody and bitter war with each side accusing the other of sabotaging Ireland's independence. The damage from this war has not yet been fully healed.

The final devastating event to hit the area was as a result of bombs dropped in 1941 from German planes. There are many theories as to why this happened but the event cost the lives of many people and destroyed a large amount of property in Ballybough. A memorial stone has been erected to those who lost their lives on 31 May 1941.

Ballybough has long been ignored in studies of local history and heritage and yet this one small area has seen so much activity throughout the centuries. At present gentrification is very much in evidence in Ballybough. Many of the derelict cottages have been revamped and a new lease of life has been given to the area. The restructuring at Croke Park, along with the extension of the Dublin Docklands Development have obvious ramifications for the greater north side of Dublin city and Ballybough will undoubtly profit from these.

For the book boundaries had to be imposed for the purpose of documenting census material etc. However people, time and place do not adhere to boundaries so where necessary the study area was enlarged.

Chapter 1

ST. MARY'S ABBEY

St. Mary's Abbey proper was founded in 1139[1] by Benedictine monks, known also as black monks. By the time Eugene III, the first Cistercian Pope, came to power, he felt that the Benedictines had become lax and had deviated from the Rule of St. Benedict, and so decreed that all Benedictine monasteries be ceded to Cistercian rule. Eight years after its foundation, St. Mary's Abbey became the property of Cistercian monks.

Details of the early years of the abbey are scanty and information on its possessions before the Anglo-Norman invasion are not available. The extent of the original grant made in 1139 is not known. In an early charter of Richard Fitzgilbert de Clare, he granted land to *"the church of St. Mary's and the white monks who serve God there, in the present and in the future, the land which is called Clonlif, with the land which is beside the sea, between the abbey of the said monks and the water which is called the Tulkan (Tolka)"*.[2] Strongbow was not in fact granting these lands but merely recognising property the monks already possessed.

Henry II dictated another charter in 1174, confirming *"all charitable grants made to the monks of St. Mary's Abbey before the coming of Strongbow and subsequently"*.[3] In this charter he mentions Clonliffe and the land near the sea as far as the Tolka. Two other charters were given by King John; one in 1185, and another in 1200 when he became King of England.

The lands of St. Mary's were divided into three sections. The area held on the north bank of the Liffey, bounded to the north by the Tolka, to the west by the Bradoge (which flows underground) and lands of Grangegorman and Glasnevin, and to the east by the sea was known as the Demesne. Crinan extended south-west from the Tolka to a point half-way between the river and the abbey and was bounded to the north by the Dublin-Clontarf Road which

1. Rev. A. Gwynn – (1949), The origins of St. Mary's Abbey, Dublin. JRSAI pp.121-122
2. John T. Gilbert – The Chartularies of St. Mary's Abbey. Vol. 1. 1884. p.78
3. ibid p.81

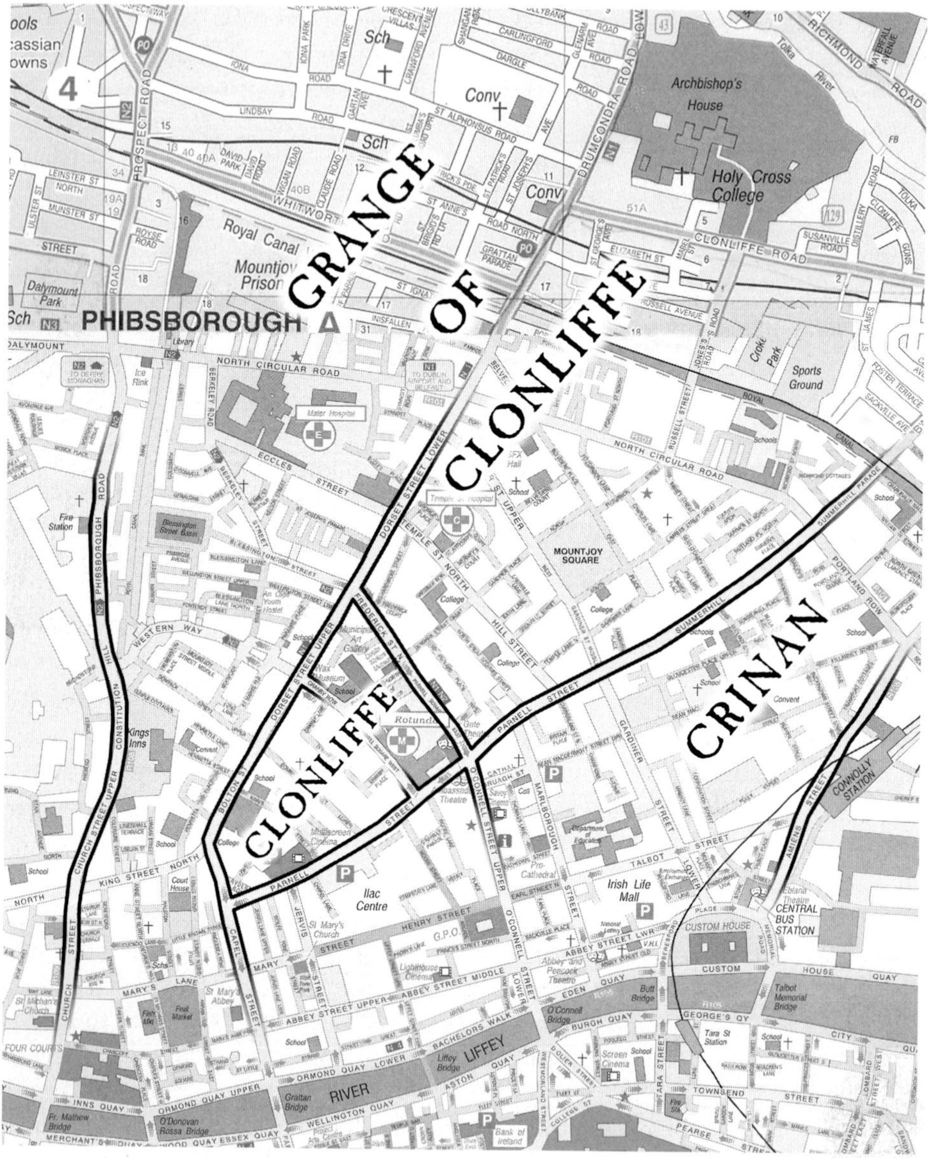

St. Mary's Abbey boundaries associated with study area. Based on Ordnance Survey Ireland by permission of the Government.
Permit No MP012501. (c) Government of Ireland

ran along the line of the present Parnell Street, Summerhill and Ballybough Road. It had obviously formed part of the lands of the abbey since the time of Strongbow, but was not named until an inquisition carried out in 1339-1340. It is described as being ravaged by the sea and therefore worthless. The name Crinan is said to mean dry or decayed wood. This area was also known as

Fyrres, as noted in a grant of 1543. The Grange of Clonliffe lay to the north and west of the said road extending to the Tolka on the north and west to the lands of Grangegorman. In 1318, the Grange is mentioned as a distinct area within the lands of Clonliffe, roughly identical with the parish of St. George. The townland of Ballybough would have been incorporated within the Grange of Clonliffe and Crinan.

Within the substantial expanse of land of the Grange, farming of an arable nature was very much in evidence. The farm buildings would have been situated here, and would have included stores, granaries and barns. As well as farm buildings, the Grange would have had other facilities such as an oratory, dormitory and refectory. These were used when distance made it impossible for the monks to return to the monastery at night. A rule stipulated that the Granges were to be arranged so as not to be more than a day's walk from the abbey. Another agricultural enterprise in which the monks were involved was the grinding of corn. A mill was mentioned in the extent taken in 1539, and is said to have been located beside the weir at Ballybough. Seasonal changes impinged on this mill, as in summer it suffered from drought and in winter was subject to flooding. Located near the mill was a large stone which delineated the boundaries of the city. An ancient salmon weir is said to have been situated at the present Ballybough Bridge, on the road from Dublin to Clontarf. Joyce, however, disagrees as to its location, stating that *"this weir occupies the site of an existing one near the Dublin Whiskey Distillery at Richmond Road"*. [4]

Cistercian abbeys were largely self-sufficient, their main economic activity being agriculture. The monks were acquainted with the skills of tailoring and shoe-making, and also brewed their own beer, but depended on overseas trade with their affiliated houses in France for a regular supply of wine. The Cistercian orders in Ireland had their own fuel and oil supply, the latter being for their lamps. The location of St. Mary's in such close proximity to a city is unusual for the order as they usually lived in more isolated areas.

The structure of the Cistercian agricultural system effectively meant that the abbot was lord of the farming families in these districts. St. Mary's Abbey was entitled from an early period to the tithes of the whole townland of Ballybough. One inventory states that the townland was

4. Weston St. John Joyce – The neighbourhood of Dublin.1939. pp.248-249

composed of two messuages (houses with attached land), 150 acres arable, 1 acre meadow, and 4 acres common pasture and gorse (iampoum).[5] The tenants paid monetary rent to the abbot. In addition, they were compelled to give customary services. This usually took the form of giving men for agricultural purposes such as reaping, ploughing and cartage of hay, corn and turf to the monastery, its granges and other places. In Ballybough, the tenants gave eight days ploughing, four days carting (three in autumn) and three hens. It was traditional that a hen be given to the Lord at Christmas.[6] Tenants on the various estates tended to grow crops on small strips of land which were scattered over unfenced fields. Gardiner's Dublin records that wheat and oats were the principal crops produced by the fertile soil.[7]

Harris notes that *"in 1313 John Decer at this time a private citizen but formerly mayor of Dublin built a bridge extending from the town of Balliboght to the causeway of the millpool at Clontarf which before was a very dangerous passage."*[8] John le Decer was reputedly an outstanding philanthropic individual. He was famed for his benevolence on both sides of the Liffey, and held the position of mayor six times between 1302 and 1326. Le Decer was first and foremost a merchant and this approach route on the north of the city would have allowed access to ships and cargo which anchored in Clontarf Pool.

Brian Boru & the Battle of Clontarf.
Courtesy of the Allen Library

Ballybough Bridge was a wooden structure, and shortly after its construction was destroyed by floods. The bridge is mentioned in the "Riding of the Franchises" in 1488 *"to Balliboght, and by the gate of Balliboght to the water of the Tulkan by the bridge of Balliboght, and over the water and so by the water southwards"*. The bridge is noted on Phillip's map of 1685 as a six-arched structure, and on Greenvile Collins' map of 1686 as on the *"road to Baldoile"*.[9]

In an historical context the bridge has been the scene of many famous battles. Some believe the Battle of Clontarf was fought there in 1014. This is based on the assumption that the battle is sometimes

5. Rev. Myles V. Ronan – The Reformation in Dublin. 1923. p.45
6. ibid
7. NCEA – Gardiner's Dublin: a history of Mountjoy Square and environs. 1991. p.15
8. Walter Harris – The history & antiquities of the city of Dublin. 1766. p.260
9. John de Courcey – The Liffey in Dublin. 1996. p.20

referred to as the Battle of the Fishing Weir, which was located close to the present day bridge. In 1534 Silken Thomas (Lord Fitzgerald) rebelled after hearing that his uncle had been executed by Henry VIII. He went to the Abbey of St. Mary where a Council meeting was being held, and threw down the Sword of State declaring war on his enemies. Ball records that during the rebellion an engagement took place *"between the insurgents and the forces of the Crown at Ballybough Bridge resulting in a great slaughter of Englishmen there and in Clontarf"*.[10] In 1937 the ancient bridge was replaced by a reinforced concrete structure which in 1985 was renamed Luke Kelly Bridge.

There were many disputes between the abbey and the city, and in 1213 an agreement was reached whereby the monks paid taxes to the city concerning lands adjacent to their own. In 1320 the city took proceedings against the abbey for murders committed by an *"insane monk"*, one William Kedenor. When the city officials and the coroner came to see the bodies, the Abbot, having been consulted on the matters, replied that the monastery was not subject to city laws but to the customs of the lands of Clonliffe in which the Abbey was situated. The city authorities again tried to exercise their juridical powers over the temporal possessions of St. Mary's in 1376. This involved an inquisition where the Corporation of Dublin attempted to hold pleas of trespass on the land which was outside their jurisdiction i.e. outside the city franchise boundaries. This action was contrary to a Royal Charter that had granted the same land to St. Mary's Abbey. The land belonged to one John Stoad, an inhabitant of Ballybough. Also in 1510, the Abbot Richard Begge, along with three of his monks, was indicted for giving sanctuary to two fugitives. John Netterville and John Penqueyt had sought asylum in St. Mary's Abbey, having committed a series of crimes including murder and larceny. William White, one of the coroners of the city, sent officers from Ballybough, including Adam Towger and John Bodenham, to stand watch over the abbey and detain the criminals therein until appropriate legal procedures took their course. The officers kept the felons until the *"Monday next after the feast of St. Margaret"*, when the abbey community compelled the guards to leave. They were later acquitted.[11]

The Act of Supremacy of 1536 was the beginning of what was to become a major upheaval in the history of Irish monasteries. St. Mary's Abbey escaped closure at this time as, according to the Act, there were some monasteries in Ireland which the King was not disposed to have suppressed or dissolved. On 3 February 1539, a Royal Commission for Suppression, under the jurisdiction of Thomas Cromwell, Keeper of the Privy Seal, was established to oversee the

10. ibid p.239
11. M. Archdall – Monasticum Hibernicum. 1786. pp.143-144

dissolution of the monasteries of Ireland, including St. Mary's Abbey. Finally, on 28 October 1539, St. Mary's Abbey was formally surrendered.[12]

In the month of its dissolution, a survey of the abbey's lands was carried out. The Grange of Clonliffe was recorded as having 1 messuage, 123.5 acres arable, 8 acres moor, 10 acres common pasture and a watermill.[13]

In relation to the population of Ballybough, Kingston states that *"a few ploughmen, a miller and their herds were settled here"*.[14] Tenants in this area were involved in the growth of arable crops. The extent taken in 1539 only mentions a few messuages. However the tenants would have had their own dwelling-houses. The people living in the Ballybough district relied on employment by the monasteries, lived relatively well and had a good supply of game, meat, ale and milk.

The assumption that *"the Abbot and monks were put in chains, cast into prison by an armed crowd and then taken to the village of Ballyboght and brutally put to death to the number fifty"* seems to be a false one. No reliable evidence for this can be obtained. However fifteen monks, including the abbot, received life pensions from the Crown. The size of these pensions was closely tied to the size of the monastery revenues. The commissioners for the English monasteries were instructed in 1537 to calculate the pensions of Superiors on the basis of a tenth of the net revenues of the monastery, with some leeway for increases, according to circumstances. The amounts awarded to Irish Superiors corresponded to these criteria. On these terms an annual pension of £50 was given to the Abbot. The rest of the community were given pensions as follows:

William Cottrell & Henry Veisen:	£3 6s 8d each
James Barret, John Festane & John Barret:	£2 13s 6d each
Walter Esmonde, Thomas Walsh, John Tirrell, John Whitrell, William Ley, William Walsh, Robert Lide, William Loghan, Patrick Bennet & Seth Peacocke:	£2 each[15]

The Cistercian brethren were left with very little following the confiscation of their lands. The monks were free to live in any way they pleased except as a religious community.

The most important issue to arise from the dissolution of the monasteries was the subsequent allocation of the vast lands. The disposable assets had already been claimed by the Crown. Now the King's favourites, including

12. Richard Sherry (ed) – Holy Cross College Clonliffe: College history and century record. 1962. p.23
13. Newport B. White – Extent of Irish monastic possessions. 1943. p.2
14. Rev. J. Kingston – Parish of Fairview. 1953. p.13
15. Rev. Myles V. Ronan – The Reformation in Dublin. 1926. p.177

some native Irish, were to benefit from the rich pickings. The extent taken in 1539 establishes that the townland of Ballyboght was held by William Leche and Agnes, wife of Richard Yonge. The abbey itself was occupied by John Travers, a Master of the King's Ordnance in Ireland, and converted into a store for munitions and artillery.[16]

Walter Peppard, described as thc *"King's farmer"*, was one of the first to benefit from the spoils. Under the Act of Parliament passed in Ireland in 1537, the King's lessee of the site of every dissolved religious house was bound to *"keep, or cause to be kept, an honest farmer's house, or household, in the same site, circuit, or precinct, according to the quantity of the demains of the same"*.[17] A patent issued by Henry VIII in 1543 leased some of the abbey lands, including the Grange of Clonliffe, to Peppard for twenty-one years. However there was a reversion of this grant in the same year by the Crown to the Earl of Desmond. With regard to Ballybough itself Kingston notes the fact that *"Peppard was advised to pass on his interest in the lands of Ballybough to Desmond"*[18]. This consisted of two messuages and 150 acres arable, 4 acres common pasture, and 1 acre common pasture and gorse, held by William Leche and Agnes, widow of Richard Yonge at 200 bushels of corn and oats, 8 days ploughing and 4 days carting and 3 hens. On 8 December 1560, Queen Elizabeth made a grant of the lands of Ballybough to James Bathe of Drumcondra, Chief Baron of the Exchequer, and they remained Bathe lands until the confiscations of the seventeenth century, when many Irish Catholic families forfeited their estates.[19]

James Fitzgerald, Earl of Desmond, was granted a lease of land which he used for the accommodation of his servants and horses when he attended parliament in Dublin. Included in his grant were the lands of Drishoge, later Belvedere, which at the time of the dissolution were tenanted by William Walsh for £4 20s per annum. They consisted of one messuage, 54 acres arable, 3 acres meadow, 5 acres pasture, 5 acres gorse, 5 acres underwood and other customs. (The tithes of both Ballybough and Drishoge were given to William Howth, one of the King's justices, and amounted to £3 12s.) Henry had been anxious to obtain support from the Irish nobility and this was a means of achieving such an end. A condition of the grant was that the Earl had to remain loyal to the King and that the lands would be forfeited were he to rebel against the Crown. In 1556 the Earl of Desmond leased the Grange and fields of Clonliffe and a mill to Matthew King of Clontarf, described as *"clerk of Check of the army and garrisons in Ireland"* during the reign of Elizabeth I.

During the lifetime of the 14th Earl of Desmond, however, rebellion broke

16. ibid p.179
17. ibid p.174
18. Rev. J. Kingston – Short history of Fairview. 1953. p.18
19. Fiants of Henry VIII, Edward VI & Elizabeth I

out and he was killed by his rivals, the Butlers, thus ensuring the immediate return of all lands and possessions to the Crown. Matthew King's lease was therefore null and void. King seems to have died by this time, as his widow Constance appealed to the Queen and regained the lease for a further thirty seven years. In 1610 Henry King, her son, acquired a royal grant of a messuage and three cottages in the Grange of Clonliffe with 123 acres arable, 10 acres meadow, 20 acres common pasture, a watermill, a watercourse and 1 acre adjoining called the Millemore to hold forever.[20]

He sold his titles of possession to Sir Garrett Moore of Mellifont and in 1619, Moore received a royal grant of the lands in perpetuity. In 1621, Moore became Viscount of Drogheda and he died in 1628. The Civil Survey of 1640 speaks of Clonliffe as follows *"ye Grange of Clonliffe – 250 acres with proprietor Charles Viscount Moore, Protestant ... upon the premises a faire stone house slated and two stone houses of office, one watermill, bounded in the east, with Ballybough, south, ye river of Dublin, west, Grange Gorman, north, with Glasnevine and Drumconragh".*

In 1729 the lands of the Grange of Clonliffe, along with the ownership of the Lordship of St. Mary's, were purchased by the Right Honourable Brabazon, Viscount Duncannon and Luke Gardiner for £11,000. The following year Brabazon sold his interest to Gardiner for £21,230.[21]

The lands of St. Mary's Abbey in the area between the Tolka and the Liffey, not including those now reclaimed, was in the region of 800-900 statute acres (using modern calculations). At the time of the dissolution the approximate size of the grange is stated to be 141.5 acres. The demesne lands were 50 acres with 30 acres of pasture and fir trees. The adjacent lands of Ballybough are estimated at 161 acres but the accuracy of these figures is open to question. It was in 1560 that James Bathe received the lands of Ballybough in a grant from Elizabeth I and thus commenced the race for land acquisition which was to last for the next two centuries. This was to see Ballybough and its surrounding areas changed forever.

20. Calendar of Patent Roll, James I
21. Registry of Deeds Memorial, 17-18 February, 1729 Memorial 10-11, 1730

Chapter 2

INFLUENTIAL PEOPLE

The fate and fortunes of Ballybough over the centuries have often been decided by the political developments and influential people of the day. In the sixteenth century Ireland constituted a nation of distinct sections and groups, many of whom had no common interests or affiliations. There seems to have been two distinct nations: the native Irish, including the Normans and the Old English, and secondly the English merchants. The townland of Ballybough was particularly influenced during this period by one notable family, the Bathes. Like other Old English families, they could be included in the former group, but yet were very far removed from the *"mere Irish"*.[1]

THE BATHE FAMILY

Although they were Catholics, the Bathe family remained loyal subjects of the English Crown throughout the reigns of Henry VIII, Edward, Mary and Elizabeth. They were isolated from the native Irish, considering themselves representatives of English nobility in the Pale. They lived in houses built in the English fashion, and married members of the Old English families; yet they had a substantial influence within the Pale over many generations. The Bathes arrived in Ireland with Strongbow and initially settled in Meath, with one branch of the family later settling in Drumcondra. By the beginning of the sixteenth century they had amassed large estates from Ballybough to Glasnevin and from Balgriffin to Artane.

Bathe Family Crest, Drumcondra Castle, present day School for the Visually Impaired, Gracepark Road

1. Nicholas Canny – The formation of the old English elite in Ireland.1975. p.2

As early as 1350, Johannes de Bathe, who was Lord Mayor of Dublin at the time, obtained a lease for land in Drumcondra from Holy Trinity monastery. The family had been in residence for at least two hundred years by the time Drumcondra Castle was built in 1560 by John Bathe and his wife Eleanor Preston.[2]

James Bathe, Chancellor of the Exchequer, and his son John, were those primarily responsible for increasing the family's lands in Dublin. James Bathe profited to a considerable degree from the redistribution of monastic estates after the dissolution of the religious houses in the mid sixteenth century. He also used his administrative position to further enhance his property by acquiring large tracts of land for a minimal financial outlay. He received leases for reallocated monastic lands in Blakerathe and Castlewaringe, Co. Kildare in 1546, and Rathcoole in 1547. He received a lease from the Dean and Chapter of Christ Church Cathedral for 60 acres in Drumcondra in 1550; then followed lands in Crumlin and a farm in Meath in 1551, and in 1555 Lords Meadow, Glasnevin.

It was under the reign of Queen Elizabeth that the former Cistercian lands of Ballybough first fell into the possession of the Bathe family. James Bathe applied successfully for a fee farm grant for 80 acres of arable ground in Ballybough. In 1539, after the dissolution of the monasteries, Ballybough consisted of 150 acres under crops, five under grass and two messuages. The grant was made to him with the proviso that the grantee should remain *"an able archer of the English nation living in these lands or his adjoining land of Drumconragh"*.[3]

When James Bathe acquired his 80 acres, the area remained sparsely populated and rural. According to Kingston, the Bathe family *"farmed wisely and employed a number of men at the historic mill near the bridge as well as herdsmen, plough men and servants"*.[4] He also implies that the local people relied heavily upon the Bathes for their livelihoods as he states that *"... the population ... must have been very small and completely agricultural and remained unchanged for a century"*.

John, son of James Bathe, was just as determined to build on the existing family fortune and managed to surpass his father in expanding land holdings. He obtained leases for land in Kildare as well as extensive property in north county Dublin, including Clonturk, Drishogue, Glasnevin and Artane. When it was built, Drumcondra Castle was considered to be among the four finest residences in the whole of Dublin. The castle originally stood on the site of

2. Francis Elrington Ball – Southern Fingal, being the sixth part of a history of County Dublin. 1920. p.158
3. Calendar of State Papers, 1509-1573
4. Rev. J. Kingston – The parish of Fairview. 1953. p.25

St. Joseph's School for the Visually Impaired, nowadays located on Gracepark Road. By 1564 John held a lease for all the former lands of St. Mary's Abbey in Ballybough.

After John's death, the estates went to his eldest surviving son, William, (1564-1614), who became a Jesuit and a very respected writer on music and the teaching of languages. William Bathe was a favourite of Queen Elizabeth at court. He played music for her and presented her with a harp, an instrument thought to be taboo at the time, which he had designed and made himself. He also wrote a number of volumes, the most celebrated of which was his *"Janua Linguarum"*, a textbook to aid the student of languages. By his own testimony he was a student at Oxford, although there is no evidence of this from the student records there. This was probably due to the fact that at that time the college disallowed Papists from graduating. According to Edmund Hogan, Elizabeth showed her favours towards young William Bathe *"by many grants of land"* but most of the leases granted to him were renewals of land already possessed by his father. Although he maintained the family estate, he could do little to enlarge it because the land bonanza which followed the dissolution of the monasteries had come to an end.

William Bathe was unconcerned with increasing the family holdings because he intended to enter a religious life and had not the same drive towards expansion as his father and grandfather before him. In fact, virtually all lands mentioned in William's renunciation in favour of his brother John can be accounted for in previous leases to his father. The Queen instructed her Lord Chancellor in 1587 to pass a lease for 41 years to William, son and heir of John Bathe, of such lands as were in the possession of John at the time of his death. However if he was unwilling to be ruthlessly ambitious, William did use his good offices and legal expertise to make sure that the bulk of his father's vast holdings would transfer to his younger brother. In the opinion of T.J. Corcoran *"if he had possessed an easy conscience and acquiesced with the new English, as many of his circle did half a century before, he would have wielded powerful influence"*.

In 1599 William formally renounced his private possessions in order to pursue a religious life, and transferred his lands to his brother John Bathe. John had two sons, James and Robert, both of whom played a very public role in Irish affairs. James participated in the Rising of 1641, while Robert was a member of the Kilkenny Confederation, which addressed a number of issues including the Catholic Question and land confiscations.

James was the eldest son of John's first marriage and was, at the time of the Rising, proprietor of Drumcondra, Drishogue and Ballybough. Charles I had essentially striven to rule England without the assistance of parliament and was staunchly supported by the Bathe family. The power struggle escalated into a military conflict and Charles I was eventually executed in 1649, when Cromwell came to power. With the fall of the King, the lands were declared forfeit by the government and sold to loyal Protestants. Colonel Michael Jones defeated the Royalist forces at Rathmines, and established a bridgehead for Cromwellian forces. This was to be the last battle fought in Dublin city until 1916. For his loyal support Colonel Jones was given Drumcondra Castle. The rising of 1641 and the wars that followed destroyed the dominance of the Bathes and impoverished the surrounding countryside.

Charles II, in 1660, was returned to the throne, and thus began the period known as the Restoration. Although the Bathes had supported the King in the struggle with parliament, they did not recover their lands in Ballybough, which passed instead to the Duke of York, brother of the King. Effectively, this ended the position of importance enjoyed by the Bathe family. During the reign of James II, the lands were granted to Giles Martin. Captain Chichester Phillips then purchased them under the lease which had been bestowed in 1677 upon the aforementioned Giles Martin. He later gave a lease of land to the Jewish community which was used to create their cemetery in Ballybough. The principal resident in Ballybough at this time was Andrew Cave. His house was rated for *"three hearths and beside it were some 5 houses rated for 1 hearth"*.[5] The next major figure mentioned in relation to landholdings in the area was Alderman Eccles who purchased 80 acres of Ballybough.

The Bathes had lost their prestigious position in Irish society and were no longer of any major relevance to Ballybough. A family crest embedded in a wall in the former Drumcondra Castle, now St. Joseph's School for the Visually Impaired, is the only physical reminder of their presence in the area.

THE COGHILL FAMILY

Another family to benefit from the Restoration were the Coghills, who had come to Ireland in search of land and wealth. Sir John Coghill was a member of an old Yorkshire family from Coghill Hall, near Knaresborough, and was to become a judge of the Prerogative Court and Master in Chancery. The Coghills married into the Cramer family and leased Drishogue in Drumcondra from James II, to whom the land had now fallen. Later they acquired property on the sale of forfeited estates. Through the Coghills, Drishogue became Belvedere, a title meaning a raised turret or summer house from which to view scenery. When Sir John died, his son Marmaduke inherited the estate, and it was this Coghill who was to make the most profound impact upon Drumcondra and the area around Ballybough.

Marmaduke Coghill was an extraordinary individual. He entered Trinity

5. ibid p.166

College at the age of 14, graduated four years later, became a member of Parliament at 19, and took over from his father as Judge of the Prerogative Court at the age of 26. He was also to become Privy Councillor, Chancellor of the Exchequer, Commissioner of the Revenue, Representative of the University of Dublin in the Irish Parliament, and one of the most important men of his day.

I sing a subject sung by no men
A common lawyer advocate or proctor
And yet he's all and is a doctor,
Common to landsmen and to seamen
Common to churchmen and to laymen,
The common and the sure resort;
Both of the country and the court,
Common to rich and poor, nay more he
is common both to Whig and Tory[6]

Marmaduke, not content with Belvedere, acquired a lease from Dublin Corporation for the former Dower-house once belonging to the Bathe family, which had at one time housed the steward of the Abbey of All Hallows. A dower-house was the widow's share of her husband's estate, a small house near a large one, forming part of a widow's dower.

Coghill Family Crest, Drumcondra House, present day All Hallows College

The Coghills had the house demolished in 1725 and a large mansion built in its place. This would become Drumcondra House, now part of the Missionary College of All Hallows. The family crest, a cock crowing up a high hill between the Pilasters, is still to be seen on the building.

In the eighteenth century the villages of Drumcondra and Ballybough were greatly influenced by the two Coghill properties of Belvedere and Drumcondra House. Marmaduke was also responsible for the manufacture of linen which gave substantial employment for many years to his tenants. There appear to have been two factories. One was constructed at a weir on the Tolka, between Ballybough and Glasnevin, and was used for the printing of linen by copper plate. This can be seen on Rocque's map of 1765. It is possible that the

6. Rev. J. Kingston – The parish of Fairview. 1953. p.46

Drumcondra House, present day All Hallows College

factory in Ballybough, located at the Ballybough end of Richmond Road, was the first bleach-green factory.

Kingston tells how a certain Miss Delaney in 1752 wrote to her sister saying *"My Companion, Miss Bushe, made me go with her to Drumcondra, half a mile away to see a manufactory that has been set up there of printing linen by copper plates; they are excessive pretty but I will not describe them as I hope to bring you a small sample next summer."*[7]

Belvedere was at one time leased by Coghill to Alexander Fitzpatrick, a wealthy linen merchant who later became one of the first Governors of the Bank of Ireland. Coghill was also a member of a committee appointed by Grizel Steevens (Madame Steevens), sister of Dr. Steevens, to found a general hospital in Dublin in around 1717. Fellow committee members included Sir William Fownes, Thomas Molyneux, Richard Helsham, Archbishop King and Colonel Thomas Burgh. In 1721 Jonathan Swift also joined the group.[8]

Marmaduke was at one time engaged to be married, but his future wife called off the nuptials because of a ruling he had made in a court case where a husband was accused of beating his wife. Marmaduke ruled that a certain amount of flagellation was acceptable and so scared his prospective bride.

He died of gout on 9 March 1738 after a long and painful illness, leaving his wealth to his sister Mary Coghill. She was responsible for the building of what was later to become the parish church of Clonturk and Drumcondra. A large and impressive monument was erected there to her brother Marmaduke seated in his robes as Chancellor of the Exchequer, flanked on either side by Minerva and Religion weeping for the departed souls. The surrounding

7. ibid
8. Maurice Craig – Dublin, 1660-1860. 1952. p.96

cemetery contains the graves of James Gandon, the Dublin architect, and his close friend Francis Grose, an antiquarian.

When Mary died in 1755, she left the estate to her niece Hester Coghill. Hester had married Charles Moore, Lord Tullamore, later Lord Charleville. He was responsible for the addition of the classical facade to the house as well as the construction of the edifice known as the temple. Hester was widowed in 1764 but remarried a younger man, Major John Mayne. The Major assumed the name Coghill but Hester was only to be married for a few years before being widowed a second time. She left Drumcondra for Twickenham where she died without children in 1789. The property was left to her cousin Sir John Cramer, who was made a baronet in 1778, and he too assumed the name Coghill.

The last occupant of Drumcondra House before the foundation of the Missionary College of All Hallows in 1842 was Sir Guy Campbell, a distinguished soldier. He was married to Pamela, daughter of Lord Edward Fitzgerald.

THE JEWISH CEMETERY

The first Jewish burial ground in Ireland is located at Fairview Strand in Ballybough. The original Jewish congregation in Dublin was formed in the 1660s and many were of Spanish and Portuguese descent. Manuel Lopes Pereira, his brother Francisco, and Jacome Faro established Ireland's first synagogue in Crane Lane, near present-day Dame Street. Both Manuel and Jacome are recorded as having fled here following the Canariote Inquisition. On arrival in Dublin, the Pereiras declared themselves as Protestants, which gives an indication as to the situation of Jews in Ireland at that time. A synagogue was later established at Marlborough Street, about a mile from Ballybough cemetery.

Jewish headstone

Ballybough was an ideal location for these Jewish immigrants and for many other foreigners in the seventeenth century. It was as such the *"Soho"* of Dublin.[9] However immigrants did not tend to settle in the area for long and soon the Jewish community had moved further north of the city centre. By the 1700s the Jewish colony was concentrated in Annadale, north of the Tolka, in the vicinity of present-day Philipsburgh Avenue.

The Jewish graveyard in Ballybough was first used in 1718, when Captain Chichester Phillips of

9. B. Shillman – A short history of the Jews in Ireland. 1945. p.19

Jewish cemetery headstones

Drumcondra Castle signed a 40-year lease with Alexander Felix, Jacob de Porto, David Michado de Sequeira and Abraham Meirs. In 1746 a sum of money was owed on the cemetery and the Dublin Jews turned to the London Congregation for financial assistance. This debt being cleared, the London Congregation expressed interest in the burial ground and so bought the plot as a leasehold in 1748, with Michael Phillips acting as a lessee on their behalf. The terms of this lease were for one thousand years at the nominal rent of one peppercorn, in addition to surrender of the 1718 lease for the sum of £34. The cemetery remained the only Jewish graveyard in Dublin until 1900 when a Jewish burial site was opened at Dolphin's Barn. The last burial in the Ballybough cemetery took place in 1908.[10]

The Portuguese Jewish congregation in London had a high wall erected around the cemetery in the 1740s to protect its graves, partitioning the graveyard from William Phillips' property. In 1919 extensive repairs were carried out. The cemetery certainly required some form of protection, as locals allegedly had taken gravestones for use in building their own homes. Legend states that in 1824 while a Jewish man visited a Gentile in the area he found the man installing a new hearthstone. When asked to read the Hebrew inscription on the hearthstone, the Jew replied that it indicated that his father was now buried in the chimney.[11]

10. ibid p.25

11. A. MacLoughlin – A guide to the history of Dublin. 1979. p.88

Caretaker's Lodge, Jewish Cemetery

Presently there are 148 headstones remaining in the cemetery. Two notable burial plots are those of Alderman Lewis Harris (1812-1876), the first Jew to enter public life in Ireland, and that of the Cohen family who manufactured pencils. The importance of Harris in Dublin is evident in the following lines from Sr. Katherine Butler's article *Synagogues of Old Dublin "Lewis Harris was buried at Ballybough and his funeral was attended, so Hyman tells us, by the Lord Mayor, by Aldermen, physicians, lawyers, clergymen of the Irish Church and every single Jew of Dublin"*.[12] The remains of a Catholic also lie in this burial ground. This individual was of Jewish ancestry and was buried there according to his wish.

The Cohens built a hut in the cemetery in 1798. This was replaced with a more permanent style of caretaker's lodge in 1857. It bears a plaque with the inscription *"anno 5618"* in the Hebrew calendar, translated as 1857. The house which stands to the left of this building was a Royal Irish Constabulary station from 1832 until 1909, when a new facility opened in Strandville. Joseph Dioderci lived on the right-hand side of the lodge and was butler to Luke Gardiner. His residence was replaced in 1845 by Elrington House which was home to Madame Josephine O'Brien, opera singer, in the 1870s.

The number of Jews living in Dublin today is much greater than in the eighteenth century. The majority now reside on the southside unlike their eighteenth century predecessors whose congregation was concentrated in the Fairview region. It is recorded that in 1746 there were forty Jewish families in Dublin. However by 1800, their numbers had dwindled significantly, and their synagogue could not be maintained as there were not even ten males available, which was necessary to constitute the house of worship. Their decrease is noted in a reference to the history of the synagogue in Marlborough Green *"The temple was converted to a glass-house, and the congregation is now reduced to two families, consisting of nine individuals, who perform their religious rites in their own houses."*[13] Today the cemetery is open to visitors and retains much of the character it had in centuries past.

12. Sr. Katherine Butler (1974) Synagogues of old Dublin. DHR Vol. 27 No. 4, p.127
13. ibid p.845

MUD ISLAND

The settlement at Mud Island, or Crinan as it was known in Irish, occurred after the Ulster Plantation in 1605. Having been dispossessed of their homes, three MacDonnell brothers fled southwards to Dublin, where one of them settled on a barren wasteland area by the sea on the north of the river Liffey. As the years passed by, a colony of mud houses was established in the vicinity. At the time of its colonisation, Mud Island lay off the sloblands along the estuary of the Liffey, and was probably accessible on foot at low water.[14] The *Irish Builder* describes it as being situated *"between the Royal Canal and the river Tolka on the north and south, and bounded east and west by the North Strand and the Ballybough Road; but we think we may with some degree of truth affirm that it received its name from its low, marshy situation, and from being at one time at no distant date under the influence of the sea."*[15]

Mud Island was one of the poorer locales in Ballybough. Its inhabitants lived in badly-constructed mud huts or shelters, and its imperfect drainage system was at the mercy of the sea at high tide.[16] The geographical outline of the region was very different when the MacDonnells arrived from that of today. It has been said that *"then, and for long afterwards, open country intervened between this place and the city, the North Strand was under water, and a rough bridle track extended along the shore some distance eastward of Ballybough Road, which was, until the building of Annesley Bridge in 1797, the highway to Malahide, Howth and Clontarf."*[17]

The following streets stand today in the area which was roughly encompassed by Mud Island: Newcomen Avenue, Clonmore Road, Charleville Avenue, Bayview Avenue, King's Avenue (named after the monarchs of Mud Island), Nottingham Street, parts of Spring Garden, Ballybough Road and North Strand Road. It was shown on Campbell's map of 1811 and by Duncan in 1821, but neither shows it as an island.[18]

The MacDonnells were the principal family on the island and by the late 1700s, the existing MacDonnell was recognised as the *"King of Mud Island"*. Thereafter the island's denizens elected a king – often a member of the MacDonnell family. Two of these renowned monarchs were Art Granger who died in 1759, and Grid Iron MacDonnell. It is said that the latter derived his name from the fact that punching him was like hitting grid iron, so great was his strength. Eventually the residents of Mud Island became proprietors of the land on which they lived by what is known as *"squatter's title"* – a title given to

14. Weston St. John Joyce – The neighbourhood of Dublin. 1921. pp.244-245
15. Irish Builder – 15 July, 1870. p.163
16. ibid
17. Weston St. John Joyce – The neighbourhood of Dublin. 1921. p.244
18. John de Courcey – The Liffey in Dublin. 1996. p.258

them for having resided there for over a century. The houses on the island were made from mud and thatched and are shown on Phillip's map of 1685.

The *Irish Times* in 1911 ran a series of articles on the area, with much of its information coming from one of the MacDonnell descendants. This family member's father and grandfather had both been kings of the Island and acted as contractors to builders in the sand trade. Residents of the island worked as labourers in its many sand pits, carting the sand by horse for the King. However many of the inhabitants subsidised their living in a less worthy fashion. The island was home to robbers and smugglers and acted as a sanctuary for highwaymen. For the most part its inhabitants remained unhindered by the authorities for their unlawful activities. The only law in the village was the King's word and that was absolute. No constable, bailiff, beadle, revenue, or other official dared, as a rule, to enter the precincts, and King George's writ did not run in King MacDonnell's territory, unless backed with horse and artillery, so to speak. Passers-by often observed dead bodies lying at the side of the road. These were the bodies of excise men, bailiffs and similar figures of the law. General practice was to pass on and not to become involved, as this could result in jeopardising one's own life – *"tis a wise man that never*

THE MUD ISLAND FUSILIERS.

(An Old-Time Topical Hit, sung by Pat Kinsella.)

[Pat Kinsella was a versatile comedian and a celebrity in Dublin in the early '90's, and no pantomime was ever complete without "Pat" in a humorous part. For some time he was proprietor of the old Harp Music Hall, in Adam Court, Grafton Street, and many good stories are told as to how he kept the "show" going when he suffered, as he himself expressed it, "from a little pecuniary embarassment." His "Pat Among the Fairies" is still remembered as a most humorous Christmas extravaganza.]

I'd like to be a sailor,
And sail across the sea,
But a man they call a gaoler
He gave me lodgings free.
He took me in and kept me,
And treated me so kind,
And he had such care for my nut-brown hair
That he cut it all off behind.

Chorus.
We're the boys to drink and fight,
Batterin' skulls is our delight,
Which is the left foot from the right
Divil a soul does know;
As soon as one of the corps appears,
Mothers to children shout, "My dears,
There's the Royal Mud Island Fusiliers,
They're doin' the sentry go!"

We are no soldier spoonies
When fighting in campaign,
We march like men to Mooney's,
And back to camp again.
We lay a tax on travellers—
We beg, we borrow, we bone;
And we are such blockheads that another man's pockets
We once took for our own.
Chorus.

They call us chicken stealers—
That isn't right, you know;
It's well known to the Peelers
We love of poultry show.
And the jury finds us guilty,
The verdict soon appears:
That a love for chickens has played the dickens
With the Mud Island Fusiliers.
Chorus.

"The Mud Island Fusiliers" taken from "Topical Hits, Humorous & Patriotic". Courtesy of the Allen Library

saw a dead one".[19] Collier, a famous highwayman, often took shelter in a MacDonnell residence when he was being pursued.

The island was noted for smuggling. A key figure in this area was Paddy Ready Penny who provided a hiding place for goods. The island's citizens would help keep watch for the boats which lay out in Poolbeg and Clontarf Pool. At nightfall the booty would be brought ashore in skiffs, passing under Annesley Bridge to an area known as the Little Sea. The goods would be deposited in Paddy Ready Penny's or another smuggling den. It was not unusual to find the bodies of officers who tried to prevent these illegal dealings floating in the sea the following day. After 1850 smuggling declined, mostly due to the establishment of a police barracks at Fairview.

There is ample evidence of the corrupt activities of Mud Island in newspaper articles from this period. In the *Dublin Gazette*, the following appeared *"On Sunday, 17 February (1765), about eight o'clock at night, four fellows armed with knives stopped a servant on horse back between Ballybough Bridge and Summerhill, but he having no money, they robbed him of his handkerchief and the saddle on which he rode". "On Monday, 25th February, (1765) at night, Mr. John Draper made a considerable seizure of tea from a smuggler at Ballybough Bridge, which with the smuggler's horse he brought to the Custom House".*

The changes which had taken place on Mud Island were outlined as follows *"civilisation is there though sanitary perfection is yet distant … and the postmaster-general forgets to remember the classic name by which Spring Garden was formerly known."*[20] Despite the unhealthy state of Mud Island, its population remained unaffected by cholera during an outbreak of the disease in Dublin during the last century, a time when more prosperous areas of the city suffered. It was thought that the fumes from the nearby vitriol works contributed in some way to keeping the dreaded illness at bay.

Isle of ire and brightest stars,
Of broken skulls and bodily scars,
Where 'Sunday men' might walk apace
Whilst bailiffs dare not show their face,
Where wakes and weddings entertained
The 'boys' that belts and buckles brained,
Where doors of knocks and names were left,
Where bounders blazed and boasters bragged
Of crimes that might have got them lagged,

19. Irish Times – Mud Island Alsatia I. 6 Feb., 1911, p.8
20. Irish Builder – 15 July, 1870

But woe to 'stag' or 'peeler' who
Would attempt to lie perdue,
If seized, the 'Madlark' all would flock
To martyr him on Ballybough,
Or perhaps with all intents
A plunge bath o'er the battlements[21]

Although Mud Island since disappeared as a result of land reclamation, it will always be remembered through stories which pass from generation to generation.

21. ibid

Chapter 3

DUBLIN PORT & LAND RECLAMATION

The shoreline of the Liffey would have run quite a different course in the eighth century than it does today and Ballybough would have been situated at an isolated position on the edge of the river, directly northwards across the bay from Ringsend. The North Strand and Amiens Street would have marked the old course of the river and there would have been no land to the east of Ballybough.

The port itself in the fourteenth century was a hazardous place for ships. The estuary of the river was much broader and boats were forced to anchor a great distance from shore. The view from Ringsend to Ballybough at the mouth of the Tolka was across a 2.1km expanse of open water, with Clontarf Island lying slightly to the east. The terrain moving away from the shore would have been of grassy tussocks changing by degrees into rough pasture. The riverbank would have been broken by guts leading into large tidal pools behind the shoreline area in Amiens Street, and by creeks in the area between the Royal Canal and the Tolka which would have converted the shore or part of it into islands at high tide.

River Tolka

The old Dublin harbour was divided by two strands; the North Bull Strand and the South Bull Strand. The area was an extensive mudflat at low tide and the two strands were separated by the combination of Dublin's drainage rivers – Liffey, Tolka and Dodder. The interaction of the rivers and the tides, and the resulting sand led to the development of the two sandbanks to the north and south of the bay.

From 1676 onwards, the city began to petition for the setting up of a ballast office. Initial refusals and legal wranglings delayed the Ballast Office Act until 1707 when it was passed under the title *"An Act for cleansing the port, harbour and rivers, of Dublin, and for erecting a Ballast Office in the said City"*.[1] The new committee held its first meeting on 20 January 1708, and thus began the programme which would irrevocably change the face of Dublin port over the next two centuries. Its functions at first were quite modest and restricted. One of its most dramatic achievements was the embankment of the north shore of the Liffey by construction of the North Wall, thus leading to the reclamation of the area east of Ballybough, and also the construction of the South Wall and the new Poolbeg Lighthouse.

In 1712 the Ballast Office began to enclose some of the north shore and had by this time laid down *"686 kishes well filled with stones piled in front and backed with gravel and shingle from Clontarfe Bar"*.[2] These were to be known as the North and East Walls. It is not known whether the stone wall replaced or merely augmented the kishes, but the wall continued along what is now East Wall Road and went as far as Ballybough Bridge. The embankment continued until the area being reclaimed was surrounded by a fairly solid structure. This method proved satisfactory, for in a report of 1713 the directories state that it had withstood the violence of the winter storms.

It was this combination of the North and East Walls which resulted in the great land reclamation to the east of Ballybough. By 1730, an area of about two square kilometres had been walled from the areas that are now the North Strand and East-Link Bridge. Ballybough Road could no longer claim the title *"thoroughfare to the sea"* and Mud Island finally disappeared. Much of the new area east of Ballybough remains below the tide levels of the river but is still protected by the wall.

The development in this area, which has continued to the present day, has resulted in a completely new face to the north bank of the river and the extension of the city to the east by about one mile in the last 500 years.[3]

NORTH LOTTS

In 1682 a survey was ordered by the City Assembly of the Strand from Mabbott's Mill to the Furlong of Clontarf, which included the water front area of Ballybough. The results were produced in map form and divided the area

1. J. de Courcy – The Liffey in Dublin. 1996. p.19
2. ibid p.272
3. John Harvey – Dublin: a study in environment. 1949. p.21

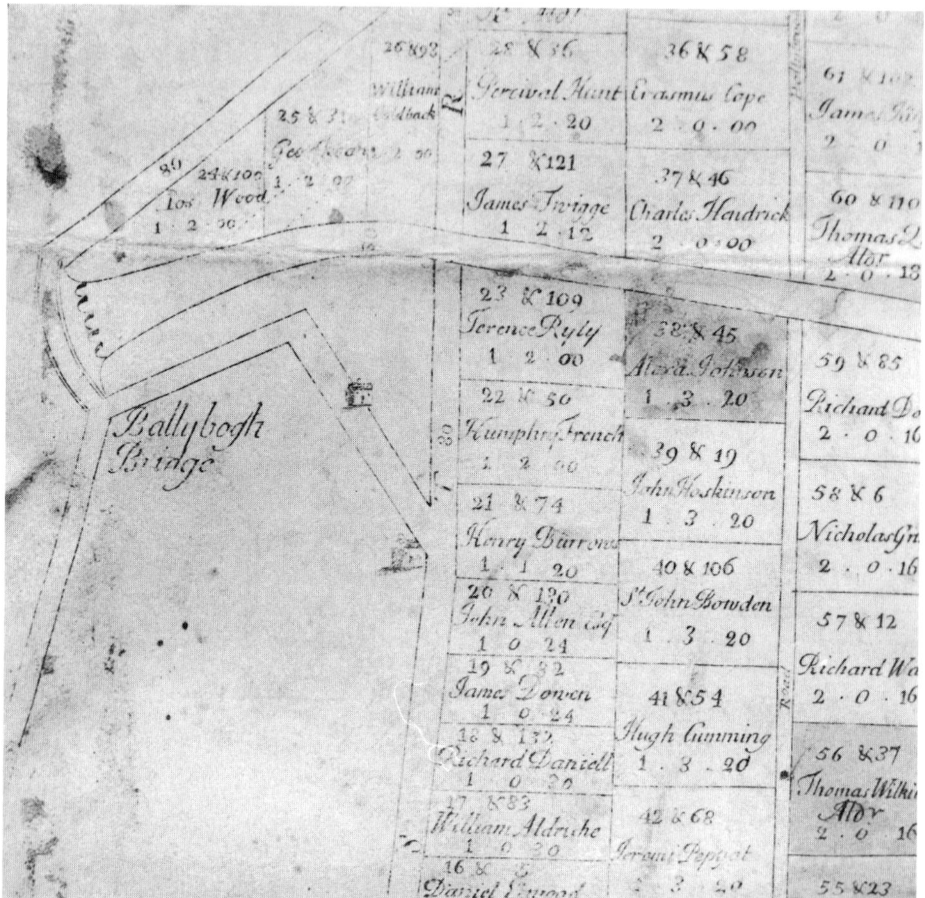

1717 map of the North Lotts. Courtesy of the Allen Library

into 152 Lotts which were to be allocated to named individuals for a fee. Included on this list were the Mayor, members of the Corporation, and other city officials. The lotts were to be drawn out of a hat at the Tholsel and if all the lotts were not selected then certain individuals would be allocated a second one. The fee per annum for a lott was 12d, and the revenue collected was given to the City Treasurer for the use of the City. The lottery took place and the list of holders was drawn up. The Lord Mayor Sir Richard Ryves received two lotts. In 1686 the allocation was annulled by the Assembly as there had been some confusion with the distribution. In 1717 a new survey of the strand was taken, with 441 acres being included between the Liffey and the Tolka, and 77 acres between the Tolka and Clontarf. There were now 132 lotts.

A bigger scheme for lott allocation was undertaken this time and a committee was set up to oversee it. The finance needed to enclose the ground in question was much greater than was initially anticipated, and the northerly scheme was not undertaken at this time. Each lott holder was now responsible for building up his own allocation. In 1728 the land north of the North Wall was marked on Brooking's map *"as yet overflowed by ye tide"*. However, in spite of this comment, much of the area had been filled in. The concept of

Title plate of 1717 map of the North Lotts. Courtesy of the Allen Library

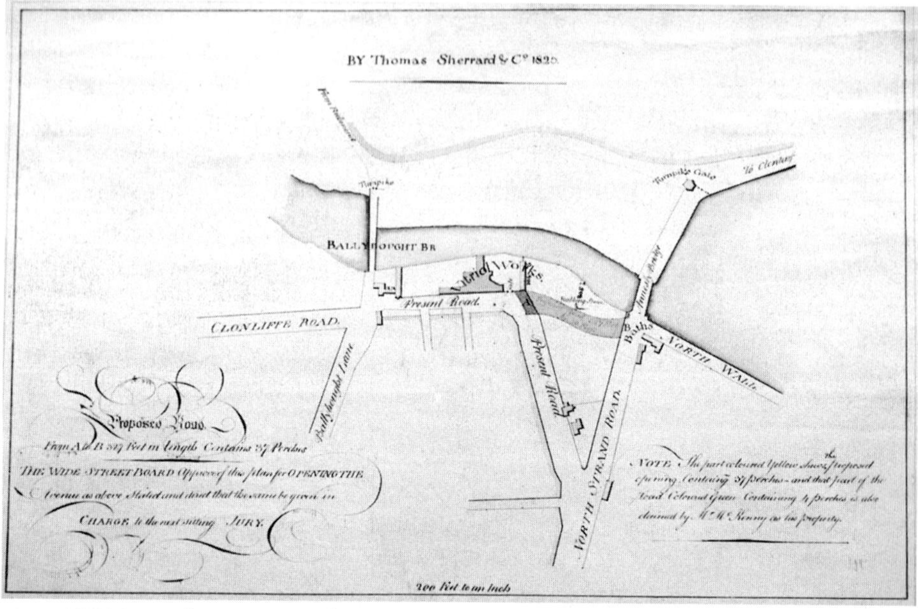

1820 Map showing turnpikes in Ballybough. Courtesy of Dublin City Archives

individuals enclosing their own lotts was later transferred by statute to the Port Authority in return for an annual fee from each lott holder. The proposed reclamation between Clontarf and the Tolka never actually took place.

The new neighbouring areas of the East Wall meant there was more land available for industrial development which in turn led to more jobs. Economically, the development at Dublin port provided much work for the the Ballybough area as increased trade and developments required more dockers and construction workers. As warehouses, boat yards and jetties were built, manpower was required to support and sustain such growth. Three generations of Matt Talbot's family, who were from the local area, worked for the Port and Docks Board.[4] The area indirectly provided employment, since the roll-on effects of increased construction and trade increased the importance of the railways and transport in general.

DEVELOPMENT OF THE NORTH INNER CITY

The eighteenth century was the turning point in the urbanisation of the north side of Dublin city. The area at the time was experiencing an economic boom. An act was passed in 1792 giving powers to city officials to borrow money to improve the neighbourhood of Ballybough Bridge. Its official title was *"An Act for enabling the Trustees for making, widening, and repairing the road from Dublin to Malahide, and the other Roads leading to Dublin over Ballybough Bridge,*

4. D. O'Carroll & S. Fitzpatrick – Hoggers, lords & railwaymen. 1996. p.30

North Strand 1815. Courtesy of the Allen Library

pursuant to several Acts of Parliament, more effectually to carry the said Acts into Execution". It is stated in this act that *"it would be of advantage to the public if that part of that space of ground overflowed by the sea at high water, lying eastward of Ballybough Bridge, between the wall enclosing the ground formerly taken in from the sea, called the north-lots, and the Weir Wall on the North Strand, were enclosed and taken in"*. Today this is the area represented by Fairview Strand, Annesley Bridge Road and the Tolka channel.

Further on, the act states *"It is intended that the said new communication shall be made nearly in a direct line from the Strand Road leading from His Majesty's Custom House, to the said ground overflowed by the sea, and across the same to the road adjoining the said Weir Wall on the North Strand, nearly at the end of the place called Fairview, on the said strand."* The act continues *"In order to make the said new and more commodious communication between the city of Dublin, and the country, on the other side of the said bridge, called Ballybough Bridge, it will be necessary to build, erect, and make a new bridge and causeway, eastward of Ballybough Bridge aforesaid"*. The bridge referred to is Annesley Bridge which was constructed in 1793. The causeway was the short portion of the North Strand Road going from Annesley Place to Annesley Bridge and from there to Fairview.

During the reign of George III, several acts were passed regarding the control of this new thoroughfare. Trustees were appointed with powers to erect turnpikes and levy tolls for the maintenance of the road. Toll gates were constructed at the northern end of Ballybough Bridge at the junction of what is now Fairview Strand and Annesley Bridge Road. There was also at one time a turnpike at the junction of the North Circular Road and North Strand Road, which is presently occupied by the Five Lamps. The turnpike system was unpopular and many went out of their way to avoid paying even the smallest sum. People had to pay anything from 1s upwards, depending on how far they had to travel. These turnpikes are often suggested as a reason why people did not move to the northern suburbs, but even after their removal under the Turnpike Abolition Act of 1855, there was no significant change in the number of new residents.

It is more probable that the lack of running water was the single most important factor in the north side area being virtually uninhabited. Dublin city was unique in having piped water, and the city's growth was in directions parallel to the original pipe line flowing west to east. It was not until much later that piped water was made available to the northern suburbs. During the mid-eighteenth century, many wealthy and influential people in Dublin lived north of the Liffey. Among them were the Gardiners.

By the beginning of the nineteenth century, many of Dublin's titled classes had begun to move either south of the river or to London, although the exodus to the latter was less significant than purported by some sources. Their once impressive homes began to fall into decay. There remained a lack of piped water. Cesspools were located in front of doors and covered in after use. The smell and filth from these added to the problem of air pollution from other sources, including chimneys. Low-lying areas were the worst affected. Health and clean surroundings were now influencing people's choice of where they wanted to reside. As a result, people moved further out into the northern and southern suburbs.

New infrastructure also diminished the relative isolation of Ballybough and linked it not only with the new neighbouring areas of north Dublin and the city itself, but also with the until-now very distant south side. Ballybough, until 1700 had been a very rural and quite sparsely populated area but in the middle of the eighteenth century, houses and intersecting streets were added to Great Britain Street, Summerhill, and Ballybough Road.[5] This must be seen as a direct result of the developments which took place in terms of land reclamation, and the astuteness of developers during the eighteenth and nineteenth centuries.

Developments and improvements in the port and its surrounds have continued in earnest to the present day. The opening of the East-Link Bridge and the Custom House Docks development have brought new life to the dockland areas. Building in this area is at an all-time peak as the economy of the port booms and interest in the area, both commercially and privately, soars.

5. D. Cosgrave – North Dublin city and environs. 1909. p.77

Chapter 4

1798 REBELLION

Political and social conditions in Ireland towards the end of the eighteenth century were in a critical state. In 1782, the Irish parliament was made *"independent"* of Westminster, but in reality parliament in Ireland consisted mainly of Protestant members who had introduced and implemented strict and severe anti-Catholic laws. These laws were slowly being removed from the 1780s onwards, but political and economic power still lay with the Protestant ascendancy.

The United Irishmen were formed in Belfast in October 1791. Many Catholics had already joined local volunteer corps. Secret Societies were growing in popularity, many being agrarian based, such as the Whiteboys and Peep O'Day Boys. The majority of these were located in Ulster.

The government established its own militia to counteract the volunteer corps but their ranks were later infiltrated by Catholics. This enabled the passage of vital information to the United Irishmen, as well as allowing access to a supply of arms. However the Society's ranks were also compromised, which proved to be one of the most significant factors in the 1798 Rebellion as the government knew all about the internal affairs of the United Irishmen Society as well as the planned assistance from France. The Dublin Rangers, one of the few groups still in existence, were approached by Alderman James in January 1793 while marching to Drumcondra House, the former home of the Coghills, to breakfast with their Colonel. They resisted the attempts of disarmament and *"gobbled up their breakfast and dispersed before the military arrival"*.[1]

The United Irishmen were suppressed in 1794 but this did not deter their activities, with Dublin becoming their new headquarters. In December 1796 an expedition force of around 14,000 men under General Hoche set sail for Ireland. The near success of this incident alarmed the government greatly and with a renewed sense of urgency they set about eliminating the discontented

1. R.B. McDowell – Ireland in the age of imperialism and revolution, 1760-1801. 1979. p.432

elements. The Insurrection Act was passed in 1796, having an automatic sentence of transportation for life for any person caught taking an oath. This period also saw the establishment of the Protestant Yeomanry.

By June of 1797 there were an estimated 7,000 United Irishmen in Dublin. A proclamation was issued to the *"citizens of Dublin, calling for unity in the fight against English rule; all sect ... remember against whom you fight, your oppressor for 600 years"*.[2]

The existence of clubs of United Irishmen throughout Dublin was widespread by 1797 as these were the only means the organisation had of meeting and practicing. Funeral societies, mourning and lottery clubs were formed for this very reason. On 24 April 1797 a group accompanied the remains of Rev. Dunne from Gardner Place, through Mountjoy Square, North Circular Road, Ballybough and eventually to St. George's Church in Temple Street. Everything appeared to be normal except for the absence of a clergyman and female mourners. Approximately three hundred men were present. A similar event occurred two days later with a procession which originated in the Liberties, passed Eccles Street and was then to have made its way to Drumcondra. The family of the deceased, a man named Ryan, all behaved normally; yet a newspaper later reported that several thousand attended and once again there were no women or children.[3] The military were called in to disperse the crowd.[4] Soon there seemed to be no need to wait for actual funerals, and mock funerals became commonplace. As suspicions grew, an order was given to the military to open coffins at any future events. These were believed to hold stores of ammunitions which would be retrieved and used at a later date. The assembled group also used the occasions to exercise marching *"by companies as regularly as soldiers"*.[5] They were closely observed following the event to ensure there were no mass meetings in neighbouring houses or fields. The government introduced strict coercion to put an end to such assemblies. These events in fact alerted the government to the danger of the United Irishmen. As spoken by a radical *"it was them damned funerals which opened the eyes of government."*[6]

The government put in place an intensive spy network to keep abreast of United Irishmen activities. This led to the arrest of many dissenters and people became suspicious. Any newcomers were distrusted. Several men were shot under suspicion of spying in the Coolock and Clontarf areas.[7] Spy letters

2. National Archives 620/28/3
3. National Archives 620/18/3
4. Finn's Leinster Journal, 30 April, 1797
5. Nancy Curtain – United Irishmen: popular politics in Ulster and Dublin, 1791-1801. 1994. p240 (620/19/3/14)
6. ibid
7. National Archives 620/10/121/66

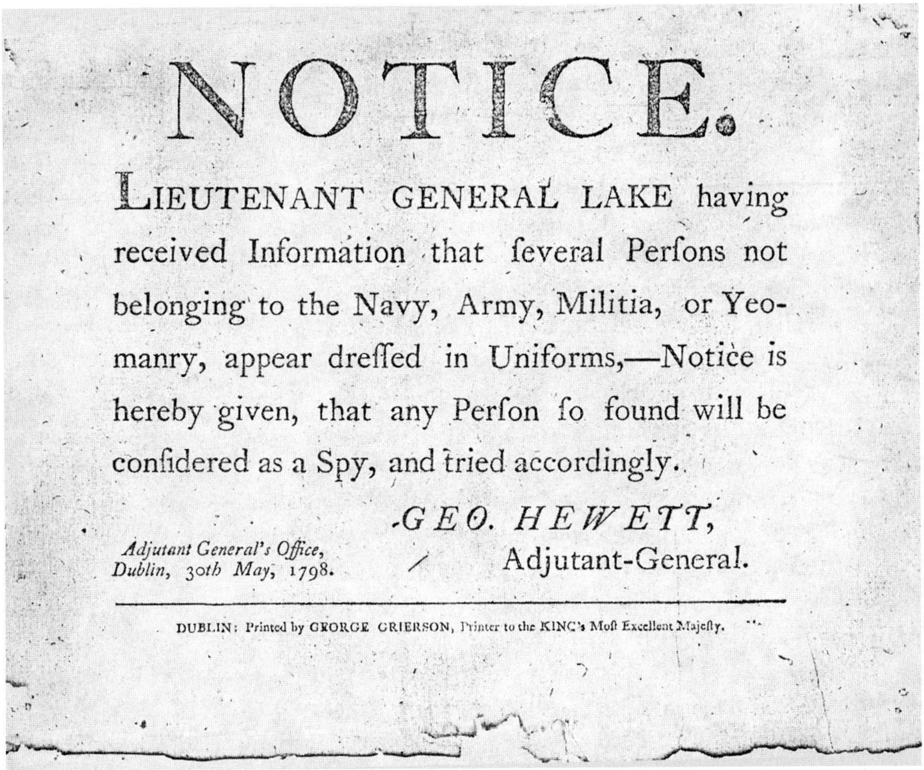

NOTICE.

LIEUTENANT GENERAL LAKE having received Information that ſeveral Perſons not belonging to the Navy, Army, Militia, or Yeomanry, appear dreſſed in Uniforms,—Notice is hereby given, that any Perſon ſo found will be conſidered as a Spy, and tried accordingly.

GEO. HEWETT,
Adjutant-General.

Adjutant General's Office,
Dublin, 30th May, 1798.

DUBLIN: Printed by GEORGE GRIERSON, Printer to the KING's Moſt Excellent Majeſty.

Notice issued by the Dublin Castle authorities prohibiting the use of uniforms by members of the United Irishmen organisation. Courtesy of the Allen Library

revealed the identities and activities of many Society members. One such letter divulged that Mr. Seagrave, a farmer from Ballybough Bridge, was treasurer of the United Baronial Committee which met in the Sheaf of Wheat and Pigeons at Finglas. Other United Irishmen in the area were also named, including Michael Walters and James Reilly, turnpike keepers in Drumcondra, McVeigh and Ramsey, publican and brick-layer of Dorset Street, and Donnelly, a gardener from Summerhill.[8] The Dorset Street rebels, believed to be led by a Mr. Wall, a pawnbroker, met in a thatched public house opposite Granby Row.[9]

Watty Cox, a Catholic gun-smith who lived at 12 North Clarence Street, Ballybough, began publishing a clandestine broadsheet known as *The Union Star*. This was run as an independent venture. Its policy was *"to establish the empire of universal benevolence and fraternity from [the] Wicklow Hills to Belfast, from the Channel to the Atlantic"*.[10] All it really did was play on the radical and

8. National Archives 620/31/149/31
9. National Archives 620/18/3
10. Thomas Pakenham –The year of liberty. 1969. p.40

religious hatreds of the submerged Catholic peasantry. The government managed to track down Cox, and T*he Union Star* was disbanded. On condition of being set free, Cox agreed to tell the government all he knew about fellow members of the United Irishmen.

By the end of 1797, hopes for French assistance had faded. Realising this, the United Irishmen decided upon Dublin as the base for attack and then worked outwards. Oliver Bond believed that *"Dublin once taken all the rest of Ireland would directly submit"*.[11]

With such a level of local unrest, it was obviously important for the government to have troops located in every area. The Rotunda Division was responsible for the protection of citizens of Ballybough in the event of a rebellion, yet their loyalty was questionable because the troops were drawn from the local community. At least 100 were from Ballybough and Summerhill. However, it is believed that most entered to screen their activities within the United Irishmen and would immediately change sides if rebellion broke out. When this eventually happened, of the 22 privates of the division infantry, 14 were proven to be sworn United Irishmen, 6 were suspected and subsequently disarmed. This left only two who were willing or able to fight against the rebels.[12]

The government prevented any great movement by arresting leaders. Most of the Leinster leaders were arrested on the 12 March 1798. This proved to be the final blow. Many followers dispersed when they realised the mission had failed.[13]

One of the most notorious hunters of rebels was John Claudius Beresford, resident of Drumcondra House from the mid 1790s. He was renowned for hunting down rebels and croppies and his cruelty used for extracting confessions knew no bounds. At the front of his townhouse in Marlborough Green *"suspected rebels were suspended and flogged until they made a "confession" true or false, or fainted away in agony"*.[14] Beresford's Bloodhounds who attended these ordeals also had a legendary position at Drumcondra House.

By the end of the conflict more than 30,000 people were dead. It did precipitate the passing of the Act of Union but Catholic Emancipation was not to be put in place due to the ill-feeling which was prevalent in both Britain and Ireland in the aftermath of the 1798 Rebellion.

11. G. O'Brien – Parliament, politics and people. 620/52/185
12. Musgrave's Memoirs p.198, 620/28/3
13. W.H. Maxwell – History of the Irish rebellion in 1798. 1845. p.58
14. Essays by Sarah Atkinson 'Old houses restored'. 1895. p.409

Chapter 5

THE ACT OF UNION

The Act of Union had an immediate effect on Dublin. It saw the departure of the politicians and their entourages to London, selling their former homes at a loss, or in some instances abandoning, them completely. This was to have significant consequences later in the century, as many of these houses became tenement slums. It was eventually realised by those in power that inclusion of some of the adjacent townships, among them Clontarf (which included the Ballybough area) and Drumcondra, within the municipality of Dublin, would to some degree reverse this stagnation. This would provide more land for building and more revenue. Proposals for the annexation of the independent townships met with opposition from all parties but it was only a matter of time before it became a reality. The townships were in dire need of sanitation and water works and could not undertake such costly investments alone. Such developments were among the greatest achievements of the city after 1800.

The population of the country had grown rapidly at the start of the nineteenth century and reached a peak of over eight million people by the 1840s. The prospects for the country's future were bright with Dublin rated as the second city in the British Isles as well as an important and vibrant commercial centre.

BOUNDARIES

Over recent centuries, the boundaries of Dublin City and its component areas have shifted and changed dramatically. The Clonturk parish maps of 1701 and 1770 mention Ballybough as a townland in Drumcondra. The Dublin Almanac of 1836, however, places it in the suburb of Clontarf. The first Ordnance Maps in 1837 record Ballybough as being in the parish of Clonturk, in the Barony of Coolock, but by 1869 it had been absorbed into the Clontarf township. Such changes were part of a larger picture of population movements, land reclamation and the extension of city limits.

During the mid 1800s, city boundaries were still located within the two canals. This meant that the availability of land for development, especially with regard to first class housing, was limited. Much of the available land tended to be low-lying and situated in areas near the port. Many believed it to be suitable only for prisons, cemeteries and workhouses, and even then, people did not want to live in their vicinities. The only housing that could be constructed in such places was that suited to the working classes. The gap, both physically and socially, was ever-widening between the professionals and working classes. By the 1911 census, Drumcondra and Clontarf had been incorporated into the city of Dublin.

The residents of the city centre had to pay higher taxes than those in any other area, as they had to subsidise the costs of hospitals, police etc. Inhabitants of the northern section of the city each paid 10 shillings in the pound in taxes, whereas those on the south side paid 3 shillings.[1] The first suggestion to extend the boundaries of the city came in 1876. It is recorded that the Corporation was almost bankrupt in 1877, and extension of the boundaries would obviously alleviate many of the financial difficulties. A Royal Commission on Municipal Boundaries came to Dublin in 1879, and the Corporation put forward a number of valid reasons for the extension of city limits, including falling valuation of city property; departure of the middle classes; and the disproportionate burden of hospitals, workhouses and improvements to city roads and tenements.

In theory this seemed like a good solution, but there was mounting opposition from both those living in the city centre and their suburban neighbours. The commission, however, recommended the extension which was to include the township of Clontarf. It also recommended a revaluation of the city, but nothing was to happen. In 1869 a bill was proposed to turn Clontarf into a township, and a petition was later put forward to have Clontarf included in the city.

The late 1880s witnessed rapid development of the suburbs but there was still a sharp decline in north-side valuations. The trend had been set very early on with the exodus of population to the southside. Drumcondra had only begun to develop in the 1870s and suburban expansion occurred mainly in areas where there had previously been villages or housing clusters. Drumcondra also had a large population of priests and theologians, as it was home to the colleges of All Hallows & Mater Dei.

The Dublin Boundaries Bill became law on 6 August 1900, and included finally the areas of both Drumcondra and Clontarf.

SOCIAL & HOUSING CONDITIONS

The population of Dublin grew from 62,000 in 1700 to 180,000 at the passing

1. Mary Daly – The deposed capital. 1985. p.227

of the Act of Union in 1801. At this time Dublin was the second largest city in British Isles and among the fastest growing cities in Europe.

As the century drew to a close, Dublin was recreated. Trade and commerce centred to the north of the city. The working class, who had resided mainly in the south-western part of the city, began moving to areas such as Ballybough in the north-east in search of work. This area was close in proximity to the city centre and the docks, thereby saving the residents the expense of tram fares.

With the arrival of trade and commerce in the city centre, the gradual disintegration of the fashionable north side was instigated. The fine Georgian residences had been abandoned. By the 1850s, people from the older established tenement areas were moving into the Gardiner estate. Ballybough would soon experience population increases, but the scale of tenements was not at the same level as in other parts of the north inner city. This was due mainly to the lack of older high-value property. Availability and quality of housing for the poor was inadequate, and they began gradually to take over the houses that the upper classes had left behind. The south-east and areas outside the city's boundaries now became the fashionable locations for the more affluent members of society.

When the wealthy departed the city centre, the new inhabitants were not in a position to maintain its upkeep. As commerce and the poorer sections of the population overran the centre, it went into decline, while the residential areas in the suburbs rapidly expanded. The Georgian terraced Summerhill close to Ballybough, gradually became tenements and often slums. The working class were forced to live in terrible conditions, a situation which was not remedied to any degree until after the passing of the Working Class Act in 1890.

Following this Act, many of the tenements inspected had rooms closed down, including kitchen areas where entire families had dwelt. In 1891, for example, a Corporation Health Report records that No. 53 Summerhill had had its kitchen and cellar area closed, due to their being totally unfit for human habitation. Such examples are numerous.

Araby, North Richmond Street

Tenement houses usually fell into two categories. First class consisted of those with

Nottingham Street

more than nine rooms and usually at least three storeys; second class houses had two storeys with some of the older ones having up to four. This is very evident in Ballybough, where respectable streets lay beside more undesirable streets, tenement streets or slum streets.[2]

James Joyce's *Dubliners* contains the story *Araby*, set in North Richmond Street, home of the Christian Brothers-run O'Connell Schools, attended by Joyce himself in 1893. The street is also said to have been home to the Joyce family in the 1890s. The opening paragraph describes the street as *"North Richmond Street, being blind, was a quiet street except at the hour when the Christian Brothers' school set the boys free. An uninhabited house of two storeys stood at the blind end, detached from its neighbours in a square ground … the other houses of the street conscious of decent lives within them, gazed at one another with brown imperturbable faces"*.[3]

The other houses on the street are mainly of three storeys. Little has changed there. It is still reasonably quiet apart from the fore-mentioned hour. In Joyce's day the cottages which lay behind the street were in sharp contrast *"The career of our play brought us through the dark and muddy lanes behind the houses, where we ran the gauntlet of the rough tribes from the cottages, to the back doors of the dark dripping gardens where odours arose from the ashpits …"*

Ballybough Road

Ballybough also had first class residential areas, including the North Circular Road and Russell Street. North Richmond Street, with its three-storey residential houses, was also considered a first class street, whilst second class areas included Ballybough Road, the North Strand and Summerhill

2. Brian Murnane – On common ground. 1988. p.196
3. James Joyce – Dubliners. 1981 (reprint) p.25

Parade. First class tenement houses were found at the rear of Summerhill and Gloucester Place North, whilst second class tenement houses lay to the east between Summerhill and Buckingham Street. Two-storey houses were to be found east of Portland Row, Dunne Street, Clarence Street, Nottingham Street, Spring Garden Street and Annesley Place. Some of the red-brick houses on these streets were constructed around 1880. These were known as artisan style houses and provide evidence of the *"philanthropic and commercial forces at work in the housing market of the 1880s in Dublin"*.[4]

It would appear that tenements also lay between Portland Row and the Royal Canal, with a few also in existence in the North Strand/Ballybough Road area. Evidence suggests that overcrowding did exist here, especially in the small cottages in and around the railway viaduct, and off Ballybough Lane.

Much of the land around Ballybough was reclaimed at a time when Dublin Corporation was desperate for building space to relieve the more squalid areas. Indeed, with the influx of working class families into the north side in the nineteenth century, and the opportunity for building ground, the area of Ballybough became a very popular locale. Areas around the city's industries and railways were undesirable regions, and only working class accommodation could viably be built there. Ballybough, close to the docks where many of the city's industries lay, along with its railway lines, could only be suitable in this period for working-class housing.

Conditions were notably better in the first class houses, as well as some of the more salubrious cottages in Ballybough. The cottages on Clonliffe Road, in contrast to those of the North Strand, had front gardens, a sign of wealth at that time. There was a great difference between the many streets, roads, avenues, courts and terraces of Ballybough. In 1896, the Dublin Corporation Private Improvement Expenses Records, state that the residents of St. James's Avenue lodged complaints about the neglected condition of the Avenue, terming it a "*... source of much annoyance ...*". The Avenue and its inhabitants were described thus *"St. James Avenue, south side of Clonliffe Road*

Clonliffe Road

4. Brian Murnane – On common ground. 1988. p.194

contains a large number of well built dwellings tenanted by a most respectable class".

Behind North Richmond Street, with its *"rough tribes"*, improvements were also needed. The same report mentions an inspection of the lane behind the street. It was the only approach to numbers 1 and 2, St. Joseph's Villas and the report states that "... *this lane, in consequence of inadequate lighting was constantly the resort of evil doers, which made the place most obnoxious to the inhabitants of the surrounding locality"*.

While detailed information on the specific conditions of housing in Ballybough is scarce, more general sources can help us to glean some understanding of the situation there. Peggy Pigott, who worked in a school in Rutland Street in the 1940s, said that areas such as Summerhill and nearby Gardiner Street were considered slum areas.[5] L.M. Cullen in *Dublin through the Ages*, discovered that according to contemporary evidence, in nearly every tenement "... *human excretia is to be found ... scattered about the yard, and in some cases even in the passages of the house itself"*. However, it must be stressed that many first-hand witnesses would dispute accounts such as Kearns', telling their own stories of the proud women of the tenements who always kept their homes, halls and stairs scrubbed and as decent as possible.

Corporation Reports state that up to 1200 houses had been built in the north of the city by 1884 with 50 new houses being built in Ballybough and the surrounding area in 1887. In 1891, this area had the lowest number of houses constructed. The housing of the working class was thoroughly investigated in 1913, and a report published the following year estimated that the area needed 14,000 extra houses and apartments to alleviate overcrowding, whilst many existing ones would have to be closed down.

Two new roads opened in 1900 and were extensions of Clonliffe Avenue and Foster Terrace. A further three new roads were to be created at the rear of Newcomen Terrace. A number of cottages were also to be constructed. In 1913 a certain Miss Jane Hughes offered to sell numbers 7, 8, 9 and 10 Ballybough Cottages to the Corporation. The engineer sent to inspect the premises noted that there were only 17 perches (one perch is equal to 5.5 yards) in the area and that a large number of adjoining cottages were in a state of deterioration. He felt that acquiring and removing these houses would provide a building site of two acres. Another site known as Friend's Field was also under investigation as a viable ground for building. It was almost four acres in size and was bounded to the north by the G.S. & W. Railway, to the east by Ballybough Road and O'Sullivan Avenue, and to the west by St. James's Avenue. It was thought to have space for up to 168 cottages. Further enquiries into the site noted that it was "... *admirably situated for working class dwellings"*. However,

5. K.C. Kearns – Dublin tenement life. 1996. p.163

O'Sullivan Avenue

a great deal of filling and levelling would need to be done. It was low-lying and below the drainage level. The time required to complete the necessary preparation of the site was estimated at 4-5 years. An area of Clonliffe Road lying at the rear of a terrace of houses joining up with Ballybough Road was also under recommendation for building. The site was bounded by the Tolka, Orchard Road and Ballybough Bridge, near to where the now redundant and filled in sewerage tank lay. This was held by the Corporation, having been taken over from the late Drumcondra Commissioners. The lease was for 400 years, a term in place since 13 July 1881, with rent set at £73 1s 6d per annum.

Very little information has been gathered for the years following 1922. Conditions in Dublin did not improve greatly with the achievement of self-government. Housing conditions actually deteriorated during the 1920s. The Dublin Civic Survey of 1925 reports that *"housing in Dublin today is more than a question and more than a problem – it's a tragedy"*.[6] The list of proposed sites selected by the Corporation for housing included five acres at Friend's Fields, Ballybough, and 89 acres at Croydon Park, Fairview.[7]

By the 1930s the city did not extend far beyond Ballybough, except along the coast. It was officially reported in 1939 that 428 houses had been erected at Marino, and 931 at Croydon Park, Philipsburg Avenue and Griffith Avenue.[8] It was only following this that any significant response to rehousing needs was witnessed. By the 1950s, however, only limited planned action had been undertaken. Housing in the area had not changed extensively for the better part of a century. Corporation policy began to shift during the 1950s, from a

6. Dublin Civic Survey Report. 1925. p.58
7. ibid p.69
8. ibid p.75

long-standing commitment to fringe areas towards development of substantial blocks of flats in the city centre. South of the Tolka awaited the 1960s for any radical changes.

Ballybough Road

During the late 1960s, the Georgian terraces of Summerhill were demolished and new Corporation flats took their place. As number 118 Summerhill was in the process of being torn down, strange occurrences were reported. Originally owned by the Hutton family, the house had later become a tenement building. Workmen in the house encountered a ghostly apparition which frightened them so much that they would work only when they were all present in the same room and left before darkness fell. The apparition was that of a man wearing a striped apron, sometimes seen with something around his neck, described by one of the workmen as a napkin. The figure was believed to be that of one Patrick Conway, a butcher who had cut his own throat in the house in 1863. The excitement caused by the ghost lasted for a few weeks, with follow-up reports in the *Evening Press*!

HEALTH

Also of concern in nineteenth century Ballybough was the issue of public health. The first Public Health Act in Ireland was passed in 1848 and allowed the Corporation to act on any report of a *"nuisance"* if made by two or more people. Nuisances included cesspools, manure heaps, swine houses and filthy buildings which could be injurious to health. The Health and City Preservation Committee was established soon afterwards but their activities were initially slow. The following year there were record mortality rates due to a cholera epidemic. An Inspector of Nuisances was appointed and prosecutions soon began.

The Dublin Corporation Sanitary Association was created so that members could have the sanitary conditions of their dwellings examined at a modest cost. Ash pits were one area of particular contention. Dr. Charles Cameron, appointed City Health Officer in 1879, stated in a Health Report for the Corporation in 1885 that *"Until lately the majority of ashpits in connection with the tenement houses were roofless, consequently rain-water generally rendered their contents more or less liquid and caused soak age into the ground to take place. The quality of air is a point of considerable importance because this air is constantly escaping upwards into our dwellings, I have long been of the opinion that the more expeditiously filth is removed from our habitations, the better it is for our health".*

Fining of landlords for unsanitary premises was in evidence but simply paying the fine was usually cheaper than improving the building. James O'Reilly, owner of 68 Ballybough Road was fined 5s in 1891 for the unsanitary conditions of his house. In 1892 Philip M'Eneny, owner of 23b Ballybough Road, was charged the princely sum of £2, and in 1898 Thomas O'Connor, owner of 37 Ballybough Road, was fined twice, first the sum of 6d and later 2s. Many houses were also closed or vacated.

In 1892, dairy yards were inspected by Dr. Charles Cameron, who was in favour of their removal to outside city boundaries, believing them to be another source of infectious diseases such as typhoid fever. Four inspectors were dispatched to enforce cleanliness on the north side. In 1887 these dairy yards numbered 149 and were subject to constant inspection. By 1892 it had been reduced to 88, many now having been paved, supplied with piped water, and having had new sheds constructed. Listed in the report of 1887 there were three premises on Spring Garden Street, one on Ballybough Road, one on Ballybough Lane, and one on Bessborough Avenue. There was also a stable on North Richmond Street. Joyce in *Araby* tells the reader of the "*... dark odorous stables where a coachman smoothed and combed the horse or shook music from the buckled harness.*"

The total number of cattle recorded was 79. An act, known as the Contagious Diseases (Animals) Act, had been in operation since 1879, and regularly led to fines on owners of premises that did not fulfil the desired sanitary expectations set down by the Corporation. In 1890, for example, Thomas Malone of Belvidere Road was fined 10s for keeping a pig in a dairy yard contrary to regulations, and in 1892 Luke Hyland of 40 Spring Garden Street was fined 10s for a breach of the regulations concerning his cowsheds. In 1896 the records also show that rubbish was carried by night in wagons on the tram lines and deposited on Fairview sloblands to assist in their reclamation for parkland.

Time for tea. Courtesy of the Allen Library

The short term effect added to the unattractiveness of this north-eastern quadrant of the city.

Dublin at the turn of the century was recognised as the unhealthiest and worst housed city in Britain and Ireland. The death rate was high, especially in the overcrowded working class areas. A report on the health of Dublin was drawn up for the local government in 1900 in response to the high death rates in 1890. Ballybough at this time was part of the North City District No. 1 East, an area covering the north-east as far as Clonliffe Road and the Tolka. It had one of the lowest death rates in the city – 26.7 per 1000, compared with 28.8 per 1000 for Dublin as a whole. The state of tenements, overcrowding and drainage were seen as the main contributors to this high rate. Ballybough was relatively tenement free and its population averaged 40.3 per acre, again the lowest in the city, compared with 124.4 per acre in the North City No. 2 district. Edgar Flinn's report in 1906 showed the population level in the Ballybough area as still below that of the remainder of the city.

The issue of public health was superseded by the more urgent matter of slum clearance and rehousing, with the 1914 report highlighting the need for the immediate break-up of the tenement system and provision of proper new dwellings. The maps included with the 1925 Civic Survey placed much of Ballybough among the unhealthiest areas, particularly the smaller streets behind main Ballybough Road, Poplar Row and North Strand area. The city's mortality rate had fallen by 1922 to an average of 17.6 per 1000, North City No. 1 East District now had a rate of 19.6 per 1000, second highest in the city, while its infant mortality rate at 4.9 per 1000 was the highest in Dublin. However, mortality rates overall fell from 20.9 per 1000 in 1914 to 14.36 per 1000 in 1940, and tubercular mortality 3.788 per 1000 to 1.63 per 1000, a situation linked to the 1930s developments in the welfare system.

SEWERS, DRAINAGE & WATER SUPPY

The city's inadequate sewage treatment and water supply was among the main factors responsible for the problems of illness and disease during the nineteenth century. Sanitation reforms were urgently required and the best means of accomplishing this was through public intervention. Following the report of Sir Edwin Chadwick in 1842, which dealt with the labouring population in Great Britain, much attention was focused on the need for removal of all forms of waste. Domestic sewage was to be carried by water carriage through drains and therefore a widespread system of drains and sewers was needed. The onus fell on the local authority to provide it.

The issue of drainage and water supply was always one of contention in Dublin. The City Engineer, Parke Neville, was the sole sanitary agent in the city and his report of 1853 emphasised the need to build new sewers to replace older ones. A general sewage scheme was undertaken during the 1850s and 1860s, but the Corporation did not have the power to compel house owners to install drains until 1861, and many houses still lacked connection to the main sewers in 1880.

By 1869 there were fifty miles of sewers emptying into the river Liffey, leading to major problems with both air and water pollution and many city dwellers feared a cholera epidemic. During the 1860s, advertisements were placed in newspapers by the Corporation seeking applications from relevant bodies on how to ultimately solve the problem. In 1871 the Dublin Main Drainage and Purification of the Liffey Act was passed. Funding remained a major obstacle and no real progress was made until 1892. Popular opinion at the time was one of ambivalence – the people wanted an unpolluted city but did not want to shoulder the cost.

The area of Ballybough was outside the municipal boundary. In June 1861, tenders of construction for various sewers including that of Bayview Avenue were to be sent to Parke Neville and the contract was eventually awarded to Joseph Enright. On July 5 Hannah Mooney of Clarke's Bridge Cottage, Summerhill, sent a letter to the Corporation stating that she intended to pursue compensation for damage caused to her dwelling and premises during excavation of sewerage works. Another complaint was later received from Mary Branagan, of Summerhill Parade, who was intending similar action.

The Drumcondra and Tolka scheme was proposed in 1875 by James Boyle who suggested an outlet at either Ballybough Bridge or east of Annesley Bridge. The residents of Fairview Strand and adjacent areas waited on the Commissioners of the Clontarf township to work in unison with the Corporation to clean the bed of the Tolka, but disagreement arose regarding responsibility for the pollution and nothing was achieved. One of the biggest obstacles, according to the Corporation, was the problem of flooding. This would in fact cleanse much of the river, and any further work could commence in the spring, with a new sewer being constructed at Poplar Row. John Costello of the Dublin Whiskey Distillery Company said in 1880 that a family had had to be rescued from their house by means of a ladder due to the severe floods. Parke Neville, in a commentary on the area, stated that much foul matter was to be found in and above the area of Ballybough Bridge, and also near Annesley Bridge, even after the flooding. (The section between the two bridges was the only part that lay within the then municipal boundaries of the City of Dublin.) He also said that there was little point in cleaning just one section of the river unless the townships involved cleaned the rest. There was just one Corporation sewer discharging into the Tolka east of Ballybough Bridge and this could be diverted to meet with the planned new sewer in Poplar Row, which would have an outlet to the tideway just below Annesley

Bridge. The only problem was that the tide would carry large amounts of foul matter back up the river and also that Glasnevin, Finglas and Drumcondra used the river for discharging sewage and other foul matter. If the scheme was to go ahead, the area between Fairview and Marino Crescent would be transformed into a putrid swamp.

At the time of the first proposal to include Drumcondra, Clonliffe and Glasnevin as one township, Drumcondra had no proper drainage system and foul matter made its way up the river. The old cesspool system was still in operation and the subsoil was saturated with filth. Less poisonous and heavier matter was carted away but the area remained heavily impregnated with sewage poison. Many believed it to be responsible for much of the illness and disease that occurred at the time. Various proposals were put forward but it seemed almost impossible to reach any agreement. The one certainty was that the townships were not in a financial position to achieve an effective end result by themselves. The laying of the first pipe for main drainage in the township occurred in 1881, and was performed by J.F. Lombard, Chairman of the Commissioners. It took place at the east end of Clonliffe Road close to the point where the principal drainage was later to be constructed. By 1887 the Tolka was a big cesspool. To add to the hardship of the area, many new housing schemes were being built. The stench from the river was now at crisis levels and the current was too feeble to remove the matter deposited in disgusting banks along both sides of the river.

In 1884 Hassard proposed a plan which would lead to the discharge of sewage at the Nose of Howth. This plan was accepted by the Municipal Corporation.

Charles Cameron, the Public Health Officer for the City, visited the area in 1887 and reported that the river was a pure and limpid stream under Drumcondra Bridge, but that less than a half mile away it turned into a foul and offensive waterway. He blamed this on the city sewer which discharged into the river. This sewer had the collections of a considerable district of the City of Dublin. The district in fact was larger than the whole of the Clontarf township and had double the population. The mouth of the sewer was covered by a tidal flap and generally closed for up to twelve hours per day, and in dry weather the more solid matter was left behind for longer periods. When the weather deteriorated and rain fell, the matter was washed away and carried back and forth on the ebb and flow of the tide until at last a considerable portion was left on the banks, which was obviously unpleasant to many of the senses. The sewage of the Clontarf township at this time discharged directly onto the strand where it lay at low water for hours until the returning tide absorbed, churned and tossed it about. After a while it became more solid and undissolved residues joined the filth from the City and helped in the contamination of the air and aspect of the district.

The Dublin Improvement Bill became law in August 1890, and by this time an Act for the Notification of Infectious Diseases had also been passed. The Dublin Corporation Main Drainage Works were designed in 1891 to take sewage of the outlying districts of Clontarf township, Drumcondra, Clonliffe and Glasnevin township, the urban district of Grangegorman and New Kilmainham, together with the City of Dublin, and convey it to the Pigeon House where it was to be treated. Clontarf drainage was to be dealt with by an intercepting sewer running along the foreshore which, together with that coming from Drumcondra, would be taken into the main drainage scheme at Poplar Row, near Ballybough Bridge, thereby cleansing not only the sea front but also the Tolka. The pumping station was to be located at the Pigeon House Road. The treatment was to take place there, and any remaining sludge was to be removed via a large specially built sludge carrier *The Shamrock*. This would be discharged not less then six miles from the Poolbeg Lighthouse outside the Port of Dublin and north of a line due east of the Baily Lighthouse. By 1897 the Dublin main drainage scheme was finished and the pollution of the Liffey and its shores abated.

On Monday 24 September 1906, the main drainage scheme for Dublin was formally declared complete. This was after several decades of tireless work by some prominent members of Dublin Corporation who faced many setbacks during that time. When completed, Dublin was as well modernised in sewage and drainage as other cities.

VARTRY WATERWORKS

Canal water had been used in the north side of the city but was often scarce due to the locking up and down of boats and it also had high quantities of lime. The Corporation had obtained deeds from the Royal Canal Company and by 1805 was ready to afford permanent and ample supply of water to the north side. The Feinaiglian Institution in 1817 requested supply of water which was granted at a cost of £30 per annum.[9]

A Royal Commission on Water Supply under John Hawkshaw was set up in August 1861. The end product was the proposal of the Vartry scheme which would bring water from Co. Wicklow. Prior to the introduction of the Vartry supply squads of men were employed solely to maintain and clean the pipes.

On the north side of the city much of the water came from wells, the Tolka and the canals. Unfortunately the Tolka and the ground water in the area were contaminated and this led to problems for individual households and for the larger institutions and industries in the area. In 1871 Clonliffe College received a supply of Vartry water and five years later the residents of Drumcondra had applied for an extension of the Vartry Water Supply. The

9. CARD Vol.xvii, p.148

Rations cards used during the Great Famine under the Soup-kitchen Act 1847. Courtesy of the Allen Library

latter was not yet readily available in the area and only the larger buildings and institutions had it by means of a special contract with Dublin Corporation. They had to bear the cost of the expense of the pipe-laying required. By 1878 the township of Drumcondra, Clonliffe and Glasnevin Act had come into effect. The following year the Corporation agreed to supply Drumcondra with Vartry water but not to houses valued under £5. The increased supply also affected the water borne sewage levels.

Water from the Vartry was eventually pumped all over the city as far as the northern suburb of Artane, the southern area of Bray and from Dundrum to the coast, an area of 22 square miles.

FAMINE & WORKHOUSES

By the time potato blight became a serious issue, the foundations for a crisis of economy, class and colony were already in place.

Dublin inevitably saw a population increase with the influx of starving beggars and unemployed farm labourers who travelled to the city in search of work. The first workhouse in the capital was located at James's Street. The institution which catered for the northern area of the city was known as the North Dublin Union Workhouse. (Dublin had been divided into two unions following a report in 1840.) The North Union was to cater for half of the city and suburbs, with a rural district composed of the Barony of Coolock and portions of the Baronies of Castleknock and Uppercross; in total almost 39,000 statute acres with a total population of 125,245. This included the area of Ballybough.[10]

From their inception, workhouses received bad publicity. The institution was officially opened in May 1840.[11] Under the 1847 Irish Poor Relief Extensions Act, following the outbreak of the Great Famine, the workhouse guardians were empowered

10. Richard Earle – Poor Law Commissioners Reports 6-7. 1840-41. p.276
11. John O'Connor – The workhouses of Ireland's poor. 1995. p261

to acquire land adjacent to their institutes for the interment of the dead. Many were buried in pauper plots without coffins. Some of the guardians introduced a system of outdoor relief by giving food to those who were not inmates. In Dublin, soup kitchens were set up and ration cards issued, entitling people to certain quantities of food. This was stopped by the Poor Law Commissioners. The only option remaining for many was emigration or public works. The latter were badly paid (in some cases unpaid due to lack of funds) and many died from starvation while trying to carry out their tasks. Those who emigrated went to England, America, Canada and Australia.

The workhouse records for 1844 show that only seven people from the Ballybough area were admitted, spending an average of 14.5 days there with only one person dying that year. The following year 32 people were listed, this time spending on average 130.9 days in the workhouse. Three people died. Two years later, at the height of the Famine, the figure had doubled and the mortality rate was running at over 20%. The average time spent there was now 226 days. By 1852, only 13 people were registered and spent less than two weeks within the gloomy walls.

YEAR	TOTAL	M	F	D	A. Days
1844	7	4	3	1	14.5
1845	32	15	17	3	130.9
1846	35	19	16	6	151.5
1847	64	34	30	15	226.1
1848	66	32	34	12	210.0
1852	13	4	9	3	68.1

T = Total admitted from Ballybough
M = Males, F = Females
D = Died while in the Workhouse
A. Days = Average number of days spent by those admitted from Ballybough

After the Famine many of the workhouses faced closure due to financial pressures. The workhouse system was finally dismantled, and the Poor Law Unions were reorganised on a county basis. New hospitals and institutions were founded, many utilising the former workhouse buildings.

The Famine was one of the most tragic periods in Irish history but it also acted as a catalyst for change in the following decades.

Chapter 6

AFTERMATH OF THE GREAT FAMINE

The advent and aftermath of the Great Famine left behind a transformed society. More than half the population had either died of starvation and illness or had emigrated. This concept of emigration and population decline was unique to Ireland in the nineteenth century. Old ways of life had also perished with the Famine and people now turned in various directions to fill the newly created vacuum. One result was the emergence of devotional piety, and a new era of church building. The removal of the Penal Laws at the turn of the century had left Catholics with much more religious and personal freedom.

One of the areas most affected by the abolition of the Penal Code was education. Many new schools were founded by religious organisations such as the Christian Brothers and the Presentation Sisters. Children from the poorest sections of society now had the opportunity to break the vicious circle of poverty in which they lived. It also provided a more skilled and educated work force.

CHURCHES & RELIGIOUS INSTITUTIONS

It was only after the Great Famine that the majority of Irish people began frequenting regular Mass. One of the fundamental reasons for this was that Catholicism was now seen as the main distinguishing feature of Irishness, and it replaced an Irish identity lost because of the Famine. As a result there was a new impetus in the building of churches, not only by Catholics, but also by other religious groups. Like many other areas Ballybough reflected this trend and witnessed the building of new churches of various denominations, as well as other associated institutions.

Church of the Visitation of the Blessed Virgin Mary

The population of the Ballybough/Fairview area increased during the

Church of the Visitation of the Blessed Virgin Mary, Fairview

nineteenth century, and it became necessary to provide a place of worship for the local populace. James Young, a pious merchant, invited the Carmelite Tertiaries of Clondalkin to establish a branch house in Fairview Avenue. An oratory, which was blessed by Archbishop Troy, was opened in 1819, and was for parochial use. The chaplain to the Brothers celebrated Masses for the people. There were two Masses on Sundays and on Holy Days. Fr. Boyle, a curate of Clontarf parish, was unhappy with the presence of the Carmelites and was anxious to build a separate parochial church and residence. He chose a site beside Annesley Bridge and collected stones and timber for the project. Unfortunately the site was unsuitable and was soon abandoned. The Carmelite Brothers left the area during the 1830s after much confrontation with the local clergy, and the parish eventually purchased their former residence. The chapel was reopened to the public and remained in use for the next twenty years until a suitable site for the new parish church was selected on Fairview Strand, facing the road between Ballybough and Annesley Bridge. This land had once belonged to St. Mary's Abbey. The building process was slow and eight years passed before the church was opened to the public. Even then it was rough and unfinished. The present building was opened on 15 January 1855, with a ceremony performed by members of the Missionary College of All Hallows.

The church itself is cruciform in shape and is of a pointed Gothic style of the Plantagenet period. It is built of massive blocks of black limestone. The facings of the doors and windows are of Wicklow Stone. It has a fine high altar, which was bought from the old church in Dun Laoghaire and erected in Fairview in 1894. The Stations of the Cross were a present from Fr. Dudley who was a curate in St. Agatha's. In later years beautiful stained glass windows were installed.

St. Agatha's Church, North William Street

St. Agatha's Church, North William Street

The convent chapel in North William Street was used from its foundation as a Chapel of Ease for St. Mary's the Pro Cathedral. The district bounded by Drumcondra Road, North Circular Road, North Strand and the Tolka formed the separate parish of St. Agatha's in 1865.

Fr. Francis Doran became the first parish priest and he set about having a new church built for the area. Unfortunately on 2 July 1877 he was drowned in a boating accident. Fr. Matthew Collier, his successor, continued with the plan for a new church and selected a site a few yards from the chapel. He decided on a classical Roman church, and Meade was chosen as the contractor. Finances were a problem from the start, and funds ran out when the walls had reached the string course, a raised horizontal band of bricks etc. on a building. Construction ceased and Fr. Collier died of old age in 1892.

Fr. John O'Malley next arrived at St. Agatha's and was permitted to borrow money from the bank to pay the contractor. He was not satisfied with the site of the church, as it was in a back street, and began searching for alternative locations. A female parishioner who died had left £8,000 towards the new church. Fr. O'Malley liked the site at 10 Richmond Place, but the Archbishop refused his consent. Much wrangling took place and the parish priest took the Archbishop to court and lost. Fr. Dudley became senior curate at St. Agatha's, and Fr. O'Malley died unexpectedly in 1904.

Canon Michael Walsh was the fourth parish priest and he returned to the original plans and location, and the church was finally completed. The Archbishop blessed the Church at 11.30 a.m. on Sunday 25 October 1908.

The church was designed by William H. Byrne and is classical Roman Renaissance in design. Its massive fabric withstood the German bombing of the North Strand in 1941. Erected in a narrow street it is difficult to appreciate its facade, with the pediment crowned by statues of the Sacred Heart, St. Patrick and St. Agatha. In the arches of the apse are three large paintings of the Agony in the Garden, The Supper at Emmaus and the

Annunciation. The Stations of the Cross in the other arches are by the Dublin artist, Charles Goodland Bradshaw. The decorative work in the Baptistery was designed and executed by Harry Clarke.

Clonliffe Methodist

For the greater part of the nineteenth century, Irish Methodism was divided into two unequal groups. In 1878 the two conferences united, forming the Methodist Church in Ireland. In the following years a process of rationalisation occurred, bringing together congregations whose work overlapped.

With the expansion of the Drumcondra/Ballybough community, the Methodists decided to locate their new chapel on Jones's Road. A parcel of ground had been acquired by building contractor Robert Worthington of Dame Street. In the latter part of 1881, building commenced. The foundation stone was laid by Bishop Matthew Simpson who was visiting from America. The congregation was more popularly known as the Clonliffe Methodists.

The chapel was built to seat 350 people and was decorated with a small neat spire on the western gable. It was dedicated on Sunday 2 April 1882. The society was part of the Abbey Street circuit, and came under the care of the ministers there, one of whom later took charge of Clonliffe. Although the chapel was situated on Jones's Road, the society used the name Clonliffe. During 1885-1888, while Samuel Boyd was minister, No. 15 Norman Terrace was acquired as a manse, and was located opposite the chapel on Jones's Road.

The society which met in this new chapel was small or in poor circumstances (or both), for the average weekly collection in the first year amounted to only 7s 8d. By the end of the century circumstances had improved, and the average collection had risen to £2 10s. By 1907 the congregation was in financial difficulties and it was necessary to cut expenses. The status of minister was reduced to a junior, with a smaller stipend. The manse in Norman Terrace was sold and the junior minister had to find his own accommodation.

Clonliffe Methodist Church, Jones's Road

During these years, the members of the Sunday congregation complained about nuisance from the nearby recreation ground, now Croke Park. No details of the exact nature of the nuisance have survived, but it may have been noise levels during hours of worship. The same park provided the venue in 1908 for an open air fete to raise funds for the society.

The social unrest of the 1920s caused some problems for the congregation. A number of people who had been in the British service, as members of the garrison, the RIC, the postal service and such, chose to go and live in Northern Ireland or England after the establishment of the Irish Free State. It became inevitable that sooner or later the Dublin Methodists would have to reassess their work. In 1940 the Clonliffe society had only 53 members. It was transferred from the Abbey Street circuit to the Clontarf circuit. The new association was to last just a short time, as the membership continued to decline with shifting population. From then on, several circuit evangelists were appointed to Clonliffe but a revival never materialised. Services were discontinued in 1949 and the chapel was sold for £6,120. The purchasers were Castle Manufacturing Company.

North Strand Episcopal Church

The original North Strand schoolhouse was situated on the site now occupied by No. 68 North Strand Road at the corner of Spring Garden Street. Some form of chapel was incorporated into the original building but it was not licensed. Divine service was conducted there and the first chaplain was Rev. James Maxwell, who died in 1799.

During the ministry of Rev. Michael Boote, the old building evolved into the present day church. For nearly fifty years the old chapel had served the North Strand area. A building committee was appointed in 1833, and in March 1836 the site of the present church was secured on lease. The foundation stone of the new chapel was laid by Rev. C.H. Minchin, chaplain of the Rotunda Hospital, on 7 September 1836, and it was opened on 20 May 1838. The architect was Joseph Welland and his design was executed by John Butler.

Rev. Richard Hemphill was appointed chaplain in September 1840 and his ministry lasted 45 years. In 1890 the district was constituted a parish and the church became North Strand Parish Church. Mr. R.D. Bluett was its first and only Rector. In 1896 the parish was united with the older parish of Drumcondra, and became known as the Union of Drumcondra and North Strand.

The church was redecorated and had electricity installed in 1911. The present organ was dedicated in May of that year, aided by funds donated by philanthropist Andrew Carnegie.

During the labour unrest and strikes of 1913, Jim Larkin rented a field at Croydon Park where he provided food and recreation for the unemployed. The rector became friendly with him and co-operated with many of his charitable efforts. At the outbreak of the First World War a number of men from the United Parishes enlisted, many of them never to return. Their names are inscribed on brass plates in the church.

The "Ivy Church" as it was affectionately known to many local people is still in use today.

Fairview Gospel Hall, Annesley Bridge Road, Evangelical Christian

At the corner of Addison Road and Annesley Bridge Road, a mission hall was erected in 1912. This is one of the oldest of eight gospel halls in Dublin. Placed as an integral part of a development of typical red brick houses of the same period, the gospel hall blends in with the local buildings. It has a course of decorative bricks under the eaves.

Fairview Gospel Hall

The Missionary College Hall of All Hallows

Fr. John Hand was the founder of All Hallows Missionary College. His aim was to train men for the priesthood, who could then go and spread the Catholic faith in foreign countries. In 1842 Fr. Hand found an *"eligible house"* for his college, namely Drumcondra House and its surrounding land.[1] Details of the negotiations for the purchase are not known, but it is certain that Daniel O'Connell, who was Lord Mayor of Dublin 1841-42, played a major role in bringing the transaction to a successful outcome. He himself contributed an initial £100 and continued to subscribe generously to the college until his death. The splendid Drumcondra House, a fine example of the early Georgian style, had been built in 1726-27 by Sir Marmaduke Coghill.

The religious needs of the neighbourhood were not ignored. Fr. Hand had the central stable converted into a chapel where Sunday Mass was said for the parishioners.

Money had to be raised to maintain the college and Fr. Hand was often seen calling door to door on Dublin's streets. He also journeyed further by pony and trap in search of funds.

1. Rev. K. Condon – The missionary college of All Hallows. 1986. p.60

All Hallows College

The student body was increasing and new missions were opening up. In September 1843, Fr. Hand reported that there were 38 students in the college. By 1848, the need for a chapel was urgent with upwards of 80 men being crowded into Fr. Hand's converted stable. Dr. Moriarty, who had been elected superior after the death of Fr. Hand, decided to build a worthy and handsome building. The design intended for the chapel was novel, with an orientation from west to east. The nave or *"ante-chapel"* at the west end was to be separated from the *"choir"* at the east end by a rood loft, surmounted by a crucifix and statues. On either side of the nave there were to be aisles, separately gabled and roofed, each with bays containing altars. The style was *"decorated Gothic"* or *"middle-pointed"*. The choir apse had a five-light perpendicular window of *"shafted mullions"*. Due to *"pressing necessities"*, only the choir of the chapel was built. This choir alone with accommodation for about one hundred remained the chapel of All Hallows for the next forty-five years. It was destroyed by fire in 1895.

Priests from All Hallows went to serve in the missions in America, Canada, Australia, India, South Africa, Mauritius, Central and South America.

Holy Cross College, Clonliffe

Clonliffe College takes in about 35 acres of the area which was once part of the Grange of Clonliffe. Archbishop Paul Cullen purchased the Red House and its lands from the Inland Revenue Commissioners in May 1858, and subsequently purchased any adjacent land which came on the market. On 1 September 1859, Holy Cross Seminary opened for the education of young men who wanted to become priests. Since 1909 the College has made a notable contribution to the teaching staff of Ireland's universities, and has been a successful centre for the theological preparation for priests of the Dublin diocese.

St. Joseph's, Portland Row

This institution was founded in 1836 by a Mr. Murphy. It initially consisted of only two rooms in a house on Clarendon Street and was a home for destitute women. It transferred to Portland Row in October 1836, and was entrusted to a community of the Poor Servants of the Mother of God. The foundress of the order, Mother Magdalen Taylor, had become a Catholic in the Crimea and worked as a volunteer alongside Florence Nightingale. She visited Portland Row in 1866 but was disappointed with the state of the building. The Sisters were inspired by her and remedied the situation by providing better furnishings and facilities.

In 1856 the church was consecrated, the first in Dublin to be dedicated to St. Joseph. Fr. Henry Young was the first chaplain, even though he was 70 years old. He was regarded as a very saintly man and soon St. Joseph's was highly frequented. He died in November 1869. The chapel was enlarged and redecorated over the years.

St. Joseph's was well known as a place of prayer and easeful old age, not only for the residents, but also for their families. The Sisters left Portland Row in 1993.

EDUCATION

Another facet of Irish life which underwent great changes was that of education. Prior to the eighteenth century various systems had operated throughout the country. The *"systems"* were in fact more a series of schools dotted around the country with no specific ethos or aims.

Many of the stricter penalties were relaxed by the end of the 1700s and were finally abolished following the Emancipation Act of 1829. The schools which operated under these laws were often designed to protestantise rather than educate the indigenous population. As in many European countries, education in Ireland received a new impetus at the beginning of the nineteenth century. The Society for Promoting the Education of the Poor of Ireland, known as the Kildare Place Society, was established in 1811. Its objective was to establish throughout the country *"a well ordered system of education for the poor; due regard was to be paid to economy of time and money; and due attention to cleanliness and discipline in the schools; and equal facilities for education were to be afforded to all classes of professing Christians, and there was to be no interference in the matter of their particular religious belief. In order, however, to bring up children as Christians, it was considered essential that the Bible should be read without note or comment, and that all books likely to lead to religious controversy should be excluded"*. Even though this requirement was not exclusive to the Society it was this controversial religious feature which eventually led to its rejection by the Catholic population and to the withdrawal of its government grant in 1831.

At least six new religious teaching congregations were established throughout Europe in the early part of the century, including the Christian Brothers which were founded in Ireland. In addition to these, schools were set up by other religious congregations, including the Sisters of Charity and the Presentation Sisters. Ballybough was the location for some of the more unique and historically significant educational ventures of this time.

North Strand School

The North Strand School was the first important educational establishment in the area. It opened as a Sunday School in 1786 for the reception and instruction of the children of the poor in the neighbourhood. It was noted that *"a total want of education, both moral and religious prevailed among the children..."*. The Governors, finding on inquiry that the children were for the most part unemployed during weekdays, soon opened for the reception of day scholars. The trustees included Arthur Guinness, Rev. Henry Irwin and Rev. Norbert Daly. It was hoped that the children might receive instruction *"suited to their station in society"*. Admission to the day school was at a nominal rate and all denominations were invited to attend. Also included was a school for female industry which was very prosperous.

The first school house was at what is now 68 North Strand Road at the corner of Spring Garden Street. It did on occasion provide clothing for children and had a distinctive uniform – grey for the boys and olive for the girls with a check apron. The senior girls wore ribbons and a cap. Some of the regulations of the schools were peculiar and seemed very well adapted to the circumstances of the time. *"As they are open to all religious persuasions, one of the masters is a Catholic, who instructs his persuasion in their own catechism, and conducts them every Sunday to Chapel. To induce an early attendance bread is distributed to those who come soonest, and after some time*

North Strand School

clothing as a reward. To prevent a child from withdrawing from the school when this was obtained, a note was passed by the parent, on which he was liable to be sued". Woollen cloaks were lent out to the most deserving girls during the winter months, and were returned in spring. Advancement in learning was considered not a task but a reward and industry was made preparatory to learning. No girl was allowed to write until she had made a shirt!

Great poverty existed among the families of those attending the North Strand Schools. An extract from the *Dublin Chronicle* on Christmas Eve 1787 noted *"It has afforded my acquaintances in the neighbourhood of Ballybough Bridge in observing nearly a hundred poor children of every persuasion, instructed every day of the week in spelling, reading etc., in the Sunday School on the North Strand. The demeanour of these children bespeaks the civilisation of their manners and I beg leave to suggest a plan of further benevolence through the medium of your valuable paper, for those pitiful objects who are half naked and shivering in this inclement weather. To effectuate this humane purpose, perhaps some worthy ladies may be inclined to make a collection at their respective card-tables and happily convert amusement into the blissful luxury of doing good to their indigent fellow creatures".* In a footnote the editor was prepared to receive *"from the affluent and well disposed, any benefactions, for the wholesale purchase of frieze, to be made into coats and distributed, as a reward, to the most deserving boys and girls, who are in the greatest necessity".*

The North Strand School flourished and the only fund available to it was the annual voluntary contributions of individuals. One hundred of the most deserving were clothed annually at an expense of £450 which was defrayed by subscriptions, a charity sermon, and by the profits of the children's works. The chief source of income was the collection at the annual Charity Sermons. The chaplain, the teachers and clothing for children had to be paid from these monies. In 1815 with a deficit of £90, it was decided to discontinue the expenditure on clothing. An effort was made to find the necessary funds by other means. A poor shop and repository were opened *"for the sale of clothing and other articles for the use of the poor"*, and to give constant employment to the working girls. The venture was not a success and was discontinued in 1819.

In 1826, there were 173 children attending the schools, 105 males and 68 females, of whom the majority were Roman Catholic. There were three teachers, one of whom, William Ward, was a Catholic. The others were William Stoyte and Rosetta Heynd. In 1829 the infants' school was founded. It occupied, according to belief, the site on Fairview Strand where Fairview Church now stands.

The North Strand school was falling into disrepair and in 1833 it was decided to erect a new school and chapel. When the new school opened in

1842, 150 pupils attended. The chaplain was Rev. Richard Hemphill of 2 Sackville Gardens. The present site was procured in 1836. The new infants' school adjoining North Strand Church opened in January 1899 and was stated to be *"well lighted, efficiently heated with hot water by the well known firm of Musgrave, and provided with the newest pattern of kindergarten desks which are much appreciated by the little ones"*. The boys' and girls' schools were reconstructed in 1943-44 with the assistance of a State grant, and were reopened on 9 June 1944 by Mr. Eamon de Valera.

North William Street

Founded by Mother Mary Aikenhead, the Irish Sisters of Charity opened their first Dublin convent at North William Street in 1815. This had previously been a Trinitarian establishment and the Sisters continued to run the orphanage set up by their predecessors. The Carmelites came to occupy the building in 1830, and in 1857 the French Filles de Charity or the Daughters of St. Vincent de Paul (otherwise known as the Vincentian Sisters) became the new residents. They immediately began visiting the houses of the poor and soon opened a school for the multitudes of children in the locale at Cardinal Cullen's request without the Educational Board's grant. This allowed them to freely teach the Catholic religion. By 1897 the school was receiving the Board's grant.

North William Street Orphanage outing, 1926. Taken from "Memories" edited by John Coughlan

It was estimated that the police used to pick up as many as one hundred abandoned children in the city each year. Of that number, one-third would be dead and the remainder were handed over to the Protestant authorities who brought them up in the Protestant religion. Many proselytising societies were organised to buy children from impoverished parents.

A new orphanage was opened on North William Street in 1858 without State aid. In the orphanage a thriving flower industry was established along with needlework, and the making of trousseaux and football gear. All the flowers for the decoration of the streets during the Eucharistic Congress Week (June 1932), were made here. Over a century approximately six thousand girls had found a home with the Sisters.

Before the establishment of vocational or technical schools, a member of the congregation ran a centre for children who had left school at an early age or who had attended irregularly. An instructress was paid to teach the children the rudiments of good house-keeping and those who were prepared were placed in suitable and safe conditions of employment. In 1893, another Sister established a Boys' School catering for up to fourth class, inside the uncompleted walls of the new church. This school was a one-storey building with rising rows of seats for infants and had three lay teachers. Among her pupils were Bishop Carroll, Bishop Kavanagh and Brendan Behan. In 1941 the German bombs fell at North William Street. They missed the convent but it did suffer the shock of the explosion. Three hundred displaced families were housed and fed there.

O'Connell Schools

Of greater historical and educational significance was the establishment on North Richmond Street of a school and novitiate by Blessed Edmund Rice, founder of the Christian Brothers. The foundation stone of the O'Connell Schools, as it was later known, was laid by Daniel O'Connell in June 1828. Education for Edmund Rice, was *"a religious work, a total formation of youth, a system, a training that would give a new morale to the children of the poor and lift them up socially"*. Edmund Rice, two assistants, a novice master and four novices moved into the residence in 1831 and on 4 July the school opened for registration. Over 500 pupils enrolled. This building was to provide a new opportunity for some of the poorer children of the city, helping them to better their own position in society. Of the 3,000 Catholic children in St. Mary's parish, 2,000 received no education whatsoever, while the remaining one-third attended non-Catholic schools.

A variety of subjects were taught, with an emphasis on religion and reading of the catechism. There were four periods of prayer each day according to sample timetables. Singing was also important, and in 1862 the

Edmund Rice House & O'Connell Schools, 1940s. Courtesy of the Allen Library

students performed for Lord Carlisle, Lord Lieutenant of Ireland, during his visit to the school. According to the Register for 1860, of the 687 pupils attending Richmond Street, 521 attended Sunday School. Here they learned sacred history, carried out religious transcription and were given religious homework.

Pupils ranged in age from 8-17 years with many leaving after a year or two, once they could read and write. Boys at the age of 11-12 years went into their father's business or were apprenticed to printers, carpenters, chandlers and so forth. Many were absent for long periods, sometimes months, and are recorded as *"doing messages"*, or absent through illness or *"want"*. In the early years prior to education being made compulsory, many pupils were dismissed for truancy, unsocial behaviour or irregular attendance. In the latter part of the nineteenth century many boys were sent away for the same misdemeanours.

Great poverty existed as is evident from teachers' remarks in the school registers entered after pupils' names such as *"stop at home, very poor"* or *"stop at home for want of care"*. Many stayed away with sore feet as families were unable to buy shoes. On the other hand boys from wealthy families left the school to attend fee-paying establishments.

The pupils of O'Connell Schools came from various backgrounds. Many of their parents were tradesmen and general labourers. There was also a significant number whose fathers were soldiers and resided in Aldborough Barracks, and many of these eventually went to live in Gibraltar. Some of the pupils were obviously influenced by their mentors as a number went abroad to join religious communities. To name but two, Ambrose Kneafsey aged 16 from Bayview Avenue went to Holland to join the Franciscans, while a 14-year-old, William Kenny from Fairview, went to England to join the Passionists.

O'Connell Schools, Preparatory Grade class, 1916-17. Courtesy of the Allen Library

The Christian Brothers produced their own set of text books which were acceptable as they contained an ethos and a culture to which the majority of Irish people subscribed. They were part of an educational system which was Catholic in tone but which believed in presenting religion not in an isolated form, but in its natural connection with science and literature. The choice of extracts in these texts had a literary quality that was, for the most part, superior to those included in the National Books. The compilations, apart from the works contributed by the Brothers themselves, were representative of authors of world-wide fame, whose works had a universal appeal and a quality of performance, while works by worthwhile native authors were also included. The books, being the produce of Irish compilers, were inevitably more suited to the mentality of youthful readers. Coming from the ranks of ordinary people themselves, with no Ascendancy connections, or dependence on government subsidy, the compilers did not feel called upon to implement any policy involving inculcation of subordination or unity of empire, other than the principles which Christianity demanded.

In 1879 the Intermediate Education (Ireland) Act was introduced, outlining a three-year course with no compulsory subjects. Pupils were allowed to pass if they were in school for at least 12 months and were able to satisfy the examiners. The Christian Brothers achieved remarkable results. In the first year of the exams six boys passed the examination. In 1883 O'Connell Schools were judged the best in Ireland in algebra, chemistry, book-keeping and music. By 1888, 130 boys from the school had passed and were accredited with thirteen exhibitions, two medals and ten book prizes. The following year 82 boys passed Irish, which was the highest number in any school in the country. Many of these became clerks in the GPO, the Board of Works, Hibernian Bank, the Castle or solicitors' offices.

A survey of the 1916 Rebellion shows that O'Connell Schools were the most highly represented among the Volunteers. One hundred and twenty five past pupils were involved in the Rising, compared with thirty each from Westland Row and Synge Street, and twenty four from Marino. Belvedere College, a short distance from Richmond Street, produced only five Volunteers. The pupils of the Christian Brothers were socialised into nationalist values. In 1919, the first Dail had many famous past CBS boys including de Valera, Griffith, O'Higgins, Brugha and twenty other past pupils. The Brothers themselves were prevented from becoming involved but had an indirect influence, and it is notable that not one member of the congregation was killed or arrested by the military or RIC during the entire Anglo-Irish war. (see Appendix 1)

Feinaiglian Institute

Education in Ballybough was not confined to the religious congregations. Pater Gregorius Feinaigle was a former Cistercian. He settled in Karlsruhe, Germany, where he supplemented his pension by giving lectures on the Art of Memory. He compiled for sale an explanatory pamphlet on his system in 1804. Two years later, accompanied by an interpreter, he appeared in Paris where he delivered a series of lectures on what he called *"a new system of mnemonics and methodics"*. The system worked on the principle of the association of ideas as an aid to natural memory.

He visited London in 1811 and gave a display at the Royal Institute. The demonstration was repeated in several British cities and he was placed on the teaching staff of the Benedictine College at Amplefort. This was extensively advertised when he came to take up residence in Dublin in 1813. He gave public experiments of his new system of mnemonics in Dublin to aid

Feinaiglian Institute, Aldborough House

charitable organisations. He also delivered a series of lectures, including two for the Royal Dublin Society as well as giving private lessons for children.

Feinaiglianism appeared to have become a popular craze in Dublin. Several who attended his lectures desired to put his system of instruction into practice but it was almost impossible to find a school which would assist. It was proposed to raise a sum of money by subscription to establish an institution. The Committee of Proprietors acquired two contiguous and most eligible houses at Clonliffe for a Feinaiglian Institute.

It was stated that pupils so educated would be qualified for the University and would pass with ease. If a degree were not required then the student would appear in Society with the information of a gentleman. The first thirty boarders paid 60 guineas per annum and the first thirty day scholars paid 15 guineas. Prices rose for further pupils. A public examination was to be held at the Institute to manifest to the public the progress made by the pupils.

The two houses taken at Clonliffe were inadequate for the accommodation of the considerable number of students who enrolled. Aldborough House was at this time unoccupied. Feinaigle advanced the sum of £4,800 towards the purchase of the magnificent building and a sum of £15,000 was expended in rendering the mansion one of the most complete and splendid establishments of its kind in Europe. A large hall and chapel were added as wings to the original building in addition to a suite of classrooms as a distinct building. Feinaigle changed the name of Aldborough House to The Luxembourg.

The new institution proved to be a great success. The pupils were examined as promised and the achievements of the Professor and his staff were highly praised. A seminar for the education of females was opened at Clonliffe in March 1814. The Feinaiglian or The Luxembourg became one of the most successful Protestant secondary schools in Ireland. Each year students from there entered Trinity College.

Feinaigle had married a widow who had two sons but he died suddenly on 24 December 1819[2]. At the time of his death Feinaiglian schools had been established in other towns in Ireland. Mrs. Feinaigle continued as matron in the school and its success continued under a new master, John Hawkesworth[3]. In succession to Hawkesworth it was unfortunate for the Institute that the Committee of Management selected Feinaigle's step-son T. Dames Gregg[4], who had finished a course in Divinity in Dublin University. Apart from the reluctance of parents to board their children in a rapidly deteriorating part of the metropolis, some were further deterred by the new master's determination to discard the accepted classical authors and to provide education in Greek

2. Interview with Dr. Colin Stray, Wolfson College, Cambridge
3. ibid
4. ibid

and Latin solely through the study of the Scriptures in these languages. He also jeopardised the Institution by his identification with a virulent religious controversy. An old Feinaiglian, writing in 1874 recorded that *"it was the folly of Tresham Gregg and not the want of success prostrated the school. He was made headmaster and because he could not carry out a crochet of his he threw up his position and so a great school fell"*. Within ten years of the death of Feinaigle, the school had closed down.

Clonliffe School

In 1842 the Commissioners of Education received an application asking them to take a new school into consideration. It had been open for three months and was described as *"standing upon part of the estate of the Roman Catholic College of All Hallows, but ... being quite distinct from and otherwise unconnected with the college"*.

It was apparently built of mud, limestone and stone and had a thatched roof and contained one room. The applicant also stated that *"I have not ... with a case this long time more deserving the patronage of the Board than the present, there being no National School near this for 2.5 miles, leaving the facilities of Glasnevin, ... Drumcondra, Ballybough Bridge and North Strand quite destitute of the means of education"*.

The teacher was a 19-year-old John Kavanagh who had a Certificate of Training. The weekly attendance was 98 even though 168 pupils were registered. These were mainly the sons of labourers and farmers from the area. The school was obviously overcrowded. Ages ranged from 5-14 years and pupils paid 1d per week. Twenty-three of the children were exempt from paying fees. The school opened for five hours per day, during which they had one hour of religious education, and six days a week. The texts used were the National School Book 1st, 2nd and 3rd Lesson Books and the General Lesson was hung on the wall. It was multi-denominational and received no aid. The school was for boys only and remained open for about 40 years.

Other Schools

In the Second Report of the Commissioners of Irish Education Inquiry (1826) there are records for the existence of both an orphan house and day school at North William Street, under the care of Mary Westman, a Catholic. The school was both free and part paying, depending on individual circumstances. It was situated in a room attached to the convent and 126 girls were enrolled. The school was affiliated to the Irish Sisters of Charity and pupils were clothed, fed, lodged and, when ready, apprenticed out. This school received monies from an annual charity sermon.

In the same report Henry Callaghan was master of a day and evening school in Spring Garden Street. The day school was fee paying varying between 6s 6d and 22s 9d per quarter. It was held on the ground floor of a private house with around 80 pupils in attendance. The evening school was free and the master had the use of the school room gratis in return for providing a day school. It was held in two rooms of a private house and had 80 pupils. It too was connected with the religious order in North William Street convent and received subscriptions from them.

Another school existed at 2 North Strand and was run by Anne Williams where pupils paid 3d per week. It was held in a small back parlour of a private house and had 20 children enrolled, of whom 19 were Catholic. The majority of pupils were female with only 4 boys in attendance.

Two other schools were located at Aldborough Court and these were organised by Catholics. Mr. Corrigan was master to 16 boys and 4 girls in 1826. The school was held in a small room but no further information can be found. At No. 3 Terence Colgan held a school where students paid a small fee. The school was located in the front parlour of a private house and had 20 boys in attendance, 4 of whom were Protestant.

There were five other known schools in the area according to the 1826 report. At No. 4-5 Russell Place Mr. & Mrs. Kirschoffer ran a fee-paying school. There was a charge of 20 guineas per annum for day students and 56 guineas for boarders. The school was located in a private house and was in very good condition. Twenty male students were enrolled there at this time.

Madame Picorgny had a school in a private house at Russell Street where pupils paid between 2-4 guineas per annum. The Protestant and Catholic Returns suggest that there were between 13-16 pupils in attendance.

Rev. Joseph Hutton had a school at 28 Summerhill where day students paid 12 guineas per annum and boarders paid 60 guineas. The school was located in a private house with 16 Protestant boys enrolled.

Rev. John Fea had another school in a private house at 10 Summerhill and students paid 2.5 guineas per quarter. Three Catholics attended and 17 Protestants of whom all were male.

Arabella Kelly was mistress of a fee paying school (2-3d per week) in the back upper room of a private house with 20 pupils, one of whom was Catholic.

When the census material for both 1901 and 1911 was examined, it showed that the literacy rate for the area was in the region of 95%.

Chapter 7

INDUSTRY

One of the principal reasons for the siting of a port for Dublin on the north side of the city was its location in relation to the English city and harbour of Liverpool. Much infrastructure was needed to ensure its growth and continuity. Census data from 1911 show that one-fifth of the male population were employed as general labourers, without any real association to a particular industry or organisation. They literally went where work was available. This however was an abnormally high number, and led to a high unemployment level because much of the work by its nature was seasonal, with workers depending quite often on the docks and railway for their subsistence. As the types of industry changed, so too did the skills required to meet the new demands of the industrial revolution, and many skilled craftsmen found themselves redundant, without any hope of future employment in their traditional trades. This unreliability of both steady work and income led to many social problems.

By 1800 Dublin had a population of about 200,000. With the departure of a large number of Dublin's gentry, a decline in the long established luxury goods industries was soon felt. However, the city had seen an evolution of new and successful industries, many of which were based in the Ballybough area, such as printing, brewing, carriage-making and engineering. The area around the docks became a focal point for the latter. As many of the new enterprises relied on imported materials, the newly reclaimed sloblands and their surrounds were much in demand as suitable locations for factories. Dublin Whiskey Distillery Company (DWD) and Dublin & Wicklow Manure Company, along with many others, opened facilities in Ballybough which was within walking distance of the port.

The port and surrounding areas were expanding with the addition of deep sea berths and an extension to the North Wall. The success of the port was further insured with the arrival of the railways, many of which had termini in Dublin and individual lines running as far as the docks. By the end the century even the boom in this sector was failing. Wages for labourers were low and added to the already appalling social conditions that prevailed throughout the city.

Distilling

Dublin Whiskey Distillery Company, Distillery Road

The Irish distilling industry was both very lucrative and productive in the nineteenth century with a growing export trade. By 1818 there were nine distilleries in Dublin. The Dublin Whiskey Distillery Company (DWD), founded in 1871, was located in Ballybough. It initially had a limited number of shareholders, with shares costing £500 each. Two of the original subscribers were W.G. Craig and R. Gardner, both accountants.[1] The company built a large plant at Jones's Road in 1872, and by the following year the distillery was in full production.

Initially the company was very successful, and large extensions were made to the building, including bonded stores and offices, covering between six and seven acres. It employed about 100 people, and within ten years its annual output was 500,000 proof gallons. This was mainly due to its distinguished quality machinery which guaranteed excellent production. The distillery also possessed a large hydraulic pump, reputed to be the most powerful in Ireland, which had been imported from Messrs. Pearn & Co., Manchester, and was capable of raising 1000 gallons of water per minute. It worked on the old "pot-still" principle. The driving machinery was an extremely powerful construction occupying an engine-house adjoining a huge chimney stack. These engines and machinery were manufactured and supplied by iron founders and engineers Messrs. Victor Coates and Co. of the Lagan Foundry and Prince's Dock Works, Belfast. It was clear that the DWD had ended the era of the family-owned and run distilling business in Dublin, one which had flourished during the previous century. The DWD advertised its product as "the finest whiskey in the world". As well as supplying an Irish market, the company exported to America, the remote islands south of the equator, and Great Britain.

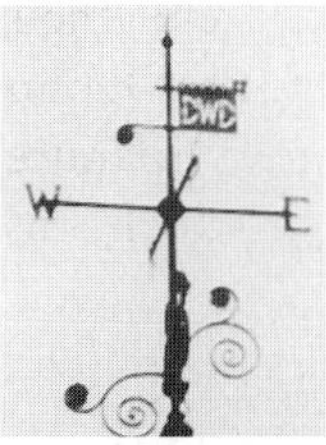

DWD weather-vane

In 1889 the DWD merged with Roe's distillery of Thomas Street, the firm responsible for the restoration of Christchurch Cathedral, and William Jameson's of

1. A. MacLoughlin – A guide to historic Dublin. 1979. p.89

Marrowbone Lane.[2] The Jones's Road distillery, so called because the original entrance to the distillery had been on Jones's Road, remained in operation until the late 1920s and the thoroughfare leading from its premises to Clonliffe Road is still named Distillery Road.

Brewing

Alexander Findlater and partners established a brewery in Russell Street and Portland Street in 1852. It consisted of three acres, one rood and seven perches and had previously been an orchard. Alexander had commenced business in 1823 as a grocer and wine merchant, and later funded the building of a Presbyterian Church at the Rotunda. He went on to found the Dublin Electricity Light Company with William Martin Murphy of the *Irish Independent* newspaper group. The quality of the stout and porter produced made it a household name. It was consumed throughout Ireland and shipped to England, Malta, Cyprus and Gibraltar. The name *"Mountjoy Brewery"* was suggested by John Lloyd Blood, one of the oldest partners in the firm, owing to its proximity to the fashionable Mountjoy Square.

The brewery consisted of many buildings, including maltings, vat-houses and cooperages, and was enclosed by a wall. The Royal Canal bounded the premises to the north. The building was made from dressed granite, limestone and ashlar. Water for the processes involved in brewing came from the Vartry Scheme, the two canals, and a well which was over 70 feet in depth.

Findlaters were the first brewers in Dublin to use Morton's horizontal refrigerators which were capable of cooling 40 barrels per hour. The brewery produced on average 100,000 barrels per annum, and had a staff of approximately 120 people. There were five houses on the estate, occupied by the head brewer, assistant brewer, head maltser, head stableman and gatekeeper.

Pottery

The first reference to the craft of fine pottery-making in the Ballybough area is found in an advertisement from the Dublin Daily Advertiser, dated 5 February 1737. According to this, the factory was situated at the World's End, near the ship buildings on the North Strand, and is referred to as a *"white pot house"*. The World's End was so called due to its proximity to the North Lotts, an area which had not yet been reclaimed. It produced blue and white earthenware as good as any imported from Britain. The proprietor was John Chambers, who petitioned parliament for assistance to carry out his pottery works, stating that he had brought workmen from abroad and had erected a kiln to bake and burn earthenware.

In 1747 ownership changed and John Crisp became the new proprietor. It

2. Irish Times, 6 May, 1889

was during this period that the industry went into a decline, alarming some sections of Dublin society. Shortly afterwards, Captain Henry Delamain, a former Captain in the army of the Prince of Saxe Gotha's service took over the site. He was an experienced man in the art of pottery making and made no attempts to conceal his ambitions for the industry. In November 1753, due to the failure of the industry in the city, Delamain forwarded a petition to the House of Commons for finance to refurbish his pottery factory. Delamain wished to offer pottery to the nation, and a week later was granted £1,000.[3]

By 1754 the earthenware factory on the Strand was complete and accommodated 200-300 people. It was known as Delamain Pottery. Workhouses, kilns and a mill to grind flint and metals were part of the factory's make-up. Delamain hired experienced staff to train school-boy apprentices, numbering 25 per year, and discharged debts affecting the old machinery. He also pursued the art of printing the earthenware with unprecedented beauty. There are some references to his work, such as a letter by Mrs. Delany who speaks of purchasing a set of earthenware and baskets for the Duchess of Portland at the World's End in 1750. Delamain's success was short-lived due to his death on 10 January 1757. Within twenty years the industry had ceased to exist.[4]

Glass Industry

A Royal Proclamation of James I in 1615 prohibited the use of wood as fuel for the glass industry thereby influencing the future locations of any new factories. Many were sited near colliers to ensure a coal supply, or near water to enable easy access for transportation and importation of materials.

The Irish glass industry dates from the second half of the seventeenth century, but the earliest reference to the industry in Dublin dates from 1690s when a round glass house was established on Mary's Lane by Captain Philip Roche, himself a displaced Catholic landowner who had gone into exile after the Treaty of Limerick in 1691. While on the Continent he learned the skills of crystal glass, and on his return to Dublin he established himself as a manufacturer. He availed of the help of itinerant traders who successfully promoted his products. When he died he left a legacy to each of his traders.[5]

The industry had a major setback in 1746 when the export of Irish glass was prohibited. The North Wall glass house was set up the following year, located close to the present Custom House. The first bottles to be blown here were in 1748, an event recorded by *Exshaw's Magazine*. This factory had a bottle-making section as well as a glass house, dwelling house and office. It had an unfortunate history as it suffered from recurrent flooding and in 1748 it

3. Mrs. A.M. Fraser (1951) – Some early Dublin potters. DHR Vol. 12. p.49
4. C. Maxwell – Dublin under the Georges. 1937. p.220
5. ibid p.219

went on fire. The *Dublin Courant* for July 16-19 records *"Sunday, about 10.00 at night, a fire broke out in one of the funnels at the glass house lately erected on the North Strand which consumed the roof and all the materials; and as the undertaking of making glass bottles in the Kingdom must tend greatly to the advantage of it, so does the unhappy accident add more to the loss of the public, as it does in a particular manner to the proprietors, whose spirit in carrying on so useful a trade makes their misfortune the more to be regretted"*. By 1754 the factory was up for sale. The following notice appeared in the *Dublin Journal "To be sold the three lots, part of the lots called foot lots numbers 1, 2 and 3, bounded to the south by the North Wall, on the East by foot lot number 4, on the north by Mayor Street and on the west by the City Ground, on which are built a glass house, with dwelling house and offices, let on a term of 99 years from March 25 1747"*. It was re-advertised in 1760 and it is not known if it had been sold during the intervening years. In 1768 it is stated that Henry Roche, a stone cutter, took over the large premises.

After 1786 restrictions to the trade were removed and there was a resurgence in the industry. John Chebsey and Partners opened a white flint glass house at Ballybough on what had been the iron foundry of Messrs. Carrothers and Wilson. It was described as *"opulent and successful"* in the *Dublin Chronicle* of 4 October 1787. Flint glass was pure and lustrous and was originally made with flint. The process had been invented in 1674 by George Ravenscroft. The Ballybough factory covered about two acres and had two fronts, one of which opened onto Annesley Bridge, and the other on the North Strand in the area today known as Poplar Row. The Custom House announced in 1788 a record exportation of flint glass to Cadiz by the Chebsey factory. The company opened a separate warehouse in Jervis Street to keep an extensive assortment of flint glass made at their new works *"Venice"* on the North Wall, which was known for excellence and elegance equal to any imports. They did, however, confine themselves to the wholesale trade.

This excellence received a further boost in 1788 when the Lord Lieutenant and Marchioness of Rockingham went there to order a set of magnificent lustres for St. Patrick's Hall and the new rooms of the Castle. The value of the glass made there was £1,996 in 1787, and reached a peak of £7,000 in 1791. However in 1798, Thomas Chebsey died and the partnership was dissolved. *The Hibernian Journal* of 24 October 1798 states *"partnership of the late Thomas Chebsey and Co. being dissolved by the death of Mr. Chebsey, the surviving partners and Mr. John Chebsey will dispose of the stock-in-trade, the warehouse at Jervis Street and the concerns at Ballybough Bridge. A large amount of every article in the flint glass trade, and a great quantity of green and flint phials, round and tincture bottles for apothecaries etc."* The Ballybough company seems to have been discontinued. A vitriol works was later erected on the site.

John Chebsey is recorded as having had an involvement with a glass house in Newry in 1880 and the proprietor of the Dublin Glass Warehouse in 1822 was a Peter Chebsey who had his premises on Sackville St.[6]

Locals benefited from the broken glass produced by the company, as they collected it and sold it to other glasshouses. By the end of the eighteenth century, the glass industry was thriving in Dublin, but it went into a decline after 1825 with the imposition of excise duties on Irish produced glass – £10-12 on every 1000 lbs. In the early 1800s another glass house is recorded, located on the East Wall not far from Annesley Bridge, known as Fort Crystal. There were also two other bottle companies, The Glass Bottle Co. and Dublin Glass Bottle Co., the latter being one of three companies who exhibited at the Cork Exhibition of 1883.

Charles Mulvany and Co. are stated to have had a glass house in the vicinity of the North Strand. He went bankrupt in 1818 and sold his interests in several lots, numbers 85, 86, 87, 88 and 103, which amounted to over thirteen acres and was to be held on terms of 999 years from September 1815. Mulvany had invested heavily in the erection of extensive glasshouses and other buildings. By 1820 he had established another glass house in Ringsend, and in 1833 he is recorded as having been in partnership with Edward Simmons Irwin with premises located between Marlborough Green and the Strand.[7]

By the end of the nineteenth century, the flint glass industry was disappearing. A report of the Select Committee on Industries in Ireland stated that this was due to the importation of cheap glass, and also the want of sufficient commercial enterprise on the part of Irish industry, such as enabled their British counterparts to keep pace with foreign manufacturers.

Iron Works

Messrs. Carrothers and Wilson established an iron works around 1785, but by the following year it was advertised for sale and removed to Thomas Street. Another iron foundry is mentioned in the area two years later, and is said to have made a wide range of goods including spades, shovels, agricultural implements and kitchen utensils, equal in quality to their imported counterparts.[8] The Carrothers & Wilson site was taken over by the glass-makers, Chebsey & Co., and eventually became home to McKenny's vitriol works.

Vitriol Works

Dublin had few chemical industries in the 1800s, and these were mainly involved in the manufacture of artificial manures. The vitriol works in

6. M.S.D. Westropp (1911) – Glass making in Ireland. PRIA Vol. xxix. Section 3 No. C. p.34-58
7. M.S.D. Westropp – A history of Irish glass-making in Ireland from the sixteenth century. 1978. p.55
8. Weston St. John Joyce – The neighbourhood of Dublin. 1921. p.246

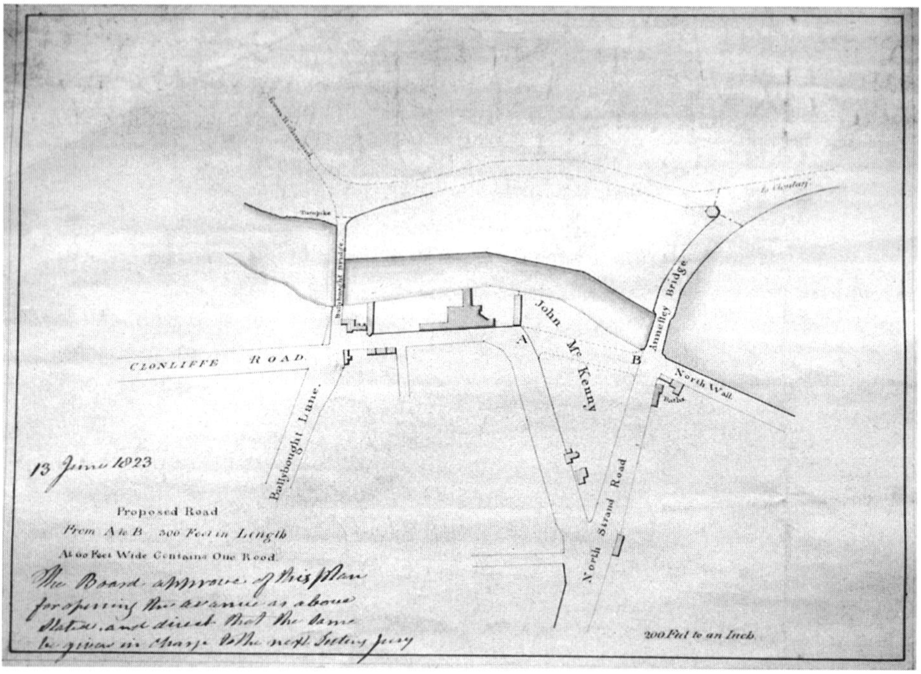

Map showing location of Vitriol Works, 1823. Courtesy of Dublin City Archives

Ballybough was located along Poplar Row and produced manures and bleaching liquids. The office of the proprietor, John McKenny, was located in Beresford Place. In 1878 the Dublin & Wicklow Manure Company is recorded as having had a factory on Poplar Row and may in fact have been the occupier of the old vitriol works. Its chairman and manager was M. MacGregor. The factory produced artificial manures and sulphuric acid as well as grinding phosphates and mixing manures. It was said to be within easy reach of the Clontarf tram-cars.[9]

John McKenny's Vitriol Works. Courtesy of Jimmy Wren

Coach Building

The firm of John Hutton & Sons, coach builders, was founded in 1799 by John Hutton at Parnell Street. He engaged the services of Rudolph Ackerman, the inventor

9. Guide to the city and county of Dublin. 1848. p.95

of movable carriage axles and promoter of acquataints and lithographic colour prints, to design a series of carriages for him. There was much attention to detail, and soon the carriages were in great demand. They are well depicted in Malton's views of Dublin. Hutton was commissioned by the Irish Post Office in 1788 to make coaches for delivering mail, which until then had been delivered by mounted postmen. He built and delivered two coaches within three months and because of this, the new mail service came into operation ahead of schedule. In 1789 Hutton moved the business to Summerhill and after the Act of Union, with many of the more affluent members of society moving to London, the business continued to prosper. Other members of the family soon became involved and brought new and innovative ideas with them. Shortly afterwards, Daniel O'Connell made his triumphal entry into Dublin in a chariot coach built by Huttons.[10]

The Famine had an adverse affect on the business, as the Irish gentry could not buy carriages whilst people were starving, and also because the Poor Law rates had been steeply increased. In times of distress, the carriage was seen as a luxury item and therefore the industry suffered.

Huttons exhibited at the Great Exhibition of 1851 in Hyde Park, London, and in the same year the factory in Dublin was destroyed by fire. The Lord Mayor's coach was rescued, however, and the factory was back in production within a year. The Irish State Coach was shown at the Dublin International Exhibition in 1853. This coach was later destroyed by another fire while awaiting refurbishment in London.

Approximately 180 men were employed by Huttons, as well as a number of women who made the carriage linings. The labourers employed in the yard received 8 shillings per week whilst the highest wage was £3 per week. The company was hit by several disputes over the years, but not one was in relation to working conditions or wages. Thomas Hutton, son of the founder, died in 1865 at the age of 76.[11]

By the turn of the century, the motor car had been developed and this heralded a new era for the company. At the 1901 R.D.S. show, 26 cars were

10. J. Cooke – Ireland's premier coachbuilders. p.4
11. ibid p.31

shown, 20 of which were supplied by Huttons.[12] They continued to make the more traditional carriages, with the outside or jaunting car being a speciality. Prince Henry of Russia purchased one of the cars in 1902. By 1908 the trade of coach building was obviously in decline due to the advent and availability of the bicycle and motor car. The firm was hit by a strike in 1913 but it was settled within six weeks. This was a period of great unrest, both in Dublin and the remainder of the country. After the 1916 Rising some family members took photographs of the destruction of the city and they also assisted with humanitarian aid for soldiers returning from the World War. They helped transport them to convalescent homes and brought many on day trips to the country.

Huttons were offered the Ford franchise for the whole of the United Kingdom, but they declined the offer in deference to Daimler. In 1925 the company had to go into voluntary liquidation as it was unable to sustain itself. The premises was sold to the Dublin United Tramway Company as a garage and works, and so ended another era in the industrial history of Dublin.

Colour Printing Works

Messers. James Walker & Co. established a colour printing works on Jones's Road. The practical adoption of lithography for colour works only commenced in 1865 with the invention of the *"Huguet"* lithographic machine, and Walkers were amongst the first colour printers who introduced lithographic machines in the British Isles. Lithography enabled art to be reproduced for the general public and also involved more creativity in designs, compared with older systems. The firm in fact pioneered this work in Ireland.[13]

TRANSPORT

The first genuine attempts were made to improve the communications network in Ireland during the eighteenth century. This was to ensure both the economic and industrial development of the country. The first major undertaking was the building of a canal system which was later replaced in importance by the railways. The roadways were also upgraded as it was imperative to have an effective infrastructure to deal with growing commercial activities and suburban growth.

Canals

From as early as 1498, the facilities for inland navigation in Ireland were well known and statutes were already in place to encourage such schemes.[14] In 1715 an act was passed which allowed for the linking of the major rivers of

12. ibid p.41
13. British Association Handbook to the Dublin district. 1908. p.420
14. J. Warburton, Rev. J. Whitelaw, Rev. R. Walsh – History of the city of Dublin. Vol. 2. 1818. p.1223

Ireland via a series of canals.

In 1755 the Corporation was awarded £20,000 for the development of a canal from Dublin to Shannon, and two proposals were submitted for consideration. After extensive debate the route travelling south of Dublin to the Shannon was chosen, i.e. the Grand Canal. The northern route, or the Royal Canal *"offered a more level ground, had good water supplies, was through firm ground, had a shorter course and fewer locks and provided a better entry port into the Shannon"*.[15] It was not heard of again until 1789, when petitions were made to the Irish parliament for aid to construct a second canal.

Lock-keeper's cottage, North Strand

The Royal Canal was not without its opponents, particularly some of those involved with the Grand Canal, who saw the new scheme as a threat. The biggest obstacle was the route chosen for the canal. The Grand Canal Company feared the new water course ran too close to their territory but was aware that *"... It could not be carried further northward, the grounds would not admit it, being placed on the very verge of the great valley in which the Finglas River runs commencing at Ballybough Bridge northward of Castleknock ... the Royal Canal, thus hemmed in on the northside by this very long ridge of high ground, is a matter of public notoriety, and therefore it could not be placed further northward from the Grand Canal"*.[16] In fact their greatest fear was loss of revenue from the competition.

Construction of the canal began in 1790. Despite the excitement and favourable reports, the work on the first stage of the canal was of a very poor standard. The engineer in charge, Richard Evans, appointed supervisors to carry out the work, as he spent most of his time working on the Boyne Navigation in Meath. The supervisors failed to identify problems with the bridges and locks early enough for them to be rectified, and several had to be demolished and rebuilt, while others needed extensive work to correct faults. Newcomen Bridge on the Summerhill Road collapsed when it was almost complete because of insufficient bonding of the stone work, and four workmen were killed in the incident. [17]

Despite showing some initial success and profit, the decline of the Royal

15. R. Delaney – Ireland's Royal Canal. 1992. p.21-22
16. An account of the rise and progress of the Royal Canal. 1797. p.13
17. Peter Clarke –The Royal Canal, the complete story. 1992. p.40

Canal Company was already imminent, with the development and introduction of the railways.

On 21 July 1845, Royal consent was given to the Midland Great Western Railway Company (MGWR) to purchase the Royal Canal Company, on condition that water and land rights were respected, the officers and staff were retained, the canal was properly maintained under a board of supervision, and that no increases in tolls or rates would be imposed without the consent of the supervising board. The majority of lock-keepers were retained on smaller wages; other canal workers were given jobs with the railway.

The condition of the canal declined considerably following the termination of the passenger service in 1849. The Royal Canal was officially closed to navigation on 6 April 1961.

Railways

The first railway route to be proposed in Ireland, in 1831, was the Dublin and Kingstown (Dun Laoghaire) line. The railway went north in 1844 with the opening of the Dublin and Drogheda line. This later became the Great Northern Railway (GNR). From Amiens Street the GNR ran north along the coast up to the North Strand. The line crossed over Sheriff Street on a cast-iron Doric colonnade. Due to the high level of the tracks, the line was carried over seventy-five arches between Amiens Street and the Royal Canal. The latter was crossed by a single-span lattice girder bridge. In 1864, two piers were placed to give the bridge added support. It was totally refurbished fifty years later. Timetable evidence shows the route from Amiens Street, like its southside counterpart, handled significant amounts of commuter traffic. Between 24 May and 31 December of its first year, 402,414 passengers travelled the route with receipts reaching a value of £19,625 18s 9d. The suburban growth of the city at this time was in the directions served by the routes south and north from the city, especially along the coast.

By the 1850s, the major railway routes to enter the city were in place, with each running to separate and unconnected termini. Although there were varied efforts by planners towards a single connecting scheme, these met with little success. The need for inter-terminus connec-

Charleville Mall from Clarke's Bridge

tions, and more importantly the desire for access to Dublin Port at the North Wall, were the central issues that brought the railways to Ballybough. The MGWR, which ran west from Broadstone Station, Phibsboro, was the first company to make a practical move. It wanted to have access to the shipping berths on the river. The railway's Liffey branch opened in 1864. It left the main line near Glasnevin and followed the Royal Canal through Drumcondra and Ballybough to the North Wall, where the large freight yards were laid out. The line was used mainly for carrying cattle which had to be transported in covered and ventilated wagons, thereby increasing the railway company's expenses.

The following letter appeared in the Corporation Reports of June 15th 1861:

> Office 45 Lower Gloucester Street
> Dublin
>
> To Rt. Hon. the Lord Mayor & Corporation of Dublin
>
> *"As contractors for the construction of the Liffey Branch Railway we beg leave to say that it is necessary for the purposes of our contract to construct a bridge under the present Newcomen or Clontarf Public Road and to excavate some 20 feet under the present road level ... the traffic at this place is very considerable more particularly the omnibus and goods traffic, the only means we can adopt to partially preserve the traffic is by erecting a temporary bridge under half the width of the present road, whilst building half the width of the permanent bridge, this plan, would be attended with considerable inconvenience and danger to the public to avoid which, we would respectfully ask you to direct the present traffic round by Summerhill for the space of one month from the receipt of order, this would avoid all chances of collisions or accidents and enable us to build the whole width of the Bridge at once and consequently occupy less time in construction.*
>
> We remain my Lord & Gentlemen
> Your obedient servants
> Moore Brothers

This was put to the meeting and carried, provided a proper footway be erected under the control of the committee.

In the 1870s, the biggest railway company in Ireland was the Great Southern and Western Railway (GS&WR), whose terminus was at Kingsbridge (Heuston Station). It too was a long distance from the port. As a railway through Dublin would have been too expensive and difficult to undertake, it proposed to build a line around the city to connect with the MGWR's Liffey

Railway bridge on the Ballybough Road, dated 1898

branch, giving it that vital link to the quays. The company raised a substantial amount of money for the project, but the greater part of the cost was contributed by the London and North Western Railway (L&NWR) as it also needed access to the port. The MGWR was in favour of the project as it would bring in much needed toll payments. Parliamentary approval was received and the new line opened for traffic in 1877. During the 1870s and 1880s, the railway line along the Royal Canal, passing through Ballybough, was being used by the Great Southern & Western Railway, the Midland Great Western Railway and the London & North Western Railway. The trains brought freight and passengers to the port, but no local passenger trains were run on the line.

In 1884 an Act was passed for the City of Dublin Junction Railways (CDJR) to connect Westland Row with Amiens Street. The two stations were linked in 1890 by a high-level bridge over the Liffey, after which the line continued to Newcomen Bridge Junction and connected with the MGWR's Liffey branch, providing the link between lines entering the city from the south, north and west. Trouble often flared at this junction, however, as relations between companies were not good and disputes arose over the exchange of traffic. All the major railway companies had stations at the North Wall. The Great Northern Railway, in particular, influenced the development of the area, affecting the conditions of the land reclamation to make way for new lines of railway and a number of railway junctions.

In 1894 Parliament sanctioned the Drumcondra and North Dublin Link Railway to run between Glasnevin and the North Wall. The promoters of this line intended it as a suburban route with stations at Glasnevin and Drumcondra. They hoped to gain financial assistance from the GS&WR, which would naturally have an interest in the venture, as their trains had to run over two miles of the MGWR's Liffey branch through Ballybough to the docks, for which privilege they had to pay tolls. The link railway was transferred to the jurisdiction of the GS&WR and construction began in 1897. The GS&WR now possessed its own tracks all the way between Islandbridge

The No. 31 tram at Howth. Courtesy of the Allen Library

and North Wall. The line passed through Ballybough, just north of the Liffey branch, and was carried over Ballybough Road on a cast iron bridge. In 1906 a curve from North Strand junction to Amiens Street was added to the link-line, giving connection to the port at Dun Laoghaire via the Loop-Line to Westland Row. The stations at Glasnevin and Drumcondra had a local train service but they failed to attract substantial amounts of passengers and both the stations and services were soon abandoned. The station at Drumcondra reopened in 1998 as part of a greater plan to encourage more people to use public transport which would in turn alleviate the problems being caused by the number of private cars entering the city each day.

Many local people were employed by the railways and the port in various positions, but predominantly as casual labourers. Over 19% were employed in public transport in 1901 and 16% in 1911. The wages of engine drivers and other skilled workers were comparable with their British counterparts but the unskilled labourers were not so fortunate. Many were provided with housing, as were tram workers, but in 1913 many were involved in what later became known as the Lock-Out.

Tramways

Prior to the introduction of other forms of transport, many people travelled as fare-paying passengers on private coaches. In 1824 the stage coach which travelled between Dublin and Howth had to have an armed escort as it travelled through Ballybough. The fare for this trip was 10s.[18]

18. Jim Kilroy – Howth and her trams. 1986. p.8

In 1870, Barrington and Jeffars proposed the construction of tram lines to various parts of the city, including Rathmines, Donnybrook, Clontarf etc. They received parliamentary approval in 1871, with the first tram going to Rathmines the following year. The fare for this journey was 3d but the demand for its services was limited and the route to Clontarf was described as disappointing.

The partnership of Barrington and Jeffars was dissolved with Jeffars keeping control of the company. His former partner established a rival company in 1875 which also received parliamentary approval. The new tram company operated to several areas, including Drumcondra. They did not have conductors, thereby enabling a reduction in fares. A third company, the Dublin Central Tram Company, was also established, and by 1880 all of these had amalgamated into the Dublin United Tramways Company under the directorship of William Martin Murphy, a prominent figure in the 1913 Lock-Out.

The new company serviced Drumcondra every twenty minutes and Clontarf every fifteen minutes. In general trams tended to follow, rather than institute, housing developments, with the exception of Drumcondra, mainly because one of the directors of the DUTC, James Lombard, was also a Commissioner of the Drumcondra Township.

The trams failed to confer equality on the labouring classes who represented a significant percentage of Dublin's population. Maurice Brookes, a Dublin employer and MP stated in 1878 that the trams were *"proving a great convenience to passengers of the genteel and well to do class"*. There was only one car in operation before 7 a.m. and one after 6 p.m., which would have suited neither the working hours nor the sheer number of labourers. The fare of 1d per mile was far too expensive and many of the routes went only to middle class areas. The only real time that the working classes used the service was on Sundays for outings to places such as the Phoenix Park. Conventional signs were used to show which route the tram was taking. The Ballybough and Parkgate route was shown as two blue diamonds with horizontal red lines. One of the DUTC trams was specially built with a high clearance to get through the flooded roads to Clontarf and was known as the "submarine".

The advent of the private motor car and other more modern and sophisticated forms of public transport ultimately led to the demise of the tram system.

Chapter 8

BALLYBOUGH FEATURES

Ballybough, like every other place, has its own unique personality and history which can be seen both through its physical architecture and its placenames. Its most famous landmark is Croke Park but the area has many other features which are less well known. It has also been both birthplace and home to some of Ireland's most famous children including authors and poets, adventurers, saints, revolutionaries and politicians who are forever immortalised in its street names.

ARCHITECTURE

Architecture in Ballybough is a hybrid of many styles and formats, from the classic Georgian houses of Ballybough Road and Clonliffe to the post-modern Corporation flats of Poplar Row. It encompasses all of the architectural forms and styles that Dublin has been subject to over the past three hundred years.

Bridges

The first important architectural structure to be erected in the area was Ballybough Bridge. It is made up of five plain low arches, and Harris records its construction in 1313 by John Decer and its destruction later the same year by a flood. It was rebuilt in 1488 and is mentioned in the Riding of the Franchises. Silken Thomas was engaged in a skirmish here during his ill-fated rebellion in 1534-35. It was described in 1858 as an ancient bridge of five rude unornamented arches and was one of the locations for toll collection on the north side of the city. The bridge was replaced by a reinforced concrete structure in 1937. It was later widened and renamed Luke Kelly Bridge.

The construction of Annesley Bridge commenced shortly after the 1792 Act of parliament which allowed for such development on the Dublin-Malahide Road *"it will be necessary to build, erect and make a new bridge and causeway, eastward of Ballybough Bridge"*. D'Alton describes it as *"a handsome erection of granite consisting of three semicircular arches and exhibiting in the*

Annesley Bridge

centre of the parapet the Annesley Arms".[1] The bridge was widened in 1928 and the new bridge consists of a three span steel beam structure with a concrete deck supported on steel troughing and surfaced with asphalt and with concrete piers, and fascia beams and metal parapets.

Newcomen Bridge was built on the North Strand to allow access over the Royal Canal. It was constructed around 1781 and was named after Sir William Newcomen, a director of the Royal Company in 1791. Clarke's Bridge on the Ballybough Road was named after Edward Clarke, another director of the same company.

Houses

One of the first important houses to be constructed in the area was the Red House, in the grounds of the Holy Cross College, Clonliffe, and was formally known as Clonliffe House. It is thought to have been built some time in the late 1700s and its first inhabitant was theatre-owner Buck Jones. It derives its name from the type of brick used in its construction which came from Tyrone. This was quite rare and not often utilised during that period. The building is a three-storey early Georgian construction typical of the era. From its front elevation it has two elongated windows which allow light to the first floor drawing rooms, above which are three smaller windows which allow less light to the bedrooms and give a sense of symmetry to the house. In the centre is the front door which is a classic panelled door with fan light arch. It is approached via granite steps. Jones had many additions made to the house including a small theatre built onto one side in which he would entertain his friends. The interior is decorated in fine Italian stucco plaster. After Jones's death, the house was occupied by the Feinaiglian Institute. When this eventually failed, it became a depot for the Custom and Excise Police before finally being bought by Holy Cross College in 1860.

Aldborough House was probably one of the last great mansions to have been built before the Act of Union. It was at that time located at the eastern end of a ridge separating the rivers Tolka and Liffey, and faced the flat, almost totally undeveloped, North Lotts. The house design has been attributed to the famous architect William Chambers, but it is more probable that it was

1. J. de Courcey – The Liffey in Dublin. 1996. p.8

designed by Pool and Cash in 1780. The builders were Sproule and Meyers. It is a brick mansion with a fine granite facade and great bulging curves in the back and side. The surviving wing has Portland Stone trimmings and a sphinx in Coade Stone. The lions on the gateposts have suffered salt damage due to the location of the house so close to the bay, which was at one time much closer than it is today. Mason Gerard Stratford, Lord Aldborough, became Earl of Amiens in 1776, and lends his name to the nearby thoroughfare. It was constructed for his wife, with work commencing around 1792. She, however, did not like the structure and never resided there. The work cost £40,000 and took six years to complete. The house also had majestically laid out gardens. It was eventually let to Pater Von Feinaigle and he later opened his famous teaching institute there. He renamed it after the country of his origin *"Luxembourg"*. According to the *Irish Builder "when Aldborough House was taken for the Feinaiglian Institute, all the statuary (some of it not decent) that adorned the gardens of Luxembourg were put in a room which was locked up, and many were the queer tales afloat about what was looked upon as a Blue-beard's chamber ..."*

Red House, now part of Mater Dei College

Nottingham House, which was also known as the Red House, stood at the corner of

Edward Terrace, Ballybough Road

Nottingham Street and was described as a singular dwelling, about five storeys high, possessing two fronts, and preserving a tablet showing the date of its erection in the eighteenth century. Jasper Wheeler Rogers resided here for a time and held trials for his first locomotive on the Malahide-Howth Road. The house also bore the name Nottingham House Collegiate Institute, an educational facility run by Nugent William Spelman. The offices of the Health of Towns Improvement Institution were also situated here during the last century. It was demolished around 1890.

The oldest houses on Ballybough Road are those of Edward Terrace and date from 1815. Each has a middle upper floor window which has been deliberately bricked over, thereby exempting the owners from having to pay a Window Tax.

The Five Lamps

STREET ARCHITECTURE

Street architecture is to be found in almost every area and yet receives very little attention. Its features contain their own unique histories, adding to and enhancing their immediate surrounds, and their origin and evolution through time can provide interesting details into many aspects of an area's development. They include lamp standards, coal hole covers, paving stones and post boxes.

The Candle Light Law was passed in Dublin in 1616, with every fifth house now having to display a light during certain hours for the guidance of street users.[2] In 1697, public lighting was undertaken in certain areas by contract. The Commission for Paving, Lighting and Cleaning the streets of Dublin, known for a short time as the Paving Board, was established by an Act of Parliament in 1774 and was abolished under Dublin Improvement Act 1849, when its powers were transferred to Dublin Corporation.[3] The first piped gas lights were used in 1825, of which some remained in operation until 1957. In 1866 the three gas companies lighting the city were amalgamated into the Alliance & Consumer's Gas Company and made responsible for lighting the city as far as Kilmainham, Fairview &

Lamp standard at Annesley Bridge Road

2. D. O'Connell – The antique pavement. 1975. p.13
3. J. de Courcey – The Liffey in Dublin. 1996. p.293

Rathmines. The first electric lights were put into operation in 1892. The opening of the Pigeon House generating station in 1906 extended the use of electric lights to almost all major city roads. Today, the city is lit by over 32,000 lamps, with standards from every era since 1825.

The lamp standards at Annesley Bridge Road are replicas dating from the years 1940-1950. They are based on earlier designs, with the shamrock being more precisely placed and with much less floral decoration. Adherence to modern lighting regulations, such as many standards now having to strain their necks, has necessitated many changes to the original designs.

Many of the streets of Georgian Dublin also contain cast iron coal hole covers (manholes) of various designs. These were delivery chutes to coal cellars located under the pavements, varying in design and date from 1760-1830. A good example can be seen near No.7, North Richmond Street.

Coal hole cover, North Richmond Street

Setts are square block cobbles, made of both stone and wood, which developed from earlier types used between the sixteenth and nineteenth centuries. Unfortunately, many setts are now covered over by tarmac including those in the Newcomen Bridge area. There was a simple vernacular law of laying setts perpendicular to direction of traffic flow. This resulted in splendid examples of sett work at street junctions.

Granite, mostly from Wicklow, was the most common stone used for making pavements, and great skill was required, as is evident from the many eighteenth and nineteenth century (roughly 1730-1840) examples found throughout Dublin. When the drop between pavement and street was too great for a single stride, a double step was often introduced, sometimes forming a pedestal to the building above. This can be seen along Summerhill Parade.

The predecessor of the Botanic Gardens was situated in 1732 near Ballybough Bridge. By 1735 the gardens had been moved to Great Martin's Lane and later to Mecklenburgh Street, before moving in 1795 to their present home in Glasnevin.[4]

Charleville Mall Library

The Young Ireland League in 1893 proposed that libraries should be provided for the North Dock, Summerhill, Trinity Ward, Arran Quay and Phibsborough

4. D. Cosgrove – North Dublin and its environs. 1909. pp.32-33

areas. Within two years a sub-committee had been appointed to examine possible sites. North William Street was selected as a viable option and it was noted by the committee that this site was accessible for the North Dock and Mountjoy areas. There were also the lower courses of an unfinished church which they believed could be of benefit with the library construction, as well as saving on capital costs. It was decided in 1895 to lease the site from the diocese for £100 per annum and to seek a report from the City Architect on the cost and feasibility of converting the existing building for library use. Problems began to arise but the biggest obstacle was the cost. A resolution was passed in July 1897 to raise a loan of £2,500 to build a new library. The City Architect was instructed to prepare plans. Tenders were invited for its construction and six were received. Joseph Pemberton & Son were awarded the contract.

The library is still referred to as the North William Street site, although it was located on the corner of Charleville Mall and Dunne Street. Work commenced in 1898 and was completed the following year. The library was opened to the public in January 1900.

It was proposed in 1908 that the Gilbert Collection be housed in the library. An extension and readjustment of the reading room was carried out to accommodate the collection, at a cost of £1,000. It was housed on a temporary basis in what was then described as the *"neat and business like Corporation free library at Charleville Mall"*.[5]

Difficulties arose over non-payment of rent for the site, and this was eventually resolved with an outright purchase of the property by the Corporation. Another extension was carried out in 1908, enlarging the basement. Windows were added to save on lighting expenses. The library had a very disruptive visitor in 1909 when records show that a large goat took refuge under a table. It was eventually expelled by staff and public, though not before overturning an old man and the table at which he sat reading. He was not seriously injured!

The library reached its present state in 1910 with the completion of the Junior Department, the first of its kind in Ireland. This is now St. Agatha's Hall. In 1923 female assistants were hired specifically to run this. The necessary qualifications for the positions included an ability to deal with children and competence in a foreign language. Their hours were different from other staff members and they received £3 per week.

5. Evening Telegraph, 8/8/1908

STREET NAMES

Addison Road

Named after Lord Addison who was Secretary of State of Ireland during the early eighteenth century.

Aldborough Place

Named due to its proximity to Aldborough House.

Annesley Avenue, Annesley Bridge Road, Annesley Place

After Richard Annesley one of the first Directors of the Royal Canal Company in 1791.

Ardilaun Road, Ardilaun Square

After Lord Ardilaun, Sir Arthur E. Guinness. He received the title baron in 1880. Ardilaun or Ardillaun is the name of an island in Lough Corrib, near Lord Ardilaun's residence.

Austins Cottages

Named during the 1950s and formerly part of Taaffe's village.

Ballybough Avenue, Ballybough Court, Ballybough Lane, Ballybough Road

Baile Bocht meaning *"poor town"* in Irish. Other explanations for the name include *"land by the sea"*. Up to some years ago there were six houses on Ballybough Road known as Edward Terrace which dated from 1815 and the name came from Edward Duke of Kent, son of George III.

Bayview Avenue

This received its name from the fact that the bay was visible from here up to the mid nineteenth century.

Brendan Behan Court

Named after the playwright Brendan Behan.

Cadogan Road

Named after the Earl of Cadogan who was Lord Lieutenant of Ireland from 1895-1902.

Charlemont Parade

This street is called after James Caulfield, first Earl of Charlemont. He was Commander in Chief of the Volunteers in 1780. He built the Casino in Marino and what is now known as the Hugh Lane Gallery on Parnell Square.

Charleville Avenue, Charleville Mall

Associated with Lord Monck who owned land in the area. His residence in Bray was called Charleville.

Clinches Court

Named after the highwayman Larry Clinch. He frequently robbed Ulster Mail coaches and met his demise at the hands of Tipperary Militia while in the process of plundering Clonliffe House. His body was left at the Suicide Plot at the end of Clonliffe Road.

Clonliffe Avenue(1866), Clonliffe Road

There are two meaning's of Clonliffe – *"Meadow of herbs"* and *"Meadow of the Liffey"*.

Dunne Street

Adjacent to Clarence Street and dated to 1840.

Fairview Passage, Fairview Strand

Located between Cadogan Road and Fairview Strand, offering a picturesque vista of the bay.

Foster Place North, Foster Terrace

Named after the last Speaker of the House of Commons, John Foster.

Jones's Road

Called after Frederick E. Jones, who was born c.1759 and known as Buck Jones. He built this road to enable him to visit the city without having to go through the dangerous thoroughfare of Ballybough. He died 1834.

King's Avenue

Named after the *"Kings"* of Mud Island, a title given to the self proclaimed monarchs of the area namely the MacDonnells who came here after the Ulster Plantation c.1610.

Mountjoy Parade

Linked to the Rt. Hon. Luke Gardiner (1745-98), Baron and Viscount Mountjoy.

Newcomen Avenue, Newcomen Court

Named after Sir William Newcomen, one of the directors of the Royal Canal Company in 1791.

North Circular Road

Northern most boundary of the city limits.

North Great Clarence Street

Named after the Duke of Clarence who later became William IV.

North Richmond Street, Richmond Cottages Summerhill, Richmond Crescent, Richmond Lane, Richmond Parade

Named after Charles Lennox, 4th Duke of Richmond or possibly after the adjoining Richmond townland, the name which existed long before the vice-royalty.

North Strand Road

In De Gomme's map of 1673 this is shown as a trackway and was deemed the *"road to Hoath"*. Prior to 1792 the Wide Street Commissioners began to use the name North Strand Road.

North William Street

Called after William, Duke of Clarence.

Nottingham Street

Dated to 1798. Named after Nottingham House, also known as the Red House, which was located here.

O'Sullivan Avenue

Possibly named after T.D. Sullivan, Lord Mayor of Dublin 1886-1887.

Poplar Row

Completed after 1823 to provide an artery between Clonliffe Road and East Wall Road.

Portland Row

Named after the 3rd Duke of Portland (1811).

Royal Canal Way

Named after the canal which is adjacent to the street.

Russell Street

Named after John Rusell, 4th Duke of Bedford and Lord Lieutenant of Ireland 1757-1761 and John Russell, 6th Duke of Bedford who was not Lord Lieutenant until 1806. Also possibly named after John Russell who was responsible for much construction in the area and referred to in the *"Encyclopaedia of Dublin"*.

Sackville Avenue, Sackville Gardens

Named after Rev. Sackville Ussher Lee, clergyman who lived in Exeter but who owned property here.

Spring Garden Street

Named after an old tea garden, a place of recreation in Dublin where people would gather to socialise.

Summerhill Parade

Was formerly known as *"Farmer's Hill"*.

Taaffe's Place

Named after a family who came over with Strongbow and were landowners in Clontarf. They later gave their lands to the Knights Templar.

Tom Clarke House

Named after the Fenian, Tom Clarke who spent fifteen years in an English prison. After returning from America he became one of the leaders of the 1916 Rebellion and was executed by firing squad.

Waterloo Avenue

Named after the famous Battle of Waterloo in 1815.

Wellesley Place

Named after Richard Colley Wellesley, Marquis Wellesley Lord Lieutenant of Ireland 1821-1828 and 1833-1834 or from Arthur Wellesley, Duke of Wellington.

Chapter 9

FAMOUS PEOPLE

Ballybough has had many famous sons and daughters reside in its streets throughout the ages. These individuals have left their mark in the areas of art, literature, politics, religion and sport. Some are still remembered and honoured today while others have slipped quietly into the pages of history.

LITERATURE, ARTS & SPORTS

Edward Smyth, *stone mason (1749 - 1812)*
Edward Smyth was the son of a stone cutter from Co. Meath. He came to Dublin c.1780 and worked with Henry Duley, a stonemason employed by Gandon in the building of the Custom House. His work so impressed Gandon that he was commissioned to execute the ornamental stone work on the external area of the building. He also worked on Lord Charlemont's Casino in Marino. On the foundation of the Royal Society's Modelling School in 1811, Smyth was appointed its first master. He died the following year.

Frederick Edward Jones, *impresssario (1759 - 1834)*
Frederick Edward Jones was more commonly known as *"Buck Jones"*. He resided in the Red House, Clonliffe, and was responsible for the construction of Jones's Road. This allowed him access to his home without having to use the main thoroughfare through Ballybough.

Jones led a varied and interesting life. At one time he challenged the notorious highwayman Larry Clinch to attack his house at Clonliffe. Clinch accepted the challenge and upon arrival was met by the Tipperary Militia and killed. His body lay unclaimed for one week before it was tossed unceremoniously into the Suicide Plot adjacent to Ballybough Bridge.

Jones was also a magistrate and dealt severely with the participants of the 1798 Rebellion. As a result of this the people of Dublin boycotted his theatre in Crow Street, thus depriving him of his main livelihood. The theatre closed and he died penniless in 1834, in a small cabin where Mountjoy Prison stands today. His ghost is said to roam Whitworth Road after 7p.m. in the evening.

Edward Walsh, *poet & translator (1805 - 1850)*

Edward Walsh was born in Derry and qualified as a school teacher. He later lived in Richmond Cottages. He began writing for the *Penny Journal* in the 1830s and also for *The Nation* in 1842. His best known books are *Reliques of Irish Jacobite Poetry with Metrical translations* and *Irish Songs*. He taught convicts on Spike Island and inmates of the Cork workhouse before his death in 1850.

Home of John O'Donovan, Bayview Avenue

John O'Donovan, *antiquarian (1809 - 1861)*

John O'Donovan was born in Co. Kilkenny and educated in Waterford. He moved to Dublin in 1823 and lived at 8 Newcomen Place and 55 Bayview Avenue. He was employed by the Irish Record Office, and in 1829 joined the Ordnance Survey. He visited every parish in Ireland and the results of his study of ancient manuscripts, along with his research into placenames, were later reproduced by Fr. Michael O'Flanagan. He founded the Irish Archaeology Society in 1840 with Eugene Curry. He also translated the *Annals of the Four Masters*, perhaps his greatest feat.

He was married and had nine sons, five of whom were involved in Fenian activity. One of his sons, Edmond O'Donovan, was educated at O'Connell Schools and later became a famous war correspondent. In 1870 he joined the French Foreign Legion and was captured during the Franco-Prussian War. He returned to Ireland and was again involved with O'Donovan Rossa and the Fenian movement. From 1873, he worked for the *London Times* and *Daily News* covering the Turko-Russian war. He was captured by the Turks and later wrote of his experiences in the widely read *Merv Oasis*. In 1883 he joined the British Army of Hicks Pasha in Sudan. At El Obeid, Hicks' army was captured by forces and all

Grave of John O'Donovan, Glasnevin Cemetery

perished, including Edmond O'Donovan or O'Donovan Pasha as he was then known. He is commemorated with other war correspondents on a plaque in St. Paul's Cathedral, London.

Timothy Daniel Sullivan, *politican & author (1827 - 1914)*

Timothy Sullivan, journalist, politician and poet, lived at 19 Richmond Place. He was editor-publisher of the *The Nation* and was also mayor of Dublin in 1887. He served time in Tullamore Jail where some of his best known works were written, including *Prison Poems* and *Lays of Tullamore, Green Leaves, Recollections* and *Speeches from the Dock*. His songs were popular throughout Ireland and America and the ballad *God Save Ireland,* written for the Manchester Martyrs, was considered the national anthem for many years.

Annie Hutton, *writer (1825 - 1853)*

Annie Hutton was a member of the famous coach-building family. She was engaged to Thomas Davis but he died after a short illness on 15 September 1845. Mrs. Hutton sent her grieving daughter abroad to help in her recovery but she did not survive him long. One of the tasks she undertook during this time was the translation of *The Embassy to Ireland of Rinuccini,* the famous Nuncio from the time of Owen Roe O'Neill. She did not, however, have the strength to finish the work which was later completed by her mother. She died on 7 June 1853 and is buried in St. George's Cemetery at the back of the old Whitworth Hospital. She was only 28 years old.

Bram Stoker, *author (1847 - 1912)*

Bram Stoker was born at 15 Marino Crescent, Fairview. His mother influenced his life with tales of death, myths and legends. As a young boy he would also have passed the Suicide Plot adjacent to Ballybough Bridge, the final resting place for those considered unworthy of a Christian burial. A common practice there was to impale the corpse with a wooden stake to ensure they would not roam and frighten the good citizens of the area. This practice was later to appear in his novel *Dracula*, the story based on Prince Vlad IV of Transylvania, published in 1897. He died in 1912 and his ashes were buried in Golders Green Cemetery, London.

General Henry Hall, *soldier*

Born near Athenry, Co. Galway, General Henry Hall fought in the Indian Mutiny as a British Officer. In his will, dated 1869, he directed his executors to construct two water fountains in the city of Dublin with a view to encouraging sobriety, and to expend a sum of not more than £200. The monument known as the Five Lamps came into existence c.1870 and was originally lit by gas. The lamp standard is made from cast iron and has at its base drinking taps and troughs suitable for human and animal alike. The Five

Headstone of Brendan Behan, Glasnevin Cemetery

Inscription on Brendan Behan's headstone

Lamps also marks the intersecting point of five roads – Seville Row, North Strand Road, Portland Row, Killarney Street and Amiens Street.

Brendan Behan, *author (1923 - 1964)*

Brendan Behan lived at 14 Russell Street and was educated at C.B.S. Brunswick Street. At the age of 17 he was sentenced to three years' borstal detention for possession of explosives in Liverpool. Returning to Ireland, he was later arrested and sentenced to fourteen years penal servitude for the attempted murder of a policeman. It was while in prison that he first began writing and his love for the Irish language was born. He was released in December 1946 and lived in various locations both in Ireland and abroad. His first play was *The Quare Fellow*, and this was followed by *An Giall* better known as *The Hostage*. His book *The Borstal Boy* was to bring him international renown but his success was also his downfall. Drinking became a problem and his health suffered as a result. He died in Dublin in 1964 and is buried in Glasnevin Cemetery. His funeral cortege was the biggest Dublin had seen since that of Michael Collins.

Fluther Good, *street character*

Fluther Good was a well-known street character in Ballybough and would often be seen sitting outside local shops soaking up the sun. He was mentioned in *The Plough and the Stars* by Sean O'Casey, whom he later sued, and received the princely sum of £10 as a result. His local was Noctor & McCanns on the Ballybough Road, and one famous brawl there left him with a steel plate in his head. Bob Brown, the well-known local barber, gave Fluther his dinner every day. He died in 1940 at the age of seventy-five, and his local was renamed in his honour.

James Hardiman, *historian (c1790 - 1855)*

James Hardiman, historian, lived and studied in Dublin and became Sub-Commissioner of Public Records in Dublin Castle and an active member of the Royal Irish Academy. *Irish Ministrelsy or Bardic Remains of Ireland,* written in 1831, remain his best known work. He lived for a period of time in the Ballybough area.

***FX Martin,** historian*

The recently deceased Rev. FX Martin was born in Ballylongford, Co. Kerry in 1922. He was the fifth child in a family of nine children. When FX was four, the family moved to Dublin. They resided at 11 Waterloo Avenue, North Strand. He attended primary school at the Holy Faith Convent in Clontarf and later went to Belvedere. He joined the Augustinians and was sent to study in UCD, where he won many awards and medals, including the Travelling Studentship on his MA results. He completed a PhD at Cambridge, a BD and L.Ph at the Gregorian University in Rome. He is best remembered for his involvement with the Viking site at Wood Quay. Prof. Martin, as Chairman of the Friends of Mediaeval Dublin, led many thousands of people in protest marches during the 1970s. He was an author, Professor Emeritus of Mediaeval History in UCD, was the first ever recipient of the Dublin Environmental Award in 1986, and also received the Dublin Millennium Medal for his defence of Viking and Mediaeval Dublin in 1988.

The family had other distinguished members, including Rev. Dr. Conor Martin who was professor of Ethics and Politics at UCD. He was also the private preserve of the Archdiocese of Dublin.

Their father, also Conor Martin, was a G.P. who later went on to become a gynaecologist. He died in October 1947 and his funeral mass was held in St. Agatha's; he was later interred in Glasnevin Cemetery. Among the chief mourners was the then Taoiseach, Eamon de Valera.

There were two other sons who became priests, Rev. L. Martin C.C. and Rev. Malachi B. Martin S.J.

***Paddy Moore,** footballer (1910 - 1951)*

Paddy Moore was born and raised in Ballybough and began his career with Richmond A.F.C. He moved on to play for his first big club, Shamrock Rovers, before moving to Cardiff. Shamrock Rovers again sought his skills and asked him to return to Ireland where he remained for two years. He then went to play for Aberdeen, before returning to Shamrock Rovers for one season. He later spent one season at Shelbourne, and then ended his career with Shamrock Rovers. His rise to fame ended prematurely, as he developed a strong taste for alcohol. Paddy gave one of the greatest individual performances ever recorded by the F.A.I., in a game played against Belgium in Dalymount Park where he scored all four goals in a 4-4 draw.

RELIGIOUS FIGURES

Edmund Rice

***Edmund Rice,** educator (1762 - 1844)*

Edmund Rice was born in Westcourt, Callan, Co. Kilkenny. He became a prominent businessman in Waterford, where he married. Unfortunately his wife died during the birth of their daughter, Mary. In 1802 he founded both the Christian and Presentation Brothers. The foundation stone of O'Connell Schools was laid by Daniel O'Connell in June 1828 and in August of the same year the foundation stone of the monastery was laid by Archbishop Murray. The O'Connell Schools opened in July 1831 and catered for 500 pupils. For seven years Edmund Rice lived with the North Richmond Street community but his health began to fail and he resigned from his position of Superior General. He retired to Mt. Sion where he stayed until his death on 29 August 1844. He was beatified in Rome on 6 October 1996.

Matt Talbot

***Matt Talbot,** labourer (1856 - 1925)*

Matt Talbot was born at 13 Aldborough Court on 2 May 1856. He was a pupil of O'Connell School for a short period of time. He left in1868 to work for the E. & J. Burke wine bottling company, but unfortunately became a chronic alcoholic. Many years later, in 1884, he took the pledge. To strengthen his resolve, he began each day by attending 5 a.m. Mass at St. Francis Xavier Church, Gardiner St. He also joined the men's sodality which he attended for over forty years. He was renowned for his devotion to the Eucharist and spent much of his day praying. He slept on a bed of wooden planks and was well known for his life of penance. On special feast days he wore chains. He worked as a labourer at T. & C. Martins until his death in Granby Lane on 7 June 1925. He was buried in Glasnevin Cemetery but his remains are now interred in Our Lady of Lourdes Church, Sean MacDermott Street. In October 1975, he was conferred with the title "Venerable Matt Talbot".

INVENTORS & ADVENTURERS

Jasper Wheeler Rogers, *inventor*

Jasper Wheeler Rogers lived in Nottingham House and was the inventor of Ireland's first locomotive. His workshop was located at the rear of his home and it is said that he often passed down O'Connell Street and along the quays and returned via the North Strand. His locomotive was said to have frightened horses and is recorded in the *Irish Builder* as being a *"fiery chariot that ran without horses with the devil as engine driver and his imps as stokers and his sinful cargo behind as tender"*. Complaints were lodged by concerned citizens regarding the locomotive and it was said the Corporation could have saved money if they utilised it as a casual stone crusher. His machine was left to rust, but its owner continued with his inventions and was involved with drainage, sewers, water supply and peat charcoals schemes. It is not known what eventually became of him or when he died.

Mr. Sadler *(1751 - 1828) &* ***Mr. Baldwin,*** *adventurers*

On 1 October 1812, Mr. Sadler made the first balloon ascent from the grounds of Belvedere House. The ascent was made at 1p.m., and within 35 minutes the mountains of Wales were visible. All was going well and he hoped to land in Liverpool but the wind shifted and the balloon fell into the sea. Mr. Sadler was rescued by a passing vessel which had in fact run her bowsprit through the balloon.

Eighty years later, in 1892, Mr. Baldwin made a parachute jump and landed in Clonturk Park.

POLITICIANS & PATRIOTS

Alfie Byrne, *politician (1802 - 1956)*

Alfie Byrne lived at 63 North Strand Road, not far from his birthplace on Seville Place. He was the landlord of the Vernon Bar on Talbot Street and it was during an after-hours session that he learned of the death of the M.P. for the Harbour Electoral Division. His companions that evening suggested that he would be an ideal candidate and so the seeds were sown for a budding political career. Alfie sold his pub, began his electioneering and was duly elected. He became a champion of children's rights, fighting continuously for playgrounds and swings. He became affectionately known as the *"Children's Lord Mayor"*. He had a charm and charisma which enabled him to mix on equal terms with kings and paupers. He was famous for his lollipops which he bought from Urney's in Tallaght and dispersed to the children in their thousands. He lost the election in 1918, but of the twenty-seven elections he fought throughout his career, this was the only defeat he suffered. He was elected to Dail Éireann as an Independent candidate in 1922 with 18,000 votes, the highest poll of any new candidate in the Free State. His career spanned a further three decades and he represented many north Dublin constituencies. He was elected Lord Mayor in 1930, the first of the newly created Greater Dublin. He was elected again in 1954.

During the Eucharistic Congress of 1932 he organised soup, sandwiches and accommodation for those travelling from the northern counties. He visited many political prisoners after the 1916 Rising and during the War of Independence, and subsequently was enlisted as a messenger. He was a keen cyclist and carried out most of his duties using this mode of transport. He died on 13 March 1956 but is still fondly remembered by those who met or knew him.

Tom Clarke, *Republican (1857 - 1916)*

Tom Clarke at one time lived at 10 Richmond Avenue. He was born in England of Irish parents and his father was in fact a British soldier. Clarke spent the first ten years of his life in South Africa. When he was 21 years old he went to America where he joined Clan na nGael. He returned to England in 1883 as a dynamiter and was subsequently arrested and sentenced to 15 years penal servitude. He was released from prison in 1898, and married Kathleen Daly in 1901. She was the daughter of John Daly, the Limerick Fenian leader. Clarke had a tobacco shop at 75A Parnell St. He revived the Irish Republican Brotherhood (IRB) and fought in the GPO in 1916. He was one of the signatories of the Proclamation and was executed on 3 May 1916.

Tom Clarke.
Courtesy of the Allen Library

Sean MacDiarmada, *Republican (1884 - 1916)*

Originally from Co. Leitrim, Sean MacDermott spent much of his youth in America and Scotland. On his return to Ireland, he lived at 16 Russell Place, Jones's Road, and joined every prominent national movement. He received his republican training from Bulmer Hobson in Belfast and became a full-time organiser, paid 30s per week. In 1908 he came to Dublin and was soon the master of revolutionary intrigue. His address is recorded in Dublin Castle in 1916 as 500 North Circular Road. He was executed on 12 May 1916.

Michael J. Molloy, *compositor*

Michael J. Molloy, who was the compositor involved in the printing of the 1916 Proclamation, lived at 45 Bayview Avenue. The Proclamation was produced with great difficulties in the basement of Liberty Hall with type on loan from West's Printing Works, Capel Street. There was not enough type available to produce the document in one printing so it had to be produced in two segments. Michael Molloy was deported to Knutsford on 3 May 1916.

Edward (Ned) Daly, *Republican (1891 - 1916)*
Ned Daly also resided for a time at 10 Richmond Avenue, with his brother-in-law Tom Clarke. He was the only son of a family of ten and was born six months after the death of his father. He joined the Volunteers in 1913 and was commandant at the Four Courts in 1916.

Edward (Ned) Daly.
Courtesy of the Allen Library

Peadar Kearney, *composer (1883 - 1942)*
Peadar Kearney was born at 68 Lower Dorset Street, and during his lifetime lived in many areas including Summerhill and Marino. He wrote the words of *The Soldier's Song* in 1907, the composer being Paddy Heeney who died shortly afterwards. With the foundation of the Irish Volunteers in 1913, the Fenian Anthem *God Save Ireland* was superseded for route marches by *The Soldier's Song*. It was sung in 1916 and later in the internment camps. An Irish priest, Victor Herbert, heard it in New York, made a musical arrangement for it and had it published. He returned to Ireland in 1917 with the royalties for Kearney. Peadar married and settled at 17 Russell Place and fought in Jacob's factory in 1916 with Thomas MacDonagh. He assisted in the reorganisation of the Volunteers after the Rising and wrote many poems in favour of Sean Treacy and other national heroes. He was property master with the Abbey Theatre and was Brendan Behan's uncle. In November 1920, he was arrested while living at 3 Richmond Parade and interned at Ballykinlar, Co. Down until the signing of the Treaty in 1921. He died in 1942 and is buried in the Republican Plot, Glasnevin Cemetery.

John O'Neill of 61 Ballybough Road was a Captain in the Irish Citizen Army in 1916 and had been educated at the O'Connell Schools. He was based in St. Stephen's Green when the Rising broke out and was responsible for seizing the railway bridge which commanded the South Circular Road. This prevented military interference until the area was consolidated. He then fell back and rejoined the others at the Green. After the Rising he was deported to Wandsworth.

Sergeant Frank Robbins lived at 39 North William Street and fought at the Royal College of Surgeons during the 1916 Rising. He was entrusted to take

The Flood Family.
Inserts from left to right : Frank, Peter, Harold, Tom, Sean, Eddie & Val.
Seated left to right : Alfie, John & Sara. Standing : Mary. Courtesy of the Allen Library

the building and was assisted by three men and three women including Countess Markievicz, Lily Kempson and Mary Hyland. They surprised the caretaker when they reached the building and managed to secure it without difficulty. Allegedly there were weapons stored in the basement but only a small number were uncovered. After the Rising Robbins spent time in both Knutsford and Wandsworth.

Eight members of the **Flood** family were involved in revolutionary activities between 1916 and the War of Independence. They lived at 19 Summerhill Parade and attended O'Connell Schools. Frank Flood (1901 - 1921) was a 1st Lieutenant in the Active Service Unit of the Dublin Brigade. He was both the leader and the victim of the Drumcondra Ambush which failed due to the activities of an informer. It was to have been a surprise attack on the Dublin Metropolitan Police (DMP) but the men were captured in Clonturk Park and Flood was arrested and court martialled. He was found guilty of high treason and sentenced to death. He was hanged in Mountjoy in March 1921, the only other student besides Kevin Barry to be executed. Demonstrations and protests marked the occasion. The hangman on the day was John Ellis from England. The bodies of Frank Flood and nine other volunteers were reinterred in Oct. 2001. Thomas Flood was involved in the burning of the Custom House and was captured and charged with treason. He had acute appendicitis on the eve of his trial and this led to its postponement. The Truce was declared before his retrial.

Oscar Traynor, *(1886 - 1963)*, lived at Clonmore Terrace. He was Commander of the Dublin Brigade during the War of Independence following the death of McKee. He was actively involved in the Civil War and was anti-treaty. He tried to attain the evacuation of the Four Courts garrison before they were fired on and failing to achieve this he later provided them with sniper fire cover. He eventually became Commander in the O'Connell Street area and ordered the evacuation of the Dublin forces in July 1922. He was later imprisoned in Dundalk. Traynor was elected T.D. for North Dublin in 1925 and held his seat until 1961. Before the outbreak of the first World War he toured Europe as the goalkeeper for Belfast Celtic and was President of the F.A.I. from 1948-1963.

Sean Russell *(1894 - 1940)* lived on North Strand Road and was Director of Munitions during the War of Independence where he organised quarry raids for explosives. He was imprisoned on a number of occasions and went on hunger-strikes. He died on board a German U-boat in 1940 and was buried at sea off the west coast of Ireland. He was not included in the Roll of Honour for 1916 because of this extreme militancy.

Sean Russell statue, Fairview Park

Cathal Brugha, *(1874 - 1922)* lived on Richmond Avenue and was founder and director of a company which made ecclesiastical candles. He fought in 1916 and was wounded in the South Dublin Union. He became a T.D. and Minister of Defence in the Black & Tan War and died during the Civil War in a hail of bullets in O'Connell Street.

Thomas Ennis was Commander of the 2nd Battalion during the Black & Tan War and was injured during the attack on the Custom House. He rose to the position of Major General during the first few months of the Free State. The first action of the Civil War began with his attack on the Four Courts. He lived at Richmond Crescent.

The **Norgrove** family lived on the North Strand and all were members of the Irish Citizen Army during 1916. George led reinforcements to help Connolly at City Hall while his wife was based in St. Stephen's Green. His daughters Annie and Emily fought at City Hall while his son Alfred was involved at the GPO.

Five of the **Ring** brothers from Sackville Gardens fought at the GPO during 1916. These were Liam, Joe, Christopher, Leo and Patrick. In December 1920 they were arrested following a raid in the area. Liam was a poet and journalist and wrote the English words for the National Anthem. He later became chief translator to the Dail.

The **Tallon** brothers, Christopher, Joseph and Seamus lived at North Richmond Street and fought in the GPO in 1916 and also in the War of Independence. Seamus was later a President of the Gaelic League and Joseph was the author of many maths text books in Irish. They all attended the O'Connell Schools.

The Byrne Family.
From left to right : Peter, Frank & John all wearing Fianna Boys uniforms.
Courtesy of the Allen Library

The **Byrne** family lived at 17 North Richmond Street and their house was used as a contact point for Volunteers as well as a delivery and collection centre for important papers. These had been taken from the British forces and were later brought to the Intelligence Office. In 1921 the Active Service Unit (A.S.U.) acquired its first Thompson gun. Collins went to the Byrne's house to hear a lecture on how it worked and later the group went to the Casino in Marino to fire off some rounds. One of the Brothers from the O'Brien Institute came out to them to tell them to stop as the gun shots could be heard all over the place.[1]

James Conroy lived at 14 North Richmond Street and was a member of 2nd Battalion F Company. He fought at the Four Courts and brought paraffin to burn the tax office at Beresford Place in 1916. He was a painter by trade and a brilliant shot according to comrades. He was later involved in the burning of the Custom House. [2]

Charles Dalton joined the Volunteers after 1916 with the help of his friend Hugh Casey who lived at 13 Clonliffe Road. Casey had fought at the Four Courts. Dalton joined at Clonliffe Hall where Harry Colley was Quartermaster

1. Statement of Paddy O'Daly p.56-57 – Allen Library
2. C. Dalton – With the Dublin Brigade. 1920

(Colley went on to become a T.D.). He had to pay a subscription fee of 3d. He went on to become sergeant of the 4th section of the Company and often in times of trouble slept in the dispensary at Summerhill and Clarence Street. He regularly attended Mass at North William Street. He was one of Collins' men and was involved in the Dublin Castle mail robbery in 1919. He went to the home of the Byrne family on North Richmond Street on one occasion and collected a black deed box. He got on the tram with the box full of papers taken from enemy agents who had been shot but managed to deliver them uninterrupted to their new owners. He was also involved in *"Bloody Sunday"* and in the attempted rescue of MacEoin from Mountjoy Jail. The nuns at North William Street sent a message to the Volunteers, after the execution of Kevin Barry, via Miss Leslie Price of the teaching staff offering dinner each night for one month in memory of Barry. Dalton was chosen to go. His own home was often broken into and both his father and brother were arrested and taken to Collinstown.

Chapter 10

THE G.A.A.

When the Gaelic Athletic Association for the Preservation and Cultivation of National Pastimes was finally founded officially on 1 Nov. 1884, in Hayes' Hotel, Thurles, it brought to an end several months of fervent work on the part of Michael Cusack. He wrote that *"the association swept through the country like a prairie fire"*. Among the most enthusiastic supporters of Gaelic games were the Irish Christian Brothers. Rules for playing of Gaelic hurling and football were drawn up at the third meeting of the executive in January 1885.

The G.A.A. became a prototype of new national movements. The Gaelic League, Irish Literary Revival and other organisations were all founded within a decade and all had links and cross references with one another. Prior to the foundation of the G.A.A., organised sport was monopolised by the minority, elitist classes. Now for the first time the nationalist majority had a sporting organisation they could belong to and play with. By recognising the necessity to fill this need, the G.A.A. became a defining body in the emergence of our national identity. The Irish as a nation were slowly emerging from years of misery and degradation and were now ready to renew their interest in not only political matters but in everything Irish.

The standardisation of rules brought order to the games. Teams were expected to play by the rules within a given timeframe. Games usually took place on Sundays and leagues and championships were organised. Venues for local events were not difficult to find but there was a growing concern that no place was large enough to accommodate a national event.

During the early 1890s there was a drop in membership mainly due to emigration. The 1892 championships were held at the City & Suburban Sports Grounds, which is now Croke Park. The finals of 1896 were played at Jones's Road. This was the first time that coloured flags were used by umpires when signalling scores.

Archbishop Croke died in 1902. The G.A.A. immediately made moves to perpetuate his memory, and in October 1907, ear-marked £100 for a memorial. From that date on, funds were set aside at irregular intervals for this purpose. Although it had never been decided what shape the memorial would take, it was presumed by the Tipperary clergy that the memorial would be situated in Thurles. However, with the fund growing, the G.A.A. began to set its sights on acquiring a stadium in Dublin where it could hold its principal fixtures.

Two sites were eventually selected – Jones's Road and Elm Park, now St. Vincent's Hospital. Ordnance Survey evidence suggests that the former site was originally a garden orchard in the suburbs of Drumcondra, prior to the building of the railway line. The Jones's Road site was owned by Maurice Butterly, later an Alderman of Dublin Corporation, and it was known as the City & Suburban Racecourse or, more popularly, the Jones's Road Sports Ground. The G.A.A. had already been frequent tenants, having held two All-Ireland finals there in 1896.

From THE GAELIC ATHLETE, *July* 22—

Football Game at Frongoch Internment Camp.

DUBLIN DEFEAT WEXFORD.

The intense Gaelicism of the Irish prisoners of war at Frongoch Internment Camp is clearly demonstrated in their eager attendance at Irish Language classes organised under the direction of capable teachers, and their zest in pursuing the Gaelic games arranged by well-known G.A.A. men in their midst. Gaelic football has been taken up with a great degree of enthusiasm, and a large number of matches are being played daily. Already a Gaelic football and athletic carnival has been held, of which an exciting game between teams representative of Kerry and Louth was the principal feature. A narrow win for Kerry by a point indicates the closeness and interesting nature of the contest.

Courtesy of the Allen Library

In 1908 a well-known Limerick journalist and G.A.A. figure, Frank B. Dineen, bought the entire site (14 acres), having procured a bank loan for £3,250. His dream was that it would become a major venue for G.A.A. fixtures. He later sold a portion of it, four acres in total, to Belvedere College, which it used as a rugby ground. It is thought that he may have run into financial difficulties by this time. On the 22 December 1913, the G.A.A. bought the site for £3,500. They did not have sufficient funds to pay for the ground so they organised the Croke Park Tournament, an inter-county event. Kerry and Louth appeared in the final and it was so well attended that they were able to complete the purchase of the site. Having appeased the Tipperary clergy with funding for local projects, the G.A.A. christened the new ground Croke Park. The G.A.A. was incorporated as a company in December 1914, and the trustees formally handed over Croke Park to the new company. The Park had two stands, one at the Clonliffe Road end, and the other near the canal. The first match played in Croke Park was the 1914 *"Southern & Western Railway Silver Cup"* with Kerry facing Wexford. Over 20,000 people attended and Harry Boland was the referee.

Stafford Jail football team. Courtesy of the Allen Library

The Rising of Easter 1916 had a huge affect on the G.A.A. and led to disruption of matches as many clubs had not enough players to field teams. While in prison, many of the deportees played G.A.A. games at recreation times. There were so many Kerry players at Frongoch that they organised a team and beat Louth in the Frongoch *"Wolfe Tone"* final. The Commission set up to investigate the Rising mentioned the G.A.A. as one of the anti-British bodies with many members being Volunteers.

Jim Nowlan of the G.A.A. Central Council had been in Wakefield Prison and was freed on 19 June. He started to reorganise games and on 23 July two matches were held at Croke Park. The senior game saw Kildare play Tipperary and the junior sides were represented by Dublin and Louth.

1918 saw a flurry of activity in the G.A.A. Games took second place to military style activities. Curtailment of trains still hampered attendance at big games. News spread that Kerry was almost ready to be back into the championships. In early July the G.A.A. was declared a dangerous organisation. The games were finally outlawed. The G.A.A. in defiance organised Gaelic Sunday for 4 August. Games were played in each county to defy the authorities. Almost 1500 games were played, with over 20 being played in Dublin. It was only in Dublin that an attempt was made to stop the games. An armed guard was set up at the entrance of Croke Park with troops in attendance. The policemen were treated to a rare sight of a camogie match being played on the road outside.[1] The Castle said it just wanted to stop those games that were being used as a political platform. The championships were eventually restored and by the end of the autumn the Provincial Championships were in full swing. In 1918 World War I ended and saw the first major elections in Ireland since the Rising.

The revolutionaries fought under the title of Sinn Fein. They gained significant results. The hurley was now used not only as a symbol of struggle

1. M. de Burca – The G.A.A.: a history. 1980. p.142

but also as a symbol of the votes of the people of Ireland. Sinn Fein won and it was seen as a victory for independence. The elected refused to enter Parliament at Westminster and established an independent Dail in Dublin instead. The military wing of the government became known as the I.R.A. Shortly after, a guerrilla campaign was launched and more oppression came in the form of the Black & Tans. Fighting took place throughout the country with towns and industries being destroyed. It took its toll on the G.A.A. who again found it difficult to field teams. The War of Independence had well and truly started. The 1920 final was eventually played in 1922 (Dublin and Tipperary). The Congress of 1919 discussed amongst other things, improvements at Croke Park and admission into the organisation.

Tomas MacCurtain, the Lord Mayor of Cork, was murdered in 1920. The G.A.A. sent a message of condolence to his family. On the night before the G.A.A. Congress, 315 evacuated police barracks were burnt and the Income Tax Office and other buildings in Dublin were raided. April saw the start of the hunger strikes and the G.A.A. cancelled matches as a token of sympathy. The championships restarted in May and continued until July when public assemblies were banned in Cork and other parts of Munster. Matches were played outside the proclaimed areas. On 25 October Terence MacSwiney died while on hunger strike in Brixton. The G.A.A. marched at his funeral. Their activities were now almost at a standstill throughout the country. The exception was the inter-county match between Dublin and Tipperary organised for 21 November.

The British intelligence system by 1920 was divided into a number of almost self-contained units. The RIC watched the movements of every known or suspected rebel, as did the G Division of the DMP. They had become less efficient, however, as many Volunteers were now on the run or were members of Flying Columns. The Volunteers had also eliminated many local spies. As a result, Michael Collins' counter intelligence unit was able to execute fourteen enemy agents in Dublin on the morning of Sunday 21 November.

Reprisals were expected but no person could have fore-told of the tragedy which would

"Bloody Sunday" match ticket bought by William Walsh of the Irish Citizen Army. Courtesy of the Allen Library

occur in its aftermath. One of the auxiliaries wounded in the operation later noted that with a toss of a coin it was decided to go on a killing spree at Croke Park rather than loot O'Connell Street. The grounds were patrolled by twenty five men from 2nd Battalion acting as stewards. Those involved in the morning's activities had been advised by Sean Russell not to attend the match for fear of recognition. Russell later learned that the British Army had targeted the football match, and hurried to Jones's Road where he met Harry Colley and Andy Doyle. They went to Croke Park, where Russell ordered Doyle to dismiss the stewards. He could not, however, convince the G.A.A. authorities to cancel the game.

A short time later the military, accompanied by the RIC, arrived and surrounded the Park. According to General Crozier, their mission was to search for weapons. A plane circled the playing field and fired a Verey light pistol which seemed to have been a signal of some sorts because within minutes, the troops began firing on the crowd and this assault continued for about ten minutes. The RIC with bayonets fixed had charged up the road outside. Many bullets were fired and several people fell down injured. Anyone who tried to go to their assistance was pushed back into the crowd. Those who managed to get as far as the gates were searched on their way out and those who remained inside had to stand with their hands over their heads. Twelve people were killed, sixty wounded and hundreds more injured.[2]

Included in the list of the dead was Michael Hogan, a player on the Tipperary team. Thomas Ryan from Co. Wexford knelt over the body of Hogan and while whispering the Act of Contrition he too was shot.[3] A Miss Doyle who worked in Speidels Pork Butchers was also killed. She had on several occasions hidden weapons in the shop for Tom Keogh, Joe Leonard and Paddy O'Daly.[4] Volunteer Thomas Ryan, who lived on the North Circular Road, was also killed. He was a member of A Company, having joined in 1918. He had taken an active part in the Collinstown Aerodrome raid in March 1919. Several children were also among the dead and injured, including 10 year old Jerry O'Leary who was shot dead, 11 year old William Robinson who was trampled to death, and J. Scott, a 14 year old, who was hit by a ricocheting bullet.[5]

The Labour Commission to Ireland held an inquiry into the events of Bloody Sunday and published their findings. They questioned several witnesses, all of whom stated that the Black & Tans arrived down Russell Street and started firing on the crowd within minutes. One witness stated that he helped a boy who fell from a tree after being shot. He took him to the

2. Dublin's fighting story. p.154
3. James Gleeson – Bloody Sunday. 1962
4. Statement of Paddy O'Daly p.44 – Allen Library
5. P. O'Farrell – Who's who. 1997

corner of the North Circular Road and gave him to someone who knew where he lived. Another told of how his fiancee was shot dead while they were standing opposite the Grand Stand. Many of those who had been sitting on the wall opposite the Grand Stand were shot and fell into Belvedere Football Ground. Another witness spoke of seeing a man in a crouched position near the Secretary's house when an RIC man went over and shot him. The witness had gone over to help the man but was stopped by the Black & Tans. While the man lay dying, he was searched by a soldier. His body was eventually taken away by ambulance.

According to Hamar Greenwood in the House of Commons on 23 November, there had been a preordained plan to search those at the match for arms. The field had been surrounded and the crowd addressed by means of a megaphone, to explain what was about to transpire and to alleviate any anxiety. In a Report of the Labour Commission to Ireland in 1921, it is interesting to note that of all the witnesses questioned about the events of Bloody Sunday, not one could recall any address or announcement by megaphone.[6] He continued to state that the officers were fired on from two corners of the field and that this was some planned signal as the crowd in the stands rose simultaneously. The officers, fearing an attack was imminent, opened fire.

Football match at Knutsford Prison, 1916. Sketched by Charles Saurin. Courtesy of the Allen Library

6. Report of the Labour Commission to Ireland. Appendix II, pp.40-41, p.120

Again no witness questioned reported hearing any shots prior to those of the troops.

Thirty revolvers were recovered during the day's operation. There may have been a planned search of the grounds organised but all the evidence implies that this was a retaliation for the execution of the British agents. An independent commission was later sent from America to ascertain what exactly happened that day. The Commission in their final report stated that there was no justification for what transpired at Croke Park on Bloody Sunday. A statement issued by the authorities following Bloody Sunday stated the following "*A number of men came to Dublin on Saturday under the guise of asking to attend the football match between Dublin and Tipperary. But their real intention was to take part in a series of murderous outrages which took place in Dublin that morning. Learning on Saturday that a number of these gunmen were present in Croke Park, the Crown Forces went to raid the field. It was the original intention that an officer would go to the centre of the field and speaking from a megaphone, invite the assassins to come forward. But on their approach, armed pickets gave warning. Shots were fired to warn the wanted men, who caused a stampede and escaped in the confusion*".

Following all this strife the finances of the G.A.A. were not good. Croke Park had large debts and the G.A.A. appealed to Dail Éireann to help. They were given a low interest loan which helped them come through this most difficult of times. With the signing of The Truce, tensions began to ease. The Leinster Hurling final of 1920 was played on 21 September 1921 at Croke Park. Over 20,000 were there to see Dublin beat Kilkenny. Michael Collins threw in the ball. The Munster counties were more cautious and the championships were not played for 1920. Instead they concentrated on reorganising the Volunteers. Rubble from 1916 was now moved from O'Connell Street and formed what was to be known as Hill 16 (also referred to as the Railway End). Financial difficulties persisted.

The next struggle was far more complex. The Treaty was negotiated in Dec. 1921 and troops left the 26 counties. A major split occurred with the foundation of the Irish Free State. The armed wing was called the Free State Army. At the start of what was to become the Civil War, many families and former comrades of 1916 and The War of Independence, saw each other on opposing sides. The G.A.A. yet again was hit. It took no part in the split which followed The Treaty.

On 18 April, Easter Sunday, the G.A.A. Congress was held at the Gresham Hotel. Croke Park now had a capacity for 60,000. By the time the war ended in 1922, the G.A.A. had become a source of reconciliation. The leaders of the different parties could now be openly seen at Croke Park.

As political tension subsided, interest in hurling, football and handball increased. The Free State Government for many was not ideal but at least it was Irish. Ideals of an Irish Ireland were now foremost in people's minds. The native language was fostered, and given equal status, Irish industry was encouraged and Irish pastimes came into their own. The Easter Congress of 1925 was held in Croke Park. Over 100 delegates, many who had been on opposing sides of the conflict sat down together, talked of sport and not politics. Finances began to improve and handball started to grow in popularity.

The first Hogan Stand was opened in 1924 and was named after Michael Hogan, one of the players killed on Bloody Sunday. The Cusack Stand opened in 1937, the Canal End in 1949 and finally the Nally Stand in 1952. These have all undergone major renovation and redevelopment over the years.

Other sporting events have also had an association with Croke Park. The Irish National Athletics Championships were held there until 1922. There was a permanent cycle track where major events took place. The Tailtean Games were held in the stadium in 1924, 1928 and 1932. The Free State Government supported these revitalised games and they were open to all amateur athletes who were Irish or of Irish extraction. At the 1928 games, over 6000 people came to see Pat O'Callaghan, the new Olympic gold medalist, in action. The National League was established in 1925 and allowed inter county football and hurling competitions to be played during the winter months. The entrance fee to matches in the 1930s was a mere 5s, and even then you could listen to the unmistakable chimes of the Artane Boys Band who had been playing in Croke Park since 1889. Croke Park is currently undergoing redevelopment at a cost of £174 million.

During mid 1998 a high technology museum opened to the public. This links the past, present and future and pays tribute to the people and events

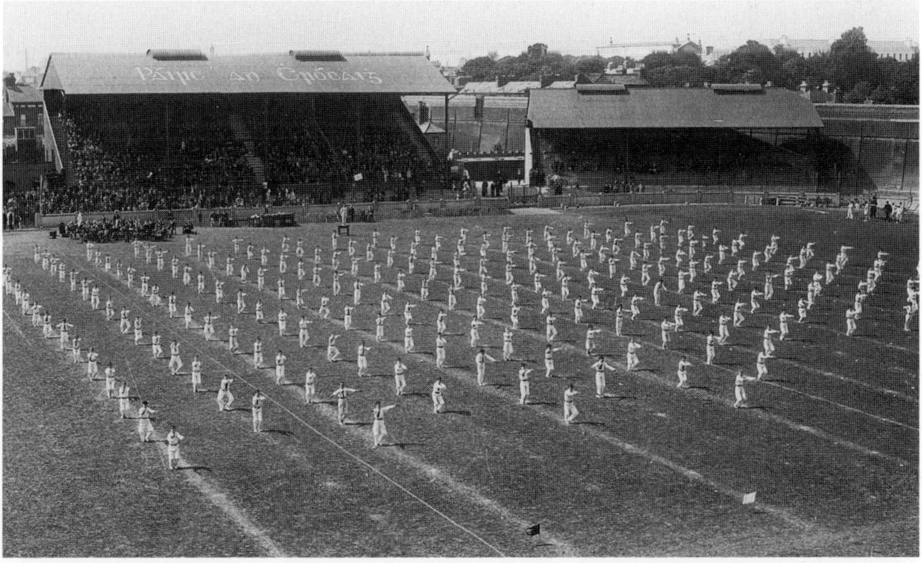

Gymnastics display at Croke Park by St. Canice's National School, a branch school of O'Connells, 1938-39. Courtesy of the Allen Library

Croke Park from Clarke's Bridge

that make the G.A.A. what it is today. The famous terracing end of Hill 16 has become an all-seater area and will make the final capacity of Croke Park 79,500 (instead of the predicted 84,000 if the area had remained standing only). Hill 16 holds a special place in the hearts of Dublin supporters particularly when their team is playing.

For the local people of Ballybough, the surrounding area takes on a carnival atmosphere during big matches. The country comes to Ballybough for the day and usually there is a genuine delight to see the colours and fans in such high spirits. There is a financial gain for local shops, pubs, restaurants and street hawkers. Rasta beads, hats, scarves and flags are available from many sources and are snapped up very quickly by the fans. During the early 1970s the locals had a great time as the Dublin team was frequently involved in All Ireland Football finals.

The G.A.A. grew in the parishes of Ireland and provided a social and cultural identity to the people during times of poverty, the ousting of the colonists and civil strife and the establishment of a new nation. From its small beginnings in 1884 the G.A.A. has grown in stature and credibility and can rightly claim a place in world sporting organisations, while still maintaining its unique identity.

Chapter 11

1900 - 1916

During the second decade of the twentieth century, Irish political and social causes encompassed several disparate traditions. Many politicians looked to England for unity, some sought Home Rule, while others wished for an independent state. The Unionists regarded any form of political or social change as a threat to their very existence and would take any measures to avoid it.

Many organisations were established with the aim of promoting various aspects of Irish life, and reviving long forgotten traditions. The Gaelic and Literary Revival evoked a new image of the Irish hero, but it appealed only to a small section of society. Conradh na Gaeilge, or the Gaelic League, founded in 1893 by Douglas Hyde, Eoin MacNeill and Eugene O'Growney, helped

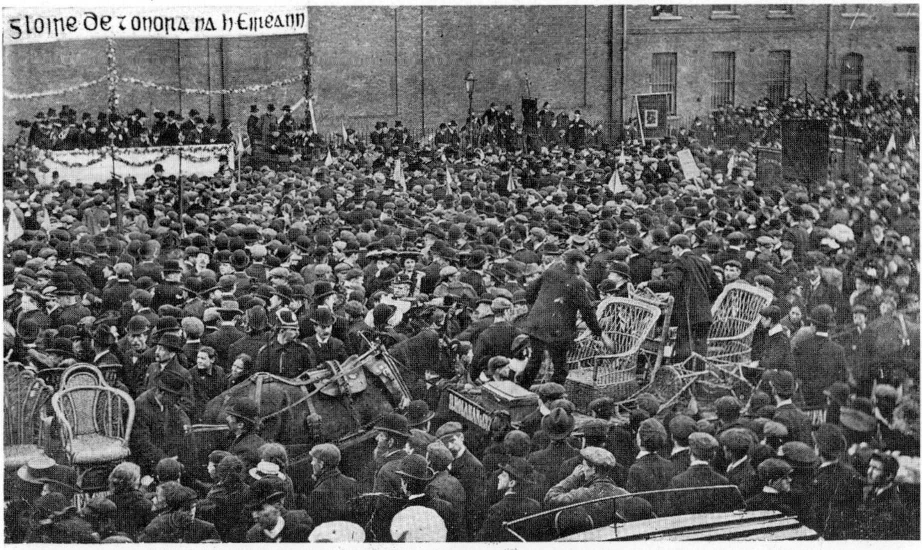

H. & M. Woods,] IRISH LANGUAGE PROCESSION.—Scene at Smithfield, Sunday, 12th March, 1905 [*Dublin.*
PORTION OF MESSRS. HOLAHAN'S WORKING EXHIBIT

Courtesy of the Allen Library

revive and encourage the speaking of the Irish language. Soon adult classes were being taught and, as part of its entertainment movement, Irish dancing and music halls began to flourish. The Gaelic Athletic Association (G.A.A.) was founded to promote and restore Gaelic games such as hurling, football and handball. These traditional pursuits gave a new-found sense of national identity.

Associations which had more political inclinations included Sinn Fein, the IRB and James Connolly's socialist movement. These wanted to establish a republic by physical force. Connolly, along with James Larkin, had founded the ITGWU and became involved with the 1913 Lock-Out, an event which was to have significant consequences for Irish labour/employer relations for future generations. The Irish Citizen Army, founded during this period, introduced the concept of militarism which was to be paramount in the subsequent rising.

Not all people were influenced by this new found Irishness. Many remained pro-English. Others felt that in order to achieve Home Rule, they would have to fight in the impending war. This group had the backing of John Redmond, who believed the future of Ireland lay within the parliamentary system. Redmond was the leader of the Irish Parliamentary Party and was opposed to any notion of armed rebellion.

By 1913, the situation in Ireland was becoming increasingly tense. The Ulster Volunteer Force (UVF) had been founded by Edward Carson, whose primary concern was to protect Protestant interests and to alleviate fears that Ireland was soon to become an independent nation. In the south, the Irish Volunteers had been formed by Eoin MacNeill. Although poorly armed and lacking significant financial backing, they soon had the support of a large number of people. The first consignment of arms to the Irish Volunteers was delivered in 1914 on board *The Asgard*. For the first time in six centuries, an Irish army paraded armed and defiant through the streets of the city.

When England declared war on Germany in 1914, loyalties were again divided. As many as 250,000 Irish men, many Volunteers, enlisted to fight for the Crown. This created a split within the Volunteer movement, and their numbers dwindling from 200,000 to 10,000. Many however believed that a show of loyalty to England at this time would in the long term oblige its government to grant Home Rule. With the outbreak of war the issue was deferred indefinitely.

DUBLIN METROPOLITAN POLICE

One arm of the British establishment in Ireland which was to hear its death knell during this period was the Dublin Metropolitan Police force (DMP) which dated from the middle of the previous century. The city was initially divided into four districts, and Dublin Castle was designated the headquarters of the new force. Ballybough fell under the jurisdiction of C/Rotunda

Division. The principal barracks were situated at Frederick Lane, Buckingham Street and Sackville Place. There was also a DMP station at Annesley Bridge, next to the Jewish Cemetery, from the 1830s until approximately 1910.[1] The total area of the C Division was 3,048 acres in 1914.[2]

The police often had difficulties in maintaining law and order in the Ballybough area. There were *"illegal societies and combinations in the city especially along Circular Road towards Phibsborough"*.[3] In 1837 it was noted that areas such as Ballybough, Kilmainham and Dolphin's Barn were *"infested by those parties"*.[4]

Not all the activities of the DMP were duty-related, and on 9 September 1893 at the DMP Sports Grounds, Jones's Road (now Croke Park), the officers were involved in a friendly tug-of-war match. Coached by Inspector Booth, the Dublin force decisively defeated the Glasgow police. The *Sport* magazine commented on how police and public relations had improved *"The scene that followed was maddening; such unbound enthusiasm, such excitement, such bewildering frantic exhibitions of delight could only be equalled by multitudes in ancient Rome witnessing the triumph of a favourite gladiator."*[5]

The Dublin Metropolitan Police had great difficulty in maintaining order during the 1913 Lock-Out. Sergeant Fergus Quinn of C Division played a major part in attempting to uphold the peace during this troubled time. Public opinion suggested that the DMP were on the side of the employers. By the time the Lock-Out ended the reputation of the DMP was in ruins, with over 200 constables injured.

1915	Leader	No.	Times	Departed	Destination
1 Jun	J. McGuinness	34	8.20-9.50	41 Rutland St	Fairview
8 Jun	J.J. Walsh		10.15-11.15	Blessington St.	Croke Park
11 Jun	F. Fahy	25		25 Parnell Sq	Fairview
22 Jun	E. Daly	34	8.50-10.10	41 Parnell Sq	Fairview
25 Jun	F. Fahy	45			Fairview
16 Jul	J. McGuinness	64			Clonliffe
23 Aug	P.T. Daly		4.00-5.00		Croydon Pk.
22 Sept	(150 Citizen Army)			Liberty Hall	Croydon Pk.

1. A. Garrett – In ages past.1985. p.51
2. Royal Irish Constabulary & Dublin Metropolitan Police: Report of the Committee of Inquiry, 1914
3. Larcom Papers 7621
4. ibid
5. Earnan Blythe –The DMP DHR Vol.xx No.3/4

The Dublin Metropolitan Police continued to restrain the extreme nationalist element in Dublin, and while some policemen were concerned with fraud, theft and traffic, others were appointed to deal with the effects of contemporary politics. Lists were drawn up of prominent IRB, IRA, Sinn Féin and Gaelic League extremists. The G men or detectives would report on their movements.[6] The Ballybough area was familiar to Sinn Féin Volunteers because they marched regularly from the Gaelic League Office at 25 Parnell Square to Fairview or Clonliffe. Some typical reports are listed on p.115.[7]

Croke Park itself attracted many Volunteers and it was noted that Major John MacBride, J.J. Walsh, Thomas Byrne and William Sheehan were among those who attended the All-Ireland Football Final between Kerry and Wexford on 8 November 1915.[8] They also attended a Central Council G.A.A. meeting the following week. D. Lynch had a brother living on Jones's Road and his visits were recorded. On the 28 June, Thomas Clarke moved most of his furniture from 75 Parnell Square to Richmond Avenue in Fairview, and J. McCartan visited him almost a month later. Police took note of those with whom local people associated. The following account was made on 10 September 1915 *"M. O'Reilly who resides at Ballybough Road is employed in the Standard Life Insurance Office and has recently been found mixing with local extremists",*

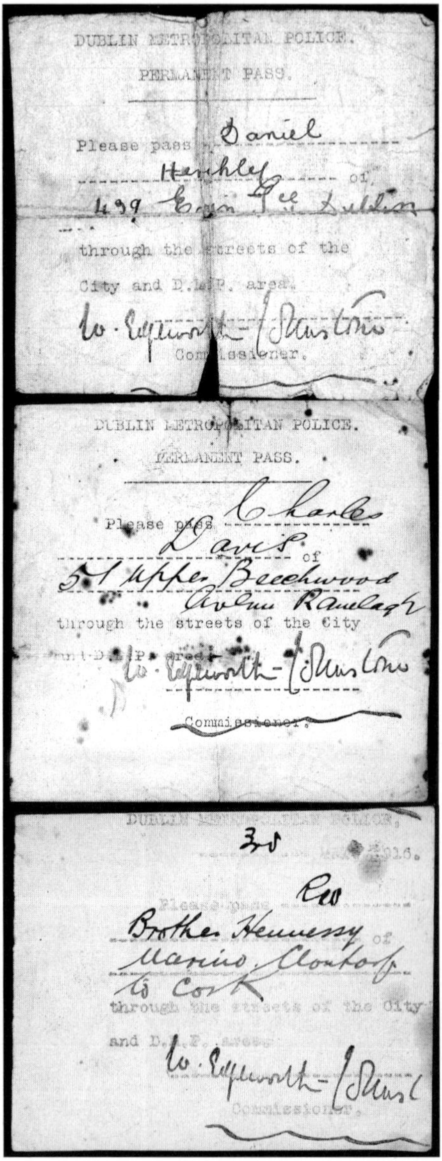
DUBLIN METROPOLITAN POLICE.
PERMANENT PASS.
Please pass Daniel Hinchley of 499 Erin Tce Dublin through the streets of the City and D.M.P. area.
W. Edgeworth-Johnstone
Commissioner.

DUBLIN METROPOLITAN POLICE.
PERMANENT PASS.
Please pass Charles Davis of 51 Upper Beechwood Avenue Ranelagh through the streets of the City and D.M.P. area.
W. Edgeworth-Johnstone
Commissioner.

DUBLIN METROPOLITAN POLICE.
3rd 1916.
Please pass Rev Brother Hennessy of Marino, Clontarf to Cork through the streets of the City and D.M.P. area.
W. Edgeworth-Johnstone
Commissioner.

DMP passes.
Courtesy of the Allen Library

6. David Nelligan – The spy in the Castle. 1968
7. Dublin Castle Reports on the movements of Sinn Féin extremists, 1915-1916
8. ibid

i.e. Beasley, Fahy, Buggy.[9] The printer John E. Lyons, of North Circular Road, was seen in the company of Pearse, de Valera and Bulmer Hobson. Amiens Street Station and the North Wall were close to the area and police kept a constant watch on new arrivals. Joseph Melinn from Sinn Féin, Tralee, arrived in Kingsbridge and drove to his brother at 107 Summerhill on 15 July 1915. Close surveillance was maintained on packages arriving from the North Wall for fear that they contained arms.

The Howth Gun-Running was somewhat of a disaster for the Dublin police. They were sent out to deal with the Volunteers but many of the police cheered as the Volunteers marched by Raheny. Closer to the Easter Rising activity on all sides increased. Seventy-six members of the Irish Citizen Army (62 armed with rifles) marched to Cross-Guns Bridge, with some heading towards Whitworth Road and others to Newcomen Bridge. They were led by Countess Marckievicz, James Connolly and James Malin.[10] The police were called in to assist in case of any disturbance of the peace. On 19 April 1916, the DMP and RIC forces in Dublin were confined to their barracks for fear of being shot. There had been an attempt on Dublin Castle and as a precaution, strong barricades were erected on the bridges over the railway on the North Circular Road and Cabra Road.[11] These were later destroyed by gunfire and 40 casualties were reported within the police force. By 2 May an order was given for all citizens to surrender arms and ammunition at their local police barracks. The following day only members of the police were allowed to carry arms. The number of policemen killed on duty between 1916-1922 numbered 32. They included William Firth and Constable Edward Dunphy, both from the C Division. Dunphy was shot by Sinn Féin Volunteers in the GPO.

THE UNEMPLOYED IN IRELAND.

The Police, having little or no duties to perform, have been lately engaged in removing anti-enlistment bills from the dead walls and telegraph poles.

Courtesy of the Allen Library

The Dublin Metropolitan Police existed for 89 years (1836-1925). There were fewer policemen per head of population compared with

9. ibid
10. Sinn Féin Rebellion Handbook – Easter. 1916
11. ibid

most European capital cities.[12] By 1925 Dublin had 25 stations and in the same year the Police Amalgamation Act was passed. The Dublin Metropolitan Police and Royal Irish Constabulary became collectively known as the Garda Síochána with the founding of the new State. (see Appendix 2)

THE 1913 LABOUR WAR

By 1911 the population of Dublin had reached 304,502. A government inquiry into Dublin's housing conditions at the end of 1913 revealed that 87,305 people, almost 30% of the city's inhabitants, lived in slums. More than 2000 families resided in one room tenements. Dublin had the highest death rate in Ireland and the worst infant mortality rate in the British Isles. The Census of 1911 placed almost one seventh of the population in the category of unskilled workers, the majority of whom were occupied with rail, road and dock work. The inevitable result was low wages and a labour force with no bargaining power to improve conditions. This was the social and economic backdrop against which the new unionism of Larkin and Connolly was to emerge. It is hardly surprising that when Larkin established the Irish Transport & General Workers Union in 1909, extending membership to all sections of general workers, its numbers grew quickly.

The creation of one big union, combining militancy in industrial action with the use of sympathetic striking, appeared to provide the general worker with his long awaited bargaining tool. Unfortunately, the very methods that empowered the union inevitably became the cause of aggressive and coordinated opposition from employers. The union enjoyed initial success which boosted its strength. As the power of the union grew, so too did the determination of the employers to destroy it. By August Dublin had witnessed no less than 40 strikes and tension in the city was mounting.

William Martin Murphy, a powerful businessman, was determined not to recognise the new union in any of his companies. By 21 August, Dublin Horse Show week, two hundred men abandoned their cars in the streets of Dublin, but despite the opportune timing, the strike was only partially effective. That night, at a meeting in Beresford Place, Larkin claimed *"It is not a strike, it is a Lock-Out"*. He criticised *"police brutality"* and warned *"if Edward Carson can call on the people of Ulster to arm, I will call upon you to arm"*.[13] Within two days, Larkin and three others had been arrested for their seditious speeches. Having been released on bail, Larkin announced at a meeting at Liberty Hall that he would be in Sackville Street on Sunday 31 August at a meeting to support the strikers. The events of the following days would never be forgotten by the people of Dublin.

12. Earnan Blythe – The DMP DHR Vol. xx No.3/4
13. 1913-1916 Intelligence notes and lists of persons sentenced by court martial. pp.38-40

The next day a proclamation was quickly issued by Mr. E.G. Swift, the Chief Divisional Magistrate, prohibiting the Sunday meeting. That night Larkin burnt a copy of the proclamation at a large meeting in Beresford Place. The following afternoon, fierce rioting broke out across the city, the worst incidents taking place in Ringsend, Great Brunswick Street, Beresford Place and Eden Quay. The police responded to the unrest with baton charges, and heavy casualties were reported. As promised, Larkin appeared the following day to address the crowd on Sackville Street. A large force of 300 police, augmented by the RIC reserve force, was deployed to prevent the meeting. Larkin was arrested quickly, and as he was being taken away *"the cheering became more intense, and then suddenly a baton charge was directed"*[14]. Many of those injured were innocent churchgoers coming from Mass in the Pro-Cathedral. Within minutes large numbers of men, women and children lay injured in the street and the reputation of the DMP lay in ruins.

Courtesy of the Allen Library

In an *Irish Times* article the following day it was reported that more than 400 civilians and 30 policemen were treated in Dublin's hospitals for injuries sustained in the weekend disturbances. At least six of those treated, two women and four men, resided in Ballybough. They were as follows:

James Dowling, Ballybough; James Saunders, 15 North Richmond Street; Mary Kelly, 15 Summerhill; Mary Wright, 51 Summerhill; Joseph Barrett, 10 Summerhill; Thomas Flood, 12 Summerhill.

On Sunday morning a man died as a result of baton blows received on Saturday night. He was thirty-three year old James Nolan, a father of five from 8 Spring Gardens, Ballybough Road. A post-mortem revealed that Nolan's death resulted from a fracture of the skull and compression of the brain. Witnesses at the inquest claimed that *"the poor man was apparently under the influence of drink, and a constable was seen to strike him a blow over the head*

14. The Irish Times. 1 Sept. 1913

with a baton. The man was not taking any part in the rioting. On being struck by the policeman he fell to the ground, and was given blows while on the ground by other constables"[15]. One eye witness, Patrick Gilligan, reported that *"there were 3 DMP and 2 RIC men and the first constable hit him on the head. Nolan then tried to get up. He struggled to his knees, and he was struck by several policemen."*[16] Despite the identification by witnesses of constables 224C and 149C, no one was ever charged with Nolan's murder on the grounds of insufficient evidence.

Nolan's funeral, attended by the Lord Mayor of Dublin and M.P. Kier Hardy, became a demonstration of working class solidarity. The Transport Union organised a procession, numbering more than 10,000 workers and over a mile in length. People travelled from all over the city to St. Agatha's Church, North William Street, to kneel and pray by the coffin. On 3 September a second man died of injuries sustained in the riots, and many of those previously unsympathetic towards Dublin's strikers were now outraged by the actions of the DMP. The Lord Mayor of Dublin, supported by M.P.s for the city, Dublin Civic League and other public bodies, called for an inquiry into the conduct of the police. The government promised an inquiry would be held when peace was restored.

Meanwhile, the labour disputes were escalating at an alarming pace. The people of Dublin faced considerable hardship in the months that followed. The arrival of *"food ships"* and financial donations from sympathetic trade unionists in Britain provided some relief but the assistance was irregular and limited and could not support 100,000 people. As the cold winter months dragged on, scenes in the city were becoming increasingly shocking.

The huge number of unemployed people on the streets inevitably increased tension and disorder. The Irish Citizen Army, established by the union to protect its workers, was also designed to occupy and discipline the strikers, and to uplift their spirits on the darkest days. The pride taken in their defiant yet orderly displays is best illustrated in the following extract *"Bea went to Croydon Park on Sunday to see the Citizen Army drilled by Captain White, and came back to Dublin with it. She says that the great game of the Army is to march as fast as ever it can. It is escorted by battalions of police 6 feet 6 each and in long skirted coats. The faster the army marches the hotter to the panting the police become, and the whole joy of the Army is to give them a run for their money"*.[17]

The Citizen Army was more than mere spectacle. Its substance was revealed later in 1916, when it played its part in transforming Irish politics.

15. The Irish Times. 2 Sept. 1913
16. The Irish Times. 2 Sept. 1913
17. Diary of Mrs. Augustine Henry, Dec. 1913

Between September and December, several attempts were made to settle the dispute but all ended in deadlock. On 12 November, the union played its trump card by closing down Dublin Port. By the end of January people had already started drifting back to work out of economic necessity.

Neither side emerged triumphant from Dublin's labour war. Indeed, the long struggle had instilled in the labour force of Dublin a sense of class consciousness and determination which would be channelled progressively under more benign market conditions. The outbreak of war in August 1914 provided a more favourable economic climate, and the labour movement reaped the benefits of its long struggle. Employers were compelled to recognise the new union and even conceded to union demands relating to wages and conditions. The Irish Transport & General Workers Union had grown from urban discontent but within a few short years had become a nation-wide union.

The long-term effects of the Dublin Lock-Out extended beyond the labour movement. The militant atmosphere in 1913 contributed to the revolutionary spirit that eventually precipitated the 1916 Rising. In the aftermath of the dispute, Connolly's focus switched to nationalism. The failure of British trade unionism to back the Irish worker, and the virtual collapse of the European socialist movement during the war, convinced Connolly that a socialist society could be achieved only through independence. The Irish Citizen Army, initially established to protect the striking workers, remained in existence after 1913 and became involved in Connolly's new agenda. In January 1916 Pearse was forced to disclose republican plans of an Easter revolt to Connolly, as he correctly feared that the Citizen Army was planning an insurrection of its own. Sworn into the IRB, Connolly henceforth played a prominent role in preparations for the Rising, and the Citizen Army fired the initial shot on Easter Monday.

The socialist element was reflected in the 1916 Proclamation with promises of *"...equal rights and equal opportunities to all it's citizens ..."* and declaring the republic's resolve *"... to pursue the happiness and prosperity of the whole nation ... cherishing all the children of the nation equally"*. Sadly the social agenda was soon submerged in the growing divisions in republican ranks. It could be argued that although the labour movement played a part in the creation of an independent Ireland, it was, in the end its first casualty.

HOWTH GUN-RUNNING

By 1914, the Volunteers and the other nationalist organisations had managed to secure a number of weapons but nowhere near a supply adequate to ensure the success of any military operation. Roger Casement, supported by other

Courtesy of the Allen Library

sympathisers of the Irish cause, raised finances sufficient to buy around 1500 rifles and 45,000 rounds of ammunition. Plans were made to transport the weapons to Ireland and, with the aid of Erskine Childers, the arsenal was conveyed to Howth on 26 July 1914 aboard the yacht *The Asgard*. Signals from Fianna Scouts announced the arrival of the vessel.

The Dublin Brigade of the Irish Volunteers, along with members of Na Fianna and the IRB, had been mobilised to retrieve the guns. E Company 2nd Battalion met at Fr. Matthew Park and, unaware of the plans, undertook what they believed was a routine march to Howth. They had to run the last half mile of the journey as the yacht had arrived. Four other battalions mobilised at Croydon Park and set off on a forced march under sealed orders. The IRB members had been instructed to go to Howth via taxi with a female companion who was to be abandoned as soon as the yacht landed.

Oak batons were distributed to be used if the police attacked. They had been made by the IRB carpenter members. The instructions were to ensure that no person be allowed to enter the harbour area. They were watched by the police who were powerless to act. It took only thirty minutes for the boat to be unloaded, leaving 2000 rounds to be transported by Na Fianna. The party marched back to Dublin, four abreast, and were unapproached until they neared Clontarf/Fairview. Fianna scouts on bicycles informed Commandant Ceannt of the situation, and the Volunteers halted and a Council of War was

Oak baton used during the Howth Gun-Running, 1914. Courtesy of the Allen Library

held. They moved off fifteen minutes later and met with the King's Own Scottish Borders who were armed with fixed bayonets, and accompanied by members of the DMP. There was an understanding among many Republicans at the time that some members of the police force sympathised with the cause of Irish freedom. John Haughey, Volunteer *"who was a young Civil Servant at the time of the Howth Gun-Running, was marching back in column to Dublin with the unfamiliar Mauser rifle awkwardly on his shoulder. One of the policemen who was marching alongside leaned over to him and said 'if you hold it this way, sonny, it will be easier'"*.[18]

A half-hearted fight ensued and lasted for about a minute before the DMP retired. The rear guard had already begun to dispose of the weapons. Realising this, the soldiers charged at the Volunteers and Ceannt amongst others began to shoot. Thomas MacDonagh and Darrell Figgis went to speak with the Chief Commissioner, Mr. Harrell. Some Volunteers tried to take the ammunition held by Na Fianna but the latter were under order from their own Commander, Padraig O Riain, not to give it to any person and they held fast. While negotiations were underway, many of those at the back dispersed and ran through the grounds of the O'Brien Institute, carrying as many weapons and rounds as they could. By the time the police and army realised what had happened, only a small number remained and these were allowed to pass unscathed. Harrell and his men went to Philipsburgh Avenue and Fairview

18. Rev. F.X. Martin – The Howth Gun-Running 1914. 1964. p.177

Fianna Éireann with laden trek-cart returning from Howth, 26 July 1914.
Courtesy of the Allen Library

Strand with a view to intercepting Volunteers there. They met with little success.

As the Volunteers raced across the grounds of the O'Brien Institute, many dropped their arms or hid them along the way. These were later retrieved by Volunteers and members of the Irish Citizen Army, the latter bringing their finds to Croydon Park. In total only nineteen guns were lost. One Volunteer reported that Mr. Newman of the lodge in Marino had a weapon and Thomas MacDonagh went to him personally to retrieve it. He later stated that the events of the day now had established the freeman's right to carry arms openly.

In general terms, the operation was very successful, as it increased the size of the arsenal of the Volunteers, as well as giving a morale boost to its members. It enabled them to commence drilling with actual weaponry and many now truly believed that the dream of revolution was fast becoming a reality.

1916 RISING

Within the Volunteer Executive there were those who believed not only that insurrection was imminent, but that as soon as Dublin engaged in battle, that the remainder of the country would join in. Tom Clarke was a key figure in the plan to precipitate the uprising. Along with Sean MacDiarmada, he began to plan how to use the Volunteers without the knowledge of MacNeill. By 1914 a major recruitment plan was in place for the Volunteers, the Irish Citizen Army and other nationalist organisations.

The Irish Citizen Army were ready and willing to take up arms and fight at a moment's notice and held their training at Croydon Park, Marino. The Ancient Order of Hibernians (AOH) were kept under observation by the DMP who recorded its having a membership of 140 and only 25 rifles. Other nationalist groups also flourished, including Fianna Éireann who were founded by Countess Markievicz in 1909 and had their first Ard Fheis the following year. Members included Con Colbert, Liam Mellowes and Sean Heuston.

The Volunteers appointed officers to command the Dublin battalions in March 1915. The Irish Volunteers were divided into a number of Battalions, which in turn were sub-divided into a number of Companies. There were five Battalions in Dublin, of which three were based on the north side of the city. The Volunteers had their training ground in Fr. Matthew Park. A lease or loan for this had been obtained from its owners, the Capuchin Order. On Saturday evenings, members of the Volunteers could practice their weaponry skills on the rifle range at the park, but this had to be curtailed due to a shortage of ammunition. It was at one of these sessions that Peadar Kearney, composer of the national anthem and member of the 2nd Battalion, was injured by a .22 bullet. He was unable to work as a result of the injury. During the spring of 1915, the Volunteers held a concert in Clontarf Town Hall during which they sold copies of *The Soldier's Song* for 1d each. The proceeds were given to Kearney and this was the first occasion on which the song had been sung in public. Cumann na mBan, the female section of the Irish Volunteers, was not organised until 2 April 1914.

The headquarters of 2nd Battalion were at Clonliffe Hall, Clonliffe Road, where a staff of instructors trained officers and NCOs. Thomas MacDonagh was Commandant, with Tom Hunter as his second in command. Hunter was later to take command of the Battalion for the duration of the Rising. There was no A Company. B Company was the parent Company of the Battalion, and initially used the Clan na nGael Hall on Richmond Road for practising before moving to the park. Many of its members came from the Fairview/Drumcondra area. C Company was made up of members from the City Centre, and D Company was a sketchy effort, while E Company covered the North Strand, Seville Place and the North and East Walls. F Company represented Clontarf and Dollymount, and G Company covered Glasnevin. The latter used the hall of the Ancient Order of Hibernians on Claude Road. The First Battalion was commanded by Edward Daly, with Eamon de Valera responsible for the third and Eamon Ceannt the fourth. Pearse, Plunkett, Hobson and O'Rahilly were commandants of headquarter staff. Initially they planned the rising for September 1915, but for several reasons this was abandoned. Eventually, Easter Sunday 1916 was chosen. Weapons were due to arrive in Kerry from Germany on Good Friday, accompanied by Roger Casement. However, Casement was arrested and the arms lost at sea. MacNeill

Gerald Keogh in full uniform, the first Irish Volunteer to die on Easter Monday 1916. He was shot outside Trinity College. Courtesy of the Allen Library

learned of the planned Rising and immediately placed advertisements in the Sunday newspapers cancelling all manoeuvres for Easter Sunday. The whole event now appeared set to become a complete fiasco, but the leaders had not yet been incarcerated and planned to go ahead with the Rising on Easter Monday. (see Appendix 3)

At noon on Easter Monday, the Rising commenced in Dublin. Pearse stated that they wanted to proclaim an Irish Republic. Slowly key buildings and positions throughout the city were taken over by the rebels, including the GPO, St. Stephen's Green, Jacob's, Boland's Mill, the South Dublin Union, City Hall etc. The military were summoned from the Curragh, and by Tuesday evening martial law had been proclaimed. For nearly a week the battle raged. On Tuesday, Pearse's manifesto to the people stated *"The country is rising in answer to Dublin's call and the final achievement of Ireland's freedom is now, with God's help, only a matter of days"*. However the support of the remainder of the country did not materialise, and on Saturday 29 April, Pearse surrendered. At 4 p.m. the troops were given the order to cease fire.

BALLYBOUGH ACTIVITIES 1916

"When big things happen like this there is often confusion of ideas and people may not always see eye to eye with each other and one warning I give you all, and that is; when you get an order, and you may get an order over this weekend, I want every man to obey it implicitly and if the orders are not carried out, you don't know what damage you could do. One thing I want to sink into your minds and that is; order, counter-order, disorder; that always happens." These words, which were to have profound significance over Easter 1916 were uttered by Thomas MacDonagh a few days prior to the Rising to the men of the Dublin Brigade 2nd Battalion.

On Easter Saturday morning the Battalion was mobilised for a long route march the following day. Volunteers were to carry ammunition, revolvers and rifles. The *Sunday Independent* carried a notice from Eoin MacNeill countermanding all orders, manoeuvres and marches for Easter Sunday. This threw everything into confusion. Many of the Volunteers of the 2nd Battalion met at Fr. Matthew Park but were dispersed by Hunter as nothing seemed to be happening. Leo Henderson, acting Captain of B Company, mounted a guard in the park to protect the arsenal which had been collected there. His watch of four men was relieved at 2:00 a.m. by four others from E Company under the command of Tom Ennis. At 7:30 on Easter Monday morning, Tom Hunter gave orders that there was to be no mobilisation at 2nd Battalion Headquarters. This occurred thirty minutes before Thomas MacDonagh gave full mobilisation orders at Liberty Hall. When news emerged that the GPO had been taken over by Pearse many Volunteers returned to the park and awaited their orders. Company Officers were ordered to have their men at St. Stephen's Green by 10:00 a.m. Many continued to assemble at Fr. Matthew Park because of all the confusion. About half the men from each company of 2nd Battalion were sent to St. Stephen's Green, the remainder stayed behind to guard the stores of munitions and other equipment and supplies.

When the mobilisation order was given Captain Thomas Weafer, E Company 2nd Battalion, headed for St. Stephen's Green. He had breakfast that morning with Sean Russell, 2nd in command to Oscar Traynor, at his house near the railway bridge on the North Strand Road and later returned to Fr. Matthew Park. He had collected medical supplies from his home at 582 North Circular Road and set about finding transport for these and the arms which were held at the park. With the earlier absence of Captain Weafer at the park, Tom Ennis had gone to the GPO to meet with Pearse and then returned with written re-mobilisation orders. Captain Weafer proceeded to order two men to secure transport for the weapons and ammunition which now lay on a big tarpaulin in the park. Seamus Daly and Charlie Saurin headed down to Summerhill and tried to break into a furniture removers. Their activities roused a yardsman who demanded to know what was

Sketch of Thomas Pugh, 9 Charleville Mall, drawn while he was a prisoner at Frongoch Camp, Wales, by T. McCartaigh. Courtesy of the Allen Library

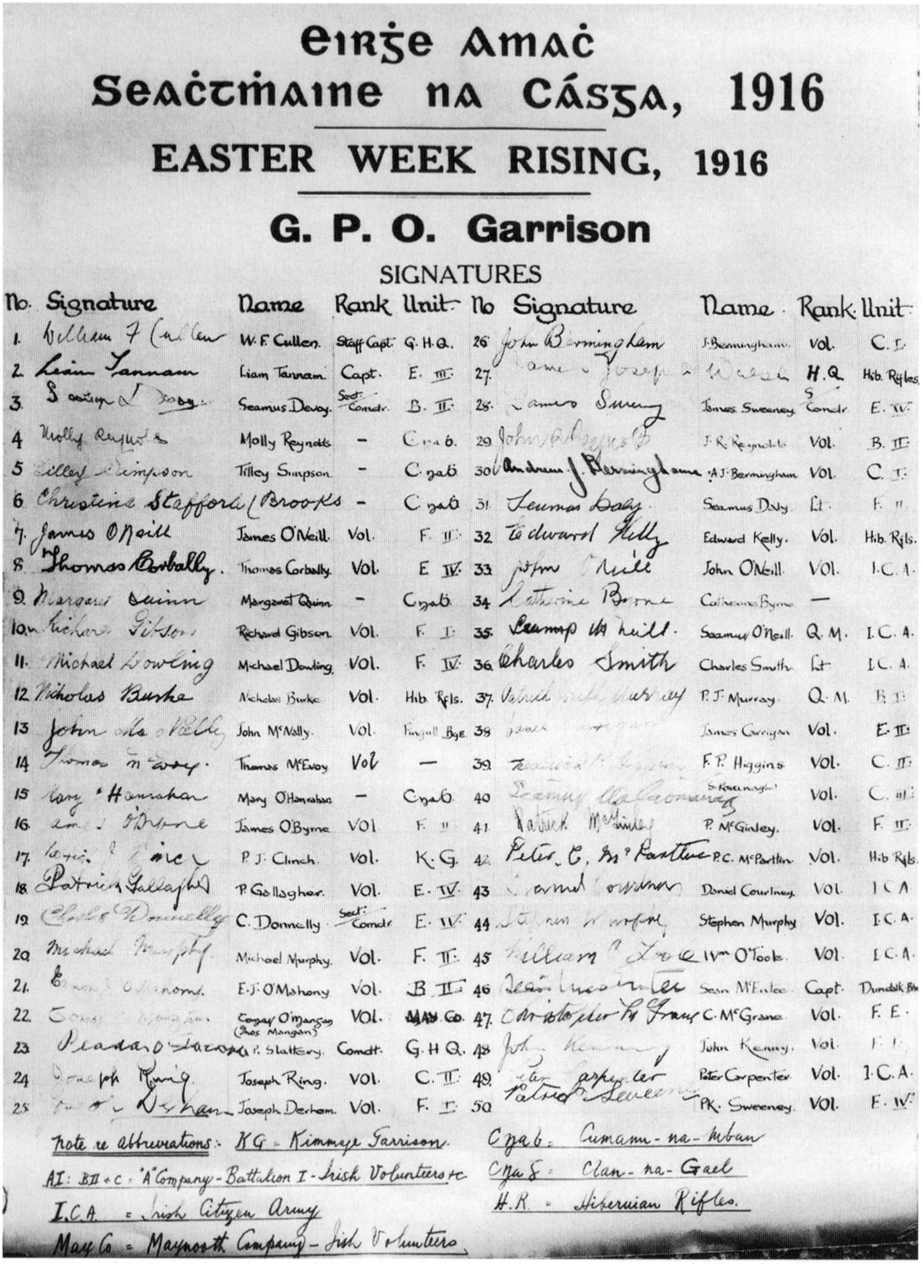

Eirġe Amaċ
Seaċtṁaine na Cásġa, 1916

EASTER WEEK RISING, 1916

G. P. O. Garrison

SIGNATURES

No.	Signature / Name	Rank	Unit	No	Signature / Name	Rank	Unit
1.	W. F. Cullen.	Staff Capt.	G. H. Q.	26	J. Bermingham.	Vol.	C. I.
2.	Liam Tannam.	Capt.	E. III.	27.	Joseph Walsh	H.Q.	Hib. Rifles.
3.	Seamus Devoy.	Sect. Comdr.	B. II.	28.	James Sweeney.	S. Comdr.	E. IV.
4	Molly Reynolds	–	C na b.	29.	J. R. Reynolds.	Vol.	B. II.
5	Tilley Simpson	–	C na b.	30	A. J. Bermingham	Vol.	C. I.
6	Christine Stafford (Brooks)	–	C na b.	31.	Seamus Daly.	Lt.	F. II
7.	James O'Neill.	Vol.	F. II.	32	Edward Kelly.	Vol.	Hib. Rfls.
8.	Thomas Corbally.	Vol.	E. IV.	33	John O'Neill.	Vol.	I. C. A.
9.	Margaret Quinn	–	C na b.	34	Catherine Byrne	–	
10.	Richard Gibson.	Vol.	F. I.	35.	Seamus O'Neill.	Q. M.	I. C. A.
11.	Michael Dowling.	Vol.	F. IV.	36.	Charles Smith.	Lt.	I. C. A.
12	Nicholas Burke	Vol.	Hib. Rfls.	37.	P. J. Murray.	Q. M.	B. I.
13	John McNally.	Vol.	Fingall Bge.	38	James Corrigan	Vol.	E. II.
14	Thomas McEvoy	Vol.	—	39.	F. P. Higgins	Vol.	C. II.
15	Mary O'Hanrahan	–	C na b.	40	S. Kavanagh	Vol.	C. III.
16.	James O'Byrne	Vol.	F. II	41.	P. McGinley.	Vol.	F. II.
17.	P. J. Clinch.	Vol.	K. G.	42.	P. C. McPartlin.	Vol.	Hib. Rfls.
18.	P. Gallagher.	Vol.	E. IV.	43	Daniel Courtney.	Vol.	I. C. A.
19.	C. Donnelly.	Sect. Comdr.	E. IV.	44	Stephen Murphy	Vol.	I. C. A.
20.	Michael Murphy.	Vol.	F. II.	45	Wm O'Toole.	Vol.	I. C. A.
21.	E. J. O'Mahony.	Vol.	B. II.	46	Sean McEntee.	Capt.	Dundalk Bn
22.	Tomas O'Mangan (Thos Mangan)	Vol.	May. Co.	47.	C. McGrane.	Vol.	F. E.
23.	P. Slattery.	Comdt.	G. H. Q.	48	John Kenny.	Vol.	[illegible]
24.	Joseph Ring.	Vol.	C. II.	49.	Peter Carpenter.	Vol.	I. C. A.
25.	Joseph Derham.	Vol.	F. I.	50.	P.K. Sweeney.	Vol.	F. IV.

Note re abbreviations: KG = Kimmage Garrison.
AI: BII + C = "A" Company - Battalion I - Irish Volunteers &c.
I.C.A. = Irish Citizen Army
May Co = Maynooth Company - Irish Volunteers
Cnab. = Cumann-na-mban
CnaG. = Clan-na-Gael
H.R. = Hibernian Rifles.

Roll of Honour, G.P.O. Garrison, Easter 1916

happening. The men managed to get two 4-wheeled lorries and two horses to pull them. When the yard man asked who was going to pay for all this the men replied *"The Irish Republic will pay for this"*. They drove back to the park via Fairview and loaded the trucks while the remainder of the Volunteers fell in. They began their procession to town and went via Ballybough. They had reached Summerhill when they were approached by an old Volunteer on bicycle from B Company who handed a communique to the Company Commander. Upon reading this the party was ordered to turn back and went at *"quick march"*. He had received a message that Infantry from the School of Musketry in Dollymount were nearing Fairview and the Volunteers had been ordered to intercept them. These were the only enemy troops located in this sector of the city.

The Volunteers proceeded down Charleville Avenue which connects Summerhill with the North Strand Road. The enemy could be seen approaching Annesley Bridge. Weafer detached an advance guard of fourteen men under Leo Henderson to intercept them at Newcomen and Annesley Bridges. A rear guard, under Frank Henderson, was deployed to Ballybough Bridge while the main body of approximately 50 commandeered houses near the canal including the house at the corner of Spring Garden Street and the North Strand Road.

The first action for these Volunteers was now imminent. Firing commenced but the troops showed no intention of wanting to become involved in any major confrontation. They in fact were more interested in reaching the docks and Amiens Street Station and securing both positions. Some troops tried to go in small groups across Newcomen Bridge but were fired upon immediately and the others dispersed down East Wall Road but again came under fire from Leinster Avenue. After a while the firing quitened down and soon died way. Two of the Volunteers captured a DMP officer but he was released and told to go home and stay there until the fighting was over. He was returning home off the North Strand after being on duty when the incident occurred. An hour or two after the commencement of the Rising, all DMP officers were ordered from the streets of Dublin by their Commissioner as several had been killed or wounded.

The Volunteers continued down the North Strand Road and neared Amiens Street. They believed that they would encounter the troops again here. They stopped in one of the side streets and it was here that their first casualties were recorded. They had placed their loaded weapons against the walls of the street and some of them fell and instantly went off. Four men were injured and Henderson ordered them to unload their weapons and make their way back towards Fairview. They took possession of a shop and public house overlooking Ballybough Bridge. They questioned any person who came along and turned back several individuals and seized the cars of others. By this time the Irish Citizen Army had taken over the Dublin and Wicklow Manure Works and they were engaged in some prolific action.

By now all the trams and trains in the city were stopped and many of those who had been enjoying a Bank Holiday had to make their way home on foot in the fear of being shot and killed. The last trains to leave Amiens Street on Easter Monday were the 2:00 p.m. to Dundalk and the 2:45 p.m. to Howth. Others were allowed to leave bringing stranded excursionists back to Belfast. Normal services were not restored until 3 May. The trams company also suffered losses of both revenue and vehicles. Two of their trams were overturned on the streets and there was some damage to overhead wires. They also suffered financially as it took about ten days to restore the service.

The British troops in the mean time were trying to use the loop-line to establish the northern end of the cordon at Amiens Street thereby securing the city. These included members of the Royal Dublin Fusiliers from Templemore, the Royal Inniskilling Fusiliers, Royal Irish Fusiliers and other Belfast troops. They came in by rail. The former arrived at Kingsbridge and the latter to a point beyond Amiens Street Station. The line at Fairview sloblands was unusable as attempts had been made to destroy the incoming line between the middle arch at the sloblands and Wharf Road and even though the rails were damaged, traffic was worked over the out-going line. A small body of 2nd Battalion Volunteers were still in action at the Tolka and the troops had to alight beyond the river. More enemy soldiers came from the Howth and Malahide Roads and the docks. The 2nd Battalion continued to fight throughout the day and caused many casualties and captured a number of prisoners. They were now however completely outnumbered.

On the Tuesday orders were received that the Volunteers should make their way to the GPO and they started out and went down the Ballybough Road and eventually arrived at Cumberland Street where they received a hostile welcome. They continued on to the GPO and were met by Pearse who congratulated them on their stand at Ballybough. The men were then given their new orders with some going across the road to assist those who held the Imperial Hotel, now Clery's and the Hibernian Bank on Lower Abbey Street. Captain Thomas Weafer was killed in action here and his body along with the building was later destroyed by fire. No

Inside the G.P.O. during Easter week 1916. Those photographed include Desmond O'Reilly, James Mooney, P. Byrne, John Doyle, Tom McGrath, Hugh Thornton, John J. Twamley & Bernard Frick. The photograph was taken by Joseph Cripps. Courtesy of the Allen Library.

Irish prisoners at an English jail, 1916, possibily Knutsford. Courtesy of the Allen Library

insurgents now remained fighting in the north east sector of the city. This was to have major consequences in the days that followed. The British established their headquarters at Amiens Street Station and completed their cordon of the city. Martial Law was proclaimed in the city that evening and the remainder of the country was affected the following day.

Despite the orders to all Companies of the 2nd Battalion to assemble at St. Stephen's Green, a considerable number of B, E and F went to the GPO.

The *Irish Weekly Independent* stated on 29 April that rebel forces held troops from Belfast at the Ballybough area from Monday to Tuesday evening. There were many snipers shooting from houses and factories in the area. The British forces managed to clear the area of rebels with close quarter fighting. One rebel who had taken the position on a roof top was shot but did not fall as he had secured himself to the chimney by a rope. He lay there for some time.

On Thursday evening sympathisers were rounded up and interned in St. Barnabas's Church and the following evening, after the arrival of General Maxwell in Dublin, all adult males were arrested and interned regardless of their political beliefs. (see Appendix 4)

CUMANN NA MBAN

The female wing of the Irish Volunteers, Cumann na mBan (League of Irish Women), was founded in April 1914 in response to a growing demand from Irish women to play some part in the nationalist struggle. Despite the fact that this was a revolutionary organisation, the role envisaged for these women reflected the traditional notion of a woman's role in society. Cumann na mBan's function was to organise Irish women *"to advance the cause of Irish liberty"* by *"arming and equipping a body of Irishmen for the defence of Ireland"*.[19] The women were also to be trained in First Aid and other skills, which would

19. Margaret Ward – Ungovernable revolutionaries. 1983. p.93

enable them to play a supporting role in any military situation. Although there was to be a separate command structure for Cumann na mBan, each branch was to be attached to an Irish Volunteers battalion and they were to have no representation on the central Volunteer council. Despite these restrictions, however, Cumann na mBan was to afford many Irish women an unprecedented amount of freedom and independence, especially during the dangerous and violent years which followed its foundation.

The Fairview branch of Cumann na mBan was among the first to be established. It was attached to F company 2nd Battalion which was under the command of Frank Henderson. Cumann na mBan had a separate commandant, Molly Reynolds. The women met in Fr. Matthew Park for drilling and training. One of the first members was Nora O'Daly, unusual in that she came from a Scots-Presbyterian background, (her maiden name was Gillies), and her father was a member of the Irish Loyal and Patriotic Union. She came to Cumann na mBan through her membership of the Gaelic League.[20] In her account of the 1916 period, she describes the women's *"principle study"* as being First Aid, as

Fairview Cumann na mBan c. 1915.
Back row left to right : Gertie Colley, Esther Wisely (later Moore), Statia Twomey & Amee MacDonald. Front row seated : (2nd from right) May Wisely (later Moore).
Courtesy of Kilmainham Gaol & Museum & Ms. Eithne O'Moor

20. Interview with Mr. Tony Roche, grandson of Nora O'Daly
21. Nora O'Daly (1926) – 'Cumann na mBan in Stephen's Green and the College of Surgeons'. An t-Óglach

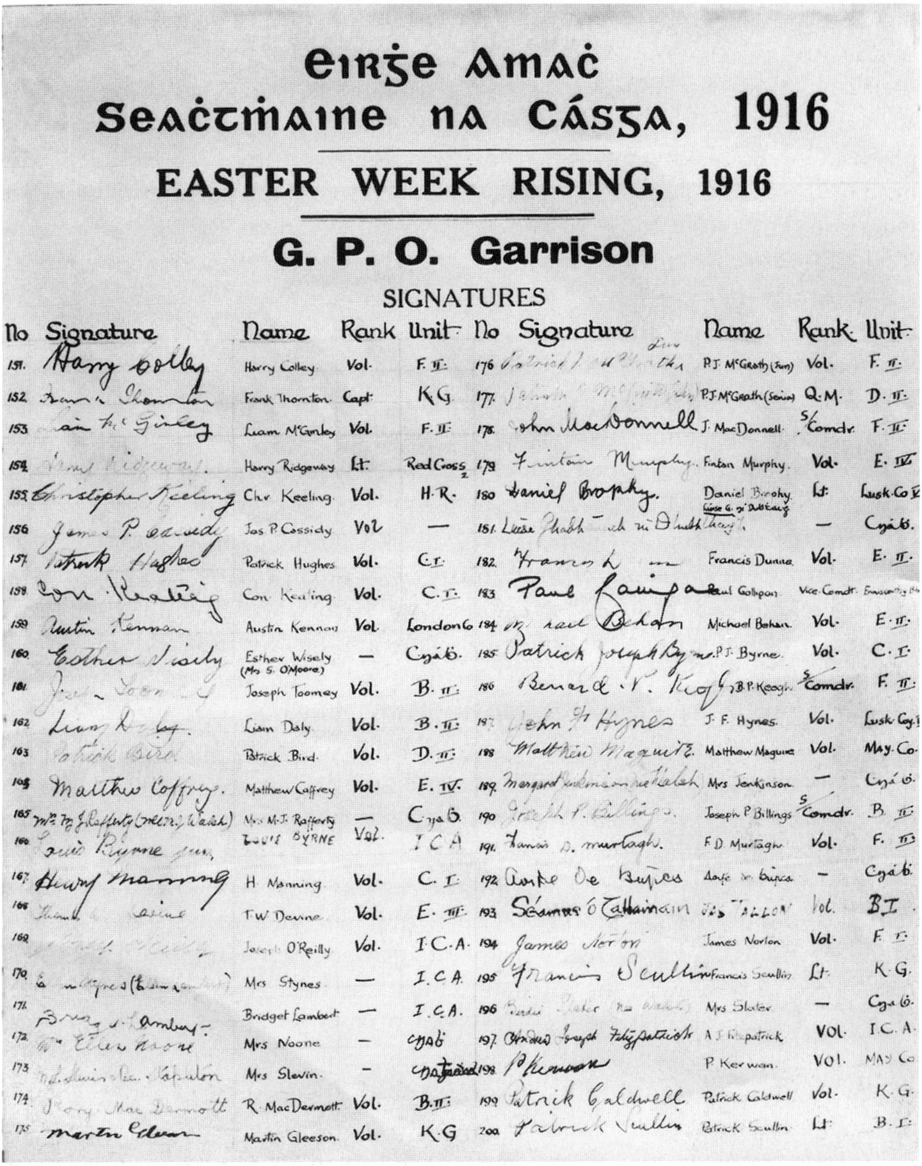

Eirġe Amaċ Seaċtṁaine na Cásġa, 1916

EASTER WEEK RISING, 1916

G. P. O. Garrison

SIGNATURES

No	Signature	Name	Rank	Unit
151.	Harry Colley	Harry Colley	Vol.	F. II.
152.	Frank Thornton	Frank Thornton	Capt.	K.G.
153.	Liam McGinley	Liam McGinley	Vol.	F. II.
154.	Harry Ridgeway	Harry Ridgeway	Lt.	Red Cross 2
155.	Christopher Keeling	Chr. Keeling	Vol.	H.R.
156.	James P. Cassidy	Jos P. Cassidy	Vol.	—
157.	Patrick Hughes	Patrick Hughes	Vol.	C.I.
158.	Con Keating	Con Keating	Vol.	C.I.
159.	Austin Kennan	Austin Kennan	Vol.	London G.
160.	Esther Wisely	Esther Wisely (Mrs S. O'Moore)	—	Cyab.
161.	Joseph Toomey	Joseph Toomey	Vol.	B. II.
162.	Liam Daly	Liam Daly	Vol.	B. II.
163.	Patrick Bird	Patrick Bird	Vol.	D. II.
164.	Matthew Caffrey	Matthew Caffrey	Vol.	E. IV.
165.	Mrs M. J. Rafferty (née Walsh)	Mrs M. J. Rafferty	—	Cyab.
166.	Louis Byrne jun.	Louis Byrne	Vol.	I C A
167.	Henry Manning	H. Manning	Vol.	C. I.
168.	[illegible]	T.W. Devine	Vol.	E. III.
169.	[illegible]	Joseph O'Reilly	Vol.	I.C.A.
170.	[illegible]	Mrs Stynes	—	I.C.A.
171.	Bridget Lambert	Bridget Lambert	—	I.C.A.
172.	Mrs Ellen Noone	Mrs Noone	—	Cyab.
173.	[illegible]	Mrs Slevin	—	Cyab.
174.	Rory MacDermott	R. MacDermott	Vol.	B. II.
175.	Martin Gleeson	Martin Gleeson	Vol.	K.G.

No	Signature	Name	Rank	Unit
176	[illegible]	P.J. McGrath (Jun)	Vol.	F. II.
177.	[illegible]	P.J. McGrath (Senior)	Q.M.	D. II.
178.	John MacDonnell	J. MacDonnell	S/Comdr.	F. II.
179	Fintan Murphy	Fintan Murphy	Vol.	E. IV.
180	Daniel Brophy	Daniel Brophy	Lt.	Lusk Co.
181.	[illegible]	[illegible]	—	Cyab.
182.	Francis [illegible]	Francis Dunne	Vol.	E. II.
183	Paul Galligan	Paul Galligan	Vice Comdt.	Enniscorthy Bn
184	Michael Behan	Michael Behan	Vol.	E. II.
185	Patrick Joseph Byrne	P.J. Byrne	Vol.	C. I.
186	Bernard V. Keogh	B.P. Keogh	S/Comdr.	F. II.
187	John F. Hynes	J. F. Hynes	Vol.	Lusk Coy.
188	Matthew Maguire	Matthew Maguire	Vol.	May. Co.
189.	Margaret Jenkinson née Walsh	Mrs Jenkinson	—	Cyab.
190	Joseph P. Billings	Joseph P Billings	S/Comdr.	B. II.
191.	Francis D. Murtagh	F.D. Murtagh	Vol.	F. II.
192.	Aoife de Búrca	Aoife de Búrca	—	Cyab.
193	Séamus Ó Cathánain	[illegible]	Vol.	B.I.
194	James Norton	James Norton	Vol.	F. I.
195	Francis Scullin	Francis Scullin	Lt.	K.G.
196	[illegible]	Mrs Slater	—	Cyab.
197.	Andrew Joseph Fitzpatrick	A.J. Fitzpatrick	Vol.	I.C.A.
198	P. Kerwan	P. Kerwan	Vol.	May Co.
199	Patrick Caldwell	Patrick Caldwell	Vol.	K.G.
200	Patrick Scullin	Patrick Scullin	Lt.	B. I.

Roll of Honour, listing some of Cumann na mBan who were in the G.P.O. Easter 1916

well as cleaning and sighting, drill and *"various other things which might prove useful in assisting the men of 2nd Battalion"*.[21] This sometimes included intelligence-gathering work. Nora O'Daly describes a trip she and one of the other women took to the Magazine Fort in the Phoenix Park on Easter Saturday 1916. Posing as two girls on a day out, they engaged the soldiers on guard in conversation while simultaneously checking guard numbers and officer visits. The two young women aroused less suspicion than would men on a similar mission.

Despite all the preparation of the Volunteers, when the Rising finally started, there was total disarray. Pearse, Connolly and the IRB had secretly planned for Easter Sunday. When this was discovered by Eoin MacNeill, the head of the Irish Volunteers, orders were issued for its cancellation. Thus when Nora and the other women arrived at Fr. Matthew Park on Easter Sunday, they were told to return home as manoeuvres had been cancelled. In an interesting stand for the independence of Cumann na mBan, Nora O'Daly refused to leave without orders from *"her own commandant"*, Molly Reynolds.[22] When Pearse and the other leaders decided to go ahead with the rebellion on Easter Monday, without MacNeill's permission, most of the Volunteers were unaware of what was happening. The Volunteer whose car was to collect the arms stored in a house owned by Nora O'Daly's husband, Seamus, had gone to the country for the holiday weekend believing that everything was cancelled. News of the rebellion had to be passed on by word of mouth.

Gertie Colley, whose brother Harry was mobilised, left her home on Clonliffe Road for St. Stephen's Green on Easter Monday. She met Amy (Esther) Wisely and Tilly (Mathilda) Simpson on the North Strand tram. They went together into the city centre, but were refused entry into St. Stephen's Green. Cumann na mBan headquarters was closed as was the GPO, the windows of which were broken. They decided to return to the park where they informed Frank Henderson of the situation in the city. While they were there, orders came from James Connolly for any available Cumann na mBan members to go immediately to the GPO.[23]

When they arrived, Gertie Colley and Amy Wisely were sent to the make-shift hospital on the ground floor. There they met their commanding officer, Molly Reynolds, and their fellow Fairview member, Statia Toomey. Gertie and Amy were then sent to the kitchen, which was being run by Louise Gavan Duffy and Desmond Fitzgerald. The women were to stay there for the next week, sleeping in relays on mattresses on the ground.

As well as First Aid and kitchen duty, the women were invaluable as dispatch carriers. In one account of the week it was claimed that *"Cumann an mBan girls did practically all the dispatch ...but none of them was unsuccessful. That was a point of honour with them – to succeed or be killed"*.[24]

Their gender was actually an advantage in bringing food and messages through British Army lines. The *"fairer sex"* were not perceived as a military threat. Gertie Colley and Amy Wisely were sent to collect messages from Mr.

22. ibid
23. Gertie Colley Murphy's unpublished account of 1916 (copy) – Kilmainham Gaol Collection
24. Sinead McCoole – Guns and chiffon. 1996. p.16
25. Gertie Colley Murphy's unpublished account of 1916 (copy) – Kilmainham Gaol Collection

W. O'Reilly in Foster Terrace and Mr. Moran in James's Avenue. As this was in their neighbourhood, it gave Gertie a chance to slip home and freshen up as well as collect some fresh clothes for Molly Reynolds.[25]

Nora O'Daly had also gone to the GPO. However, when she arrived 2nd Battalion were not there. She was told that nurses were needed at St. Stephen's Green, so she and her companions, May Moore and Bridget Murtagh, set off to see if they could be of assistance. On arrival at the Green they were greeted by the daunting figure of Countess Markievicz, the second in command. Their initial wariness of the *"rebel Countess"* was eased by Madeline ffrench-Mullen who seemed much more down-to-earth. She had established a field hospital in one of the summer houses. Nora O'Daly was not impressed by the outpost *"the Green, even to a mind untrained in military matters, looked like a regular death-trap, and although I am quite willing to die to help free Ireland, I saw no reason for doing so if I could help it before I had accomplished the purpose which had brought me hither, namely, to render assistance to save life wherever possible"*.[26]

This uneasiness was to be borne out by the events of the week. The park itself was slowly surrounded by British Army snipers. Eventually the Volunteers were forced to retreat to the College of Surgeons. The Volunteers were effectively trapped in the building. Margaret Skinnider was forced to *"run the gauntlet"* of machine gun fire every time she left the building to bring messages to the GPO. One day she saw them shooting at some of the First Aid women *"who made excellent targets in their white dresses, with large red crosses on them. It was a miracle that none of them was wounded. Bullets passed though one girl's skirt and another had the heel of her shoe shot off"*.[27]

A native of Glasgow, Margaret Skinnider was a member of both Cumann na mBan and the Irish Citizen Army. In line with socialist philosophy, the women in the Irish Citizen Army were treated as equals rather than just auxiliaries to the men. During Easter week Margaret Skinnider saw an opportunity to remove a British Army sniper by blowing up the Shelbourne Hotel. At first Michael Mallin, the commanding officer in St. Stephen's Green, was rather reluctant to allow a woman to be involved in such an operation. Skinnider answered his reservations by pointing out that *"we had the same right to risk our lives as the men; that in the constitution of the Irish republic, women were on an equality with men. For the first time in history, indeed, a constitution had been written that incorporated the principle of equality of men"*.[28]

She was allowed to take part in the operation but was badly wounded, the only woman to be seriously injured in open battle. In the years that followed

26. Nora O'Daly (1926) – 'Cumann na mBan in the GPO'. An t-Óglach
27. Margaret Skinnider – Doing my bit for Ireland. 1917. p.28
28. ibid

the Rising, Margaret moved to Fairview and joined the local Cumann na mBan branch.

By Wednesday evening all hope seemed lost in the Green. The leaders gave the women the option to return to their homes but they refused to do so. When they finally surrendered, they were brought up York Street to Ship Street Barracks. From there they were brought to Richmond Barracks and Kilmainham Gaol. Nora O'Daly shared one of the cells in the gaol with three others, surviving on meagre rations of cocoa, inedible biscuits, thin stew and potatoes. In her account of her part in the Rising, she describes being awakened by the shots which executed the leaders of the Rebellion.

As the week progressed, conditions deteriorated in the GPO also. On Thursday Gertie Colley was asked to go with Brigid Connolly to bring food to the men in Henry Street. On her way through the bombed out building, Gertie Colley became visibly upset. She saw what appeared to be a girl with her head blown off. She was relieved to discover that it was just a wax model. The men to whom they brought supplies were led by Captain Henderson, one of the officers from Fairview. They had to serve the food under gun fire. When they had finished, Captain Henderson asked them to bring one of the wounded Volunteers back to the GPO. This soldier was also from Ballybough, and he asked Gertie Colley to write a letter to his father for him, despite the fact that no messages could be dispatched at that time.[29]

When the time came for the women to depart from the GPO they were divided into a number of groups. The first party of about twenty or so left on Friday morning, and included Amy Wisely, Gertie Colley and Mary O'Hanrahan. After thanking the women for their contribution, Pearse handed Gertie Colley a Red Cross flag. With the help of Amy Wisely and Brigid Connolly she led the women as they climbed over the barricades on Henry Street on their way to Jervis Street Hospital. They were refused access there, and so they headed along Capel Street, where they encountered a line of British soldiers. They were sent up Parnell Street and headed home. They were finally stopped at the corner of Summerhill and the North Circular Road by a detachment of troops and brought to Broadstone station for questioning. Eventually they were released with passes home.[30]

Molly Reynolds was a member of the second group of women to leave the GPO. They were ordered to bring the wounded to Jervis Street Hospital. Together with a priest, the British military doctor and supplies of food and water, they set off through the building around the GPO. *"The going was necessarily slow because we had to make our way through the holes in walls, and you can not imagine what it was like trying to carry wounded men in blankets,*

29. Gertie Colley Murphy's unpublished account of 1916 (copy) – Kilmainham Gaol Collection
30. ibid

carry the stuff we had with us, and get through the holes, some of which were near the ground, others necessitating a little climbing".[31]

They decided to go through the Coliseum Hotel on Prince's Street. However the lane at the corner of *The Freeman's Journal*, which should have led them onto Abbey Street, was blocked by a burning barricade. They were effectively trapped, unable to go back and the way ahead blocked by fire. Eventually they managed to mount the barricade and trample down the fire.

When they reached Jervis Street, the British military doctor gained admission for the wounded. The help of the women was not needed, however. Unsure of the situation in the city, the women refused the offer of military passes and spent the night in the dispensary instead. The whole experience had taken its toll. Molly Reynolds describes one of the girls going into hysterics the following Saturday morning. When she was eventually calmed down, they left for home. On their first foray out they got only as far as Parnell Square before being sent back to Jervis Street. On their second attempt they reached the Parnell monument. They described themselves as Red Cross nurses and, after some debate, were allowed to pass. While this interrogation was taking place, the leaders of the Rising were lined up on the opposite side of the street. The women said nothing to them because they *"were afraid of giving ourselves away and perhaps landing them into further trouble"*.[32]

They were stopped once again at Portland Row. Molly Reynolds was particularly worried when one of the soldiers suggested she be searched. In her bag were several Cumann na mBan badges and copies of the Proclamation. Luckily the search was not carried out. One of the women was made return to Jervis Street to seek confirmation of their claim to be Red Cross nurses. On her return, they were allowed to continue on their journey. By then it was growing dark and many of the women were afraid that they would not make it home before curfew. They decided to go together to the house of one of the women who lived nearby. Molly Reynolds was arrested the following Saturday and brought to Richmond Barracks in Inchicore. She was released later the same day and no charges were brought against her.

In the aftermath of the Rising, the value of the contribution of the women was undeniable. It was with some confidence that a correspondent in *Leabhar na mBan*, the official organ of Cumann na mBan, wrote in 1915 *"It is recognised that Ireland needs a national army of defence – the Irish Volunteers – and the co-operation of the women of Ireland with the army is necessary for its efficiency"*.[33]

Many members of Cumann na mBan were involved in the Irish National Aid Association and Volunteer Dependents Fund, which was coordinated by

31. Molly Reynolds (1926) – 'Cumann na mBan in the GPO'. An t-Óglach
32. ibid
33. Leabhar na mBan 1915

Aftermath of 1916 Rising, Church Street. Courtesy of the Allen Library

Kathleen, the widow of Thomas Clarke. Money was raised for the families of those who were killed or imprisoned during the Rising. Public manifestations of support for Sinn Fein, such as the crowds on the streets of Dublin when Countess Markievicz was released, or at the funeral of Thomas Ashe, owed a lot to the organisation of the women.

Despite the undoubted role of Cumann na mBan in 1916, the nationalist leaders retained their conservative attitudes towards their female counterparts. When the Sinn Fein executive was first convened, there were no female members. While the Volunteers were automatically given representation on the executive, Cumann na mBan, supposedly its equal, was ignored. Eventually, after much lobbying and pressure, four female representatives were co-opted. When the Sinn Fein Convention which selected the candidates met in 1917, only twelve out of four hundred delegates were women. Countess Markievicz, President of Cumann na mBan, and Winnie Carney, another 1916 veteran, were the only women selected as election candidates.[34]

Around this time, another member joined the Fairview branch, or the Four Martyrs branch, as it was to become known. Her name was Florence McCarthy[35] or Blathnad Ni Charthaigh. She had moved with her family from Limerick following the death of her father. As well as working for the Prisoner's Dependents Fund, she distributed leaflets on prison conditions outside Arbour Hill and other jails where IRA men were being held. As part of

34. Margaret Ward (1996) – 'The league of women and Sinn Fein'. History Ireland
35. Eithne Coyle's unpublished account of Florence McCarthy – UCD Archives

Cumann na mBan's Irish Manufacture Campaign, she and the other members canvassed various shops in the city, encouraging them to sell Irish-made goods. When one department store refused, Florence threw a brick through its plate glass window. A few days later a sign appeared on the shop proclaiming *"we sell Irish manufacture goods here"*. Florence also managed to obtain a stand at the RDS Spring Show at which Cumann na mBan sold *An Phoblacht* and nationalist books, much to the displeasure of the RDS committee. Her greatest propaganda coup, however, was a campaign to remove any Union Jacks displayed as part of the Armistice Day commemoration. The largest flag was flying from the Kildare Street Club. Along with Sighle Humphries, Maura Deegan and Eileen Barry, she made her way up to the offending flag and burnt it, closely pursued by the doorman. His attempts to hold them until the police arrived were frustrated when Florence McCarthy produced a bottle of petrol which she pretended was vitriol. He was forced to release the women. It was because of such activities that Florence was nicknamed "the tough one".

NORTH RICHMOND STREET 1916

Michael Peter Mogan was a coadjutor Brother at the North Richmond Street monastery during the conflict of 1916. He wrote to his sister, a nun at the Presentation Convent, Castleisland, and told her of the terrifying events which occurred during Easter Week as well as highlighting the plight of those who were not directly involved.

Food supply was critical during this period as all shops were closed. The military were constantly present on the streets and people were not allowed to pass. Br. Mogan had to venture out on several occasions to procure food. On one occasion he only managed to obtain two dozen loaves and another time he got some meat. This was not a very substantial quantity of food to feed a starving monastery. Another time he had better fortune and got six dozen eggs and a few pots of jam. Butter was impossible to obtain. He stated that if the conflict had lasted much longer then the Brothers would have starved.[36]

Five shells exploded at the Novitiate in Marino but no damage was caused to the buildings or their residents. Some of the novices however were mistaken for Volunteers and were subsequently fired on by the British troops. Barriers were placed across the street in front of North Richmond Street and it was possible to see Volunteers and soldiers firing at each other. Some of the Brothers opted to sleep on the floor while others barricaded the windows for fear of being shot accidentally. This continued for the duration of the Rising until normality was restored to this otherwise peaceful community.

36. J. Anthony Gaughan – Easter Week 1916. The Kerry Magazine. Allen Library

Chapter 12

1917 - 1945

Following the 1916 Rising, many Irish prisoners were interned in prisons throughout Ireland and Britain. By August 1916, 600 prisoners had been released; many others were freed by Christmas.

Following their release Volunteers travelled by boat to Dun Laoghaire and then made their way to the city centre by train. When Seamus Daly of the 2nd Battalion arrived at Westland Row Station, his first ambition was to see the city centre and the destruction which had been caused as a result of Easter week. He then made his way home on the tram to Dollymount, and for the first time began to notice the change in attitude of the ordinary people of Dublin towards the Volunteers. The people of Clontarf gave *"their boys"* a cheery welcome home. He recalled a tram conductor who was known for his dour nature, and who had never previously spoken to Volunteers, deliberately shaking the men's hands and bidding them a warm welcome.

Sketch of Lower Compound, Frongoch, 1916, by Eoghan O Briain. Courtesy of the Allen Library

After 1916 Cathal Brugha set about reorganising the volunteer movement. Under the guise of dancing classes, one nationalist organisation met at a new premises adjoining Clonliffe College Wall on Clonliffe Road. Many of the older Volunteers attended here on a few occasions but eventually stopped as they did not recognise many of the members. A Gaelic League Branch was

Courtesy of the Allen Library

established in Clontarf Town Hall until the general release of prisoners was announced in 1917. Among its members were the Tallon family. F Company reconvened in Clonliffe Hall and Frank Henderson took control, with Oscar Traynor and Pat Sweeney as Lieutenants. The Company started drilling and began preparations for their new war.

RETURN OF I.R.A. PRISONERS, MONDAY, 18th JUNE, 1917.
ARRIVAL AT WESTLAND ROW.

Courtesy of the Allen Library

The newly reformed Volunteer Corps had weekly training sessions where they wore uniforms and learned how to march. In August they were prohibited by law from carrying weapons, or articles capable of being used as such. They continued to march and the numbers arrested rose. By this time it was estimated that there were approximately 60,000 Volunteers.[1]

Sinn Féin, which had almost faded out of existence by 1916 was also witnessing a revival, and by 1917 a new nationwide organisation was evolving.

The first Volunteer Convention was held in Croke Park on 27 October 1917, two days after the Sinn Féin Ard Fheis, with 2nd Battalion supplying a portion of the armed guard. Almost all of those present at the Convention had been delegates at the Ard Fheis, showing how closely linked both organisations had become.

1918 GENERAL ELECTION

Only two weeks after the end of the first World War, on 25 November, the House of Commons was dissolved and a general election called for Saturday 14 December. The election in Ballybough saw two of the more famous names of the Irish Free State begin their political careers. These were Alfie Byrne and Richard Mulcahy. They fought on opposing sides on this occasion but their political affiliations were the same during the Civil War and afterwards. Alfie Byrne was elected Lord Mayor ten times and became one of the most famous and popular characters around Dublin, having the distinction of being the only politician in the city to have a soccer club named after him. Mulcahy later became a government minister and eventually leader of his party.

Home Rule had been a casualty of the war but still remained on the statute books awaiting implementation. The Irish Parliamentary Party, whose raison d'être had been the introduction of Home Rule, had seen their dreams almost become a reality. However, the 1916 Rising had brought much sympathy for the republican cause in its aftermath.

The 1918 election recorded a number of significant *"firsts"*. It was the first United Kingdom election in which all three Kingdoms voted on the same day. It was also the first in which the votes were not counted immediately but instead transported to safe locations where they were guarded until counting commenced. A third and even more crucial change, which was to have ongoing implications for politics, was the enfranchisement of women. The 1918 contest saw the first female candidates in a British general election; in fact, an Irish woman, Countess Markievicz became the first female M.P. Not everyone was happy about this. John Dillon was criticised in Republican and Labour circles for allegedly stating that in his opinion, the granting of votes to women *"would be the end of our whole western civilisation"*.

1. Capuchin Annual. 1967. p.384

Most of the Ballybough area was in the Mountjoy and North Dock Wards, with the area north of Clonliffe Road in the Drumcondra Ward. These had been regarded as safe nationalist seats in previous municipal elections, but nationalism had taken on a new mantle after the events of 1916, and a new type of voter no longer satisfied with the nationalism of the Home Rule movement had emerged.

The election became a referendum between Unionism and Nationalism in those constituencies where there was a Unionist candidate (effectively the North East and parts of Dublin), or a contest between total independence and devolution in the rest of the country. This had major implications for the outcome of the contest, particularly in districts such as Ballybough, as it ensured the working-class nationalist vote would not be split.

For the purposes of the 1918 election, Ballybough was divided into two constituencies: Dublin Harbour and the new Dublin Clontarf, with Summerhill/Summerhill Parade and the Royal Canal as the dividing line. The Clontarf constituency included Clontarf, Drumcondra, East Wall and that part of the Mountjoy Ward north of Summerhill.

The Harbour constituency straddled the Liffey and included the South Dock and North Dock Wards, and that part of the Mountjoy Ward south and west of Summerhill and the canal.

The Alderman for the North Dock Ward and outgoing MP for Harbour was Alfie Byrne, representing the Irish Parliamentary Party. He had sold his public house in Talbot Street to raise funds for the 1915 by-election. He was defending his seat against Philip Shanahan, a Tipperary man and fellow publican, who had a premises on Foley Street. The two men knew each other well and were on friendly terms; Shanahan had worked as election agent for Byrne in the previous by-election. However, while Byrne had continued to favour Home Rule, Shanahan

General Richard Mulcahy, (head turned), reviewing the Dublin Brigade Irish Volunteers on the occasion of taking over the military barracks from the British after The Treaty. Courtesy of the Allen Library

had been active during the 1916 rebellion and had been interned for his participation.

On the other side of Summerhill, in the Clontarf constituency, Richard Mulcahy was the nominated Sinn Féin candidate. He too was a veteran of 1916 and had seen action under Thomas Ashe in Ashbourne. Indeed his experience in 1916 was to have a profound influence on the IRA's military strategy. In Ashbourne the volunteers had adopted aggressive, mobile tactics as opposed to the defensive stance taken by the other units in the Rising. Mulcahy, who was later to become Chief-of-Staff of the IRA, saw at first hand how effective guerrilla tactics could be against a better-armed enemy. All forces did not have to act at once, they had greater mobility, and there was more effective use of limited ammunition.

He had worked as a clerk in the Post Office until the Rising and at the time of the election was studying medicine at University College Dublin, surviving on a subsistence allowance paid by the Prisoners Dependents Fund administered by Tom Clarke's widow, Kathleen. He was running against Sir Patrick Shortall, the Nationalist candidate.

As neither contest in the Ballybough constituencies involved a Unionist, the candidates were looking for votes from the same base. This caused considerable friction between candidates. Sinn Féin appealed to people's patriotic emotions, while the *"Party"* appealed to voter loyalty for the party of Redmond and Parnell. Both claimed to be the true representatives of the Irish people.

Polling Stations in Ballybough were located in St. Columba's National School, North Strand, for Clontarf, and in St. Patrick's National School for Harbour. In Clontarf, supporters of both camps were well supplied with vehicles to transport old and infirm voters to the booths. Two-thirds of the electorate were voting for the first time, and at times it showed; one man posted his ballot sheet through a slit in the wood of the polling booth. One of the personating officers noticed and invited the man to recover his ballot paper and drop it in the box. The Archbishop of Dublin, Dr. Walsh, voted early in Clontarf and then handed his voting card to one of Mulcahy's election agents before departing to vote in Dublin North where he also had a vote.

In the evening, however, there were difficulties transporting the ballot boxes to the count centre in Green Street Courthouse. In addition to motor cars occupied by police and party workers, a private automobile which happened to be passing was pressed into service and manned by police.

In the Harbour constituency *"utmost friendliness prevailed between rival parties and police said that they had rarely seen an election so free from disorder and disturbance"*. No doubt this was helped by the fact that opening hours were restricted to between 11 a.m. and 5 p.m., especially considering the contest involved two publicans. Nonetheless, a certain friction had developed during the campaign. Unsubstantiated reports tell of Republican supporters accusing Byrne of distributing bags of coal in an attempt to bribe voters. They composed a song declaring *"We don't want your coal"* and in the next line, which rhymed, told Byrne where he could put the above-mentioned fuel, before urging voters to *"vote, vote, vote for Shanahan"*.

A group of workers entered the station bearing a large scroll stating *"We won't vote for Byrne"*. The Dublin Dockyard workers, many wearing Sinn Féin badges, also came to vote together, led by a pipe band and carrying a banner which said *"The dockyard workers demand freedom not slavery."*

The Harbour constituency was typical of the whole country in the turnout of women recorded there. Female voters, anxious to avail of the opportunity to vote, registered an 85-90% turnout, but not one charge of personation was brought against any woman. There were no reported incidents of children being left unwashed and families going unfed, contrary to some predictions, although one party election agent complained of being ignored by his wife and daughter as they brought sandwiches to the Sinn Féin agents. Indeed the majority of women voting in Harbour openly supported Sinn Féin, which also seemed to be typical of the whole country.

Towards the end of the day, Alfie Byrne alleged that there had been an illegality in one of the polling stations, and said that he would demand a new election if he lost. When Philip Shanahan came to cast his own vote, he was objected to by one of Byrne's agents and had to prove his identity to the officer in charge before being allowed to proceed. Leaving aside these incidents, the final verdict given by most contemporary observers was one of order and discipline. One periodical declared *"The most momentous General Election ever held in Ireland has also been one of the most dignified"*.

The election was decisive. The electorate had to choose between candidates who all wanted self-rule for Ireland. The results were kept secret until after Christmas. Sinn Féin claimed victory from the moment the polling booths closed. The following day even the newspapers most loyal to the Parliamentary Party cause admitted that the final result would show a Sinn Féin victory.

When the results were published on the 29 December, they showed a resounding triumph for Republicans. Out of the 103 seats contested, 73 candidates were returned. On the other hand there was a crushing defeat for Nationalists. Only six of their candidates won seats. The Unionists increased the number of seats they held from 18 to 26, in what was for them a bitter-sweet victory. They could no longer prevent some form of self-government for

Ireland, but the result improved their position for keeping the North-East in the Union.

Constance Markievicz was elected in Dublin. The only other female to contest the election in Ireland, Winifred Carney in Belfast, was easily beaten by the Unionist candidate, T. Donald.

Ballybough reflected the vote of the greater part of the country when it returned Sinn Féin candidates in both constituencies; Mulcahy defeated Shortall by 5,974 votes to 3,228, and Shanahan defeated Byrne by 7,708 to 5,368.

Alfie Byrne, speaking at the count centre said that it was the fifth time in his life to go before the electorate *"and the last time"* shouted a heckler who was then booed by many of those present. Alfie Byrne continued his speech without further interruption. He declared that the organisation he was up against was second to none, and he hoped that one day they would stand on the same platform to achieve the objectives which all Irishmen desired.

The heckler was as incorrect as he was unpopular. This turned out to be the only election that Alfie Byrne was to lose in a long political career which would see him become Lord Mayor of Dublin on ten occasions. He gained the respect of many republicans during the War of Independence by visiting prisoners, often conveying secret messages at great personal risk. Although he was elected to Dáil Éireann as an independent member, he was an ally of W.T. Cosgrave, first Taoiseach of Saorstát Éireann.

Richard Mulcahy, speaking after his election, said that the Parliamentary Party had paid the price for ignoring the huge national movement encompassing the G.A.A., the Gaelic League and the Volunteers. He criticised it for ridiculing *"the development in the minds of an Irish Republic"* and endeavouring to *"crush the Volunteer movement"*.

Sinn Féin decided to convene a parliament in Dublin and extended invitations to all elected representatives, including Unionists, to attend the first Dáil which was held in the Mansion House on 21 January 1919. Only the Sinn Féin deputies arrived, among them Richard Mulcahy and Philip Shanahan, but many other representatives could not be present as they were still detained in prison. Cathal Brugha was the speaker on this occasion and presided over the Declaration of Independence.

On the same day, an explosives lorry was attacked in Soloheadbeg, Co. Tipperary and two policemen were killed. Richard Mulcahy was reportedly annoyed to hear about such activities on the same day as the first meeting of the Dáil. It was his first real taste of the conflict between political and military action which was to become central to his life, as he went on to hold the simultaneous positions of democratic representative and Chief of Staff of the Volunteers. Soloheadbeg heralded the start of the War of Independence and Mulcahy's military, as opposed to representational skills, became increasingly important.

He became an effective but highly controversial Minister for Defence in the first government of the Irish Free State, held various other ministerial portfolios and became leader of Fine Gael. He retired from public life in 1959.

WAR OF INDEPENDENCE

During the War of Independence, 2nd Battalion were involved in many attacks and ambushes, including several at Ballybough Bridge against British troop lorries which carried 15-20 armed soldiers and police. As a result of one such attack, a cordon was established around the Summerhill-Mountjoy district for three days during which every man was interrogated and every house searched.

On 19 December 1919, members of the Battalion were involved in the ambush of Lord French. The operation was not a success and one of those involved, Dan Breen, was injured. He was taken to the home of Jack and Joe Toomey on the Phibsborough Road. These men had fought in 1916 and had lived at Clonmore Terrace. Breen had been instrumental in the first incident of the War of Independence at Soloheadbeg, Co. Tipperary. He was active in Dublin during 1920-1921 and was later injured in Drumcondra. The following year on 3 April, the Volunteers set fire to and destroyed the Tax Office at Beresford Place.

Frank Flood.
Courtesy of the Allen Library

The Battalion's strength, however, was being reduced. Many Volunteers went to join the Active Service Unit (ASU) or the Flying Columns, while numerous others were captured. GHQ was raided and enemy forces obtained the names of many Volunteer members who were subsequently arrested and jailed. Reinforcements were sent from other Battalions, among whom was section Commander Michael Magee. He was to die from wounds received during a failed ambush at Clonturk Park. Frank Flood and Patrick Doyle were also captured during this incident and were executed in Mountjoy Jail for their endeavours.

Frank Flood was 19 years old when

Patrick Doyle.
Courtesy of the Allen Library

he was arrested. He was a past pupil of the O'Connell Schools and had won a scholarship to UCD where he was studying engineering. At the time of his capture, he was a Lieutenant with H Company, Dublin Brigade. Three of his brothers were also actively involved in the struggle. Flood was executed 14 March 1921.

Patrick Doyle was born at Portland Row and also attended the O'Connell Schools. He became a carpenter and was a founding member of the Amalgamated Society of Carpenters, Cabinetmakers and Joiners. He married Louisa Herbert, from Glasgow, in 1916 and their daughter was born a year later. Patrick was a member of F Company, 1st Battalion, Dublin Brigade. His brother Sean was also actively involved and died during the attack on the Custom House. Patrick too was executed on 14 March 1921, a few weeks after the birth of his twin girls. He was 29 years old.[2]

Attacks and reprisals became a way of life. The DMP raided Clonliffe Hall in January 1919, and twelve Volunteers who were at drill practice were arrested. Two months later Alfred Pearson of 146 Richmond Road was shot dead in his home. The barracks came to life at night and it became a common occurrence to hear soldiers in full kit with bayonets fixed knocking at doors in the middle of the night. There were no warrants for these searches and no apologies made when the soldiers left. Alfie Byrne's residence on North Strand Road was raided on 12 November 1920. The following month saw the arrest of C. Lonergan at Jones's Road and Charles Murphy at his home on the North Strand.[3] Between 1917 and 1919, there were 12,589 raids on private houses in Dublin by the Crown forces, and up to 4,000 per month by the end of the struggle.

Arms had been secured from some British soldiers but attacks on magazines were common practice. In February, the IRA attempted to capture an arms train at Newcomen Bridge but the operation was unsuccessful and the signalman, Michael Geraghty was injured. On 20 March 1919, there was a very successful raid on Collinstown Aerodrome. The entire British guard were held prisoner while arms were being secured. Two of the Volunteers destroyed

2. T. Carey – Hanged for Ireland. 2001. pp.100-101
3. Acts of Aggression – Allen Library

all the transport lorries so they could not be followed. They managed to obtain 75 rifles and ammunition, which were brought to the IRA dumps at Clonliffe Road and the Naul, North County Dublin.[4]

Sir Nevil Macready was appointed Commander-in-Chief of Forces in Ireland in March 1920, and advertisements appeared for English recruits to come to Ireland. This led to the formation of the Black & Tans and the Auxiliaries, the latter being ex British Army Officers. Many people were now arrested and several of these went on hunger strike. The Trade Union movement organised strikes to demand the release of prisoners. All factories and shops closed down, and the Corporation and transport service were at a standstill. The government eventually released the prisoners after 10 days of hunger strike.

By 1921 the Army Council decided that it needed a decisive action for Dublin. The barracks at Beggar's Bush was the initial target but this was soon abandoned. Oscar Traynor set about examining other possibilities especially that of the Custom House. He asked Tom Ennis of 2nd Battalion to do the same. They both agreed that it was a viable target. Plans were put into operation. 1st Battalion were given the task of protecting the outside area from any surprise attack and they also had to deal with the fire stations. They were

Black & Tans outside Amiens Street Station, their first appearance since their arrival on 25 March 1920. Courtesy of the Allen Library

4. Iris Drong. 1939. p.18

assisted with the latter task by 3rd and 4th Battalions. The 5th Battalion was given the task of cutting off all communications. (see Appendix 5)

5th Battalion (Engineers) was the best organised unit in the country. This was established by GHQ and was attached to Brigade Headquarters. Up until now each Battalion had been responsible for the destruction of communication equipment in their own area but this was to change. Twenty five suitable men from each of the other Battalions were chosen to form 5th Battalion. They came from all backgrounds. Each section within the Battalion was divided into Companies. These were responsible for the following areas – telephone, telegraph and electrical supplies; bridge and building demolition; railways; road destruction and general mining work. They were involved in the destruction of transport at the Great Southern Railway at the North Wall, the appropriation of telephone and telegraph equipment from Aldborough House,

Civilians being stopped near the Custom House. Black & Tans can be seen in the foreground.

Courtesy of the Allen Library

Some members of the I.R.A. being arrested by the Black & Tans following the attack on the Custom House. Dead comrades can be seen in the background.

Courtesy of the Allen Library

the seizure of relevant equipment from the Dublin Dockyard Company and the stealing of motor lorries and motor cycles wherever possible. [5]

Black & Tans with captured guns after the attack on the Custom House. Courtesy of the Allen Library

Tom Ennis was in charge of the Volunteers inside the Custom House on the day of the attack. However he received an injury earlier in the day and had left for home. Oscar Traynor made his way to Ennis' home and immediately sent for Michael Collins' driver as Ennis needed to be seen by a medical team. He was taken to the O'Donnell Nursing Home on Eccles Street and had to pass two police cordons en route, one at Ballybough Bridge and the other at Jones's Road. They were allowed to pass without question.

The Black & Tans arrived at the Custom House by 1:25 p.m. The building was on fire and continued to burn for ten days after the event. The Fire Department could not get close to it because of the parafin used. It was a type which ensured total destruction. Many members of the Irish Citizen Army were employed by the Fire Brigade service and they helped remove evidence of those who fled the building, some

The arrival of the horse drawn fire brigade during the burning of the Custom House, 1921.

Courtesy of the Allen Library

5. ibid p.57

Sean (John) Doyle.
Courtesy of the Allen Library

of whom were their comrades in arms. The operation was a huge success.

It was not however without its casualties. Sean Doyle, brother of Patrick and a member of the ASU, died after being shot in the lung. He had lived near North Richmond Street. In total five people died and over 80 were taken prisoner.

Two of the Volunteers arrested were Tommy Kilcoyne and Paddy Swanzy. They were taken to Kilmainham but as they did not want to reveal their identities they called themselves Lewis and gave an address at 17 North Richmond Street, home to the Byrne family. Tommy got word while in jail that his mother was very ill and would probably die in a matter of days. It was imperative for him to see her before this happened. As he was using a false name Oscar Traynor and Paddy O'Daly arranged to find someone willing to pretend to be his dying mother. Mrs. Byrne was approached and agreed to the ruse. She got a friendly doctor to give her a false medical certificate saying she had a very bad heart condition and was close to death. This was sent to Kilmainham but all involved knew that enquiries would be made to ensure its validity. It was important that if the DMP did call that Mrs. Byrne would be in bed. They eventually arrived while she was baking in the kitchen and had to make a quick dash upstairs. She was a plump woman and by the time the police reached her bedroom she looked none too well after the ordeal and having smeared flour on her face they believed she would soon be with her maker. It was arranged for her to be sent to the Mater. The staff knew who she really was but again agreed to assist. In the meantime, Mrs. Lewis did in fact die and Tommy received this news from his sister. While debating now what to do, the DMP called to pay their condolences and the two men were released from jail. Mrs. Byrne left the Mater that evening and the ruse was never discovered and the identity of the men was preserved.[6]

Bloody Sunday took place on the morning of Sunday 21 November. Reprisals were expected following the execution of the *"Cairo Gang"*.These occurred at a football match between Dublin and Tipperary at Croke Park the same afternoon. As a result twelve people were killed, sixty wounded and hundreds more injured.[7]

6. Statement of Paddy O'Daly – Allen Library
7. Dublin's fighting story. p.154

Shortly after the events at Croke Park, Dick McKee, Commander of the Dublin Brigade, along with his Vice Commander Peadar Clancy and Conor Clune were arrested and shot dead in the Guard Room at Dublin Castle. An inquiry into this atrocity found that they had been shot while trying to escape. Later reports said that the men had been tortured in order to provide the authorities with the names of their comrades. Their families confirmed that this was the case.

The Dublin Brigade later organised an Active Service Unit (ASU) on 1 January 1921 at Oriel Hall, Seville Place. It was prepared to engage in street fighting, ambushing patrols and destroying transport. The same day the British adopted officially a policy of reprisals.[8] Fifty Volunteers were selected and withdrawn from their ordinary occupations and paid £4 10s per week.

In the meantime a curfew came into operation in Dublin, and the streets were to be cleared by 8 p.m. Armoured cars roamed from dusk until daylight. Many areas were cordoned off and then ransacked.

The resourcefulness of Cumann na mBan was again put to the test during this period. Women were involved in smuggling arms and dispatches. They gathered supplies of information as well as providing safe houses. Nora O'Daly served as a judge in one of the Sinn Fein courts which were set up as part of the party's policy of boycotting all aspects of British rule. Women also provided safe houses in which men on the run could shelter, often at great risk to themselves and their families. House burning by the Black & Tans was a regular occurrence. By the time this war broke out, Amy Wisely had married Sean Moore (May Moore's brother). With a young family and a husband sometimes on the run, she was not always able to actively take part. Instead she provided a safe house and hid guns. At that time she lived with her aunt in Northbrook Avenue. Her aunt, Miss Wisely, had been a housekeeper in the Royal Victoria Hotel, Killarney. During one raid on the house, the Black & Tans were searching through a trunk when they discovered a picture of Edward VII, which the King had presented personally to Miss Wisely following a visit to the hotel. Following their discovery, the soldiers abandoned the search and never found the guns that were hidden there.[9]

In February 1921, P. Kennedy and James Murphy were arrested and brought to the Castle. At midnight they were taken by the Auxiliary Company Commander, a man by the name of King, and two of his cadets, to a field near Drumcondra. Kennedy was found dead there the next morning and Murphy was dying, but managed to recount their ordeal. King had ordered the men to stand against a wall and have buckets placed over their heads. They were then shot.[10] Captain King was tried by British court martial in 1921 regarding these

8. Dublin Brigade Review. 1939. p.79
9. interview with Eithne O'Moore, daughter of Esther Wisely Moore
10. Dorothy Macardle – The Irish republic. 1951. p.428

murders but was found not guilty.[11] The daily newspapers began printing lists of those killed by the Crown forces. In *The Independent* of 12 April 1921, Mrs. Mary Patterson of 15 Clonmore Terrace was listed amongst those shot dead in Dublin. In May a man by the name of Redmond was shot dead on North Strand Road.[12]

The guerrilla war continued into 1921. Attacks on both troop and RIC lorries were commonplace at Newcomen Bridge, Ballybough Bridge and Tolka Bridge. One such incident at Newcomen Bridge led to the death of a civilian, C. Cox.[13] On 7 February the IRA attempted to lure the RIC cadet force into battle positions at Seville Place. Over 100 Volunteers were involved but they eventually had to retreat, as the British forces and other RIC members arrived and lit up the area. A group of DMP officers were disarmed by Volunteers at Fairview in March. One of the final local encounters in the area was in June 1921, when Volunteers engaged in battle with British forces, in civilian dress, at Bayview Avenue.

CIVIL WAR

"We have brought back the flag; we have brought back the evacuation of Ireland after 700 years by British troops and the formation of an Irish army ... we have brought back to Ireland equality with England, equality with all nations which form that Commonwealth ..."[14]

On 6 December 1921, the Anglo-Irish Treaty was signed by the plenipotentiaries Griffith, Collins, Duggan, Gavan-Duffy and Barton. From the outset, the delegations had been unevenly matched. The British team in the negotiations included some of the most able politicians of modern times with long experience of government. The Irish, on the other hand, were lacking any such experience and were also unused to working together. Above all, they were under immense emotional pressure, shouldering as they were responsibility for the destiny of the whole country of Ireland.

None of the delegation was entirely happy with the Treaty they had signed. Returning to Ireland, they were all too aware that it was not going to be acceptable to the entire population of Ireland. Indeed they were prepared for a great deal of hostile feeling. On the day he signed the Treaty, Michael Collins wrote to a close friend *"Will anyone be satisfied at the bargain? ... early this morning I signed my death warrant ...a bullet may just as well have done the job five years ago ... These signatures are the first real step for Ireland. If only people will remember that ..."*[15]

11. Roinn Cosanta – Chronology. Part 3 Section 3. p.388
12. ibid p.424
13. ibid
14. F.S.L. Lyons – Ireland since the Famine. 1973. p.442
15. Mark Tierney – Europe since 1870. 1985. p.246

The delegates pleaded with the Irish people to look upon the Treaty as a stepping stone which provided them with the *"freedom to achieve freedom..."*.[16] When Griffith persuaded a majority of the Dail to support the Treaty, he declared that the Treaty settlement had *"no more finality than that we are the final generation on the face of the earth."*[17]

The initial reaction in Ireland to news of the Treaty was one of great relief. It was generally believed that the men in London had obtained an honourable agreement with Britain. However the signatories were soon to become aware of the split even within the Dail. *"Ideology, conviction, accident, personality and geography all helped to divide much of the country into Treatyites and anti-Treatyites, and into different camps within the blocs."*[18]

The Treaty was approved in the Dail by 64 votes to 57 on 7 January 1922. Three days later, de Valera resigned as president and led his followers out of the Dail. He was replaced by Griffith, who then appointed a cabinet which included Collins in finance and Mulcahy in defence. At this point much greater splits began to develop.

Divisions within the army were emerging, as the majority of the Headquarters staff followed Collins in accepting the Treaty, but a minority, including Rory O'Connor and Liam Mellowes, rejected it. The army was now becoming more prominently divided into pro- and anti-Treaty units. A military struggle was beginning to appear more likely. On the political front, the Sinn Fein Ard-Fheis took place in February. However, it was adjourned for three months to give people more time to consider the Treaty. In March, de Valera and his supporters formed Cumann na Poblachta. His language during the months to follow was ominous *"If they accepted the Treaty ... they would have to wade through Irish blood ... perhaps the blood of some of the members of the government in order to get Irish freedom."*[19]

The content of de Valera's anti-Treaty speeches was extremely vehement. It seemed to many of his followers that he was encouraging them to commence a military struggle. Despite this, it was without the support of de Valera that the anti-Treaty army officers took control of the Four Courts on the 14 April. They acted completely independent of de Valera. The occupation of the Four Courts was a clear challenge to the Provisional government. Furthermore it created conflict, as Collins and Mulcahy wanted to avoid any outbreak of fighting with men who had not long beforehand been their closest friends and allies. Griffith and O'Higgins felt it necessary to control the army. By the end of April, Brugha, de Valera, Collins and Griffith had failed to reach

16. T.W. Moody & Rev. F.X. Martin – The course of Irish history. 1967. p.325
17. ibid p.325
18. Dermot Keogh – Twentieth century Ireland: nation and state. 1994. p.3
19. John A. Murphy – Ireland in the twentieth century. 1975. p.50

agreement. Many attempts were made to prevent the bitter conflict becoming a military war. The pact signed between de Valera and Collins on 20 May 1922 was one of the last desperate attempts to maintain peace. This pact was a basic agreement that in the coming general election the Treaty would not be an issue, and that the candidates returned would form a National Government which would work towards the avoidance of Civil War. Both men were criticised by their respective followers for having even considered such an option. Elections were held in June with results favouring the pro-Treaty group.

Any hopes of maintaining peace were now becoming more dim. On 22 June, Sir Henry Wilson was assassinated in London. The British government concluded, not unnaturally, that the assassins, two London based IRA men, had received their orders from the army executive based in the Four Courts. Some believe that these orders had in fact, been issued by Michael Collins. In any

The explosion at the Four Courts during the Civil War in 1922 led to the destruction of the Public Records Office. This was the greatest loss the nation suffered at this time, in its struggle for independence. Courtesy of the Allen Library

Four Courts during Civil war, 1922. Courtesy of the Allen Library

case this event brought British attention to events in Ireland. They were aware that the Four Courts, as well as many other buildings in Ireland, were garrisoned by anti-Treaty forces. This brought declarations of dissatisfaction from Lloyd George and Churchill. If the occupation of the Four Courts was not brought to an end soon, the British government would regard the Treaty as having been violated.

It was not, however, British pressure that led the Provisional government to act, but the daring abduction on 26 June by the Four Courts garrison of General O'Connell. This was a defiance which would not go unchallenged. Collins and others had been reluctant all along to move against old comrades but Griffiths' arguments were now unanswerable. On 28 June the Provisional government, in an ultimatum, demanded immediate evacuation of the Four Courts by its garrison. Within an hour, the National Army attacked the building with artillery borrowed from the British forces still in the Dublin area. The Civil War had begun.

The shelling of the Four Courts lasted for two days. When it ended, the building, along with many valuable records were in flames. The garrison inside the Four Courts had been urged to surrender by their comrades on the outside. On 30 June a statement by Oscar Traynor had been published in a Stop Press edition of *Poblacht na hEireann "I have gone into the whole situation re your position and have studied the same very carefully ... to help me carry on the fight outside you must surrender forthwith ... As senior officer outside ... I am entitled to order you ... This order must be carried out without discussion...".*[20] On the same day the garrison, numbering approximately 200 men, surrendered. Fighting continued in the centre of Dublin mainly on O'Connell Street, as in

Aftermath of the explosion at the Four Courts in 1922.

Courtesy of the Allen Library

20. Irish Independent, July 3 1922

the 1916 Rising. They occupied prominent buildings, and once again their enemies methodically blasted them out of their fixed positions. *"There was a certain symbolical aptness in the fact that when this phase of the war ended after a week of fighting it ended with the shooting down of Cathal Brugha ... as he emerged, gun in hand, from the ruins of a burning building."*[21] Traynor had sent a dispatch to Brugha urging him to surrender *"...but Brugha continued to fight ... two days later he died."*[22]

The strength and camaraderie which had characterised Cumann na mBan during the 1916 Rising and the years immediately following it did not prove strong enough to withstand the split over the Treaty, and the Civil War which followed. Women who had supported each other through the most desperate of times now found themselves on opposing sides. When Cumann na mBan voted to reject the Treaty, those women who supported what was to become the Free State side left the organisation. Henceforth Cumann na mBan was to become an exclusively Republican organisation. It was banned by the Free State, and membership was punishable by arrest and imprisonment. Nora O'Daly was among those who left. Her husband, Seamus, was a Free State soldier, and it was his brother Paddy, one of Michael Collins' *"Twelve Apostles"*, who led the attack on the Four Courts which began the Civil War.

On the night the shelling of the Four Courts commenced, Nora Connolly-O'Brien (James Connolly's daughter) and her husband were staying with Margaret Skinnider in Fairview. They went to Barry's Hotel, which was the Republican headquarters at the time. Margaret Skinnider was working as secretary to Austin Stack, Minister for Home Affairs in the first Dail. She was arrested early on in the war. Nora Connolly-O'Brien took over her post and she too was arrested.[23] There were regular raids on Cumann na mBan offices. Possession of republican literature or Cumann na mBan insignia resulted in arrest under the Emergency Powers Act. Clearly the preceding years of conflict and rebellion had taught the Free State leadership the danger of under-estimating the military importance of women. Women such as Margaret Skinnider were no longer considered *"just a girl on a bike"*.[24] They were treated instead as a serious security threat. It was a huge blow to the Republican communication network, and contributed to the fragmentation which characterised Republican military actions during the Civil War.

Members of the Fairview branch who were arrested included Tilly (Mathilda) Simpson, Crissie (Christina) Stafford and May Moore. Simpson and Stafford were sent initially to Kilmainham Gaol. Simpson was transferred to

21. F.L.S.Lyons – Ireland since the Famine. 1973. p.462
22. Meda Ryan – Michael Collins and the women in his life. 1996. p.171
23. Uinseann Mac Eoin – Survivors. p.211
24. Margaret Skinnider – Doing my bit for Ireland. 1917. p.95

the North Dublin Union in July 1923, where May Moore was also a prisoner.[25] Life in the various prisons and detention centres was bleak. Many of them had been abandoned for several years, rations were short and heat was often non-existent. Crissie Stafford suffered quite badly from sciatica during her time at Kilmainham and had to be nursed first by Mrs. Stack and later by a nurse brought in from St. Bricin's Hospital. Despite recommendations from both her doctor and the Governor, she was not released.[26]

The senior women organised classes in history, French, Irish and dancing. Even the ordinary criminal prisoners who were brought to Kilmainham from Mountjoy to work as orderlies began to say *"Ta an tae istigh"* when they brought the women their meals.[27] They put on pageants and held ceilís to lift their spirits. Among the prisoners was Grace Gifford Plunkett. She had married Joseph Plunkett, one of the signatories of the Proclamation, the night before his execution. Although she was not a member of Cumann na mBan, she was arrested along with her sister Catherine Wilson at their home at 49 Philipsburgh Avenue, Fairview. Grace like many other of the women, painted murals on the walls to commemorate the seventh anniversary of the execution of the 1916 leaders. Many women had autograph books in which they collected signatures and musings of their fellow prisoners. May Moore wrote a poem in which she prays;

May God above send down a dove
with wings as sharp as razors,
to cut the hands of every man,
who murdered our Irish leaders.[28]

When the Civil War ended, the women were gradually released. Disappointed, weakened by the harsh conditions and sometimes hunger strike, they returned home to try to resume their lives. For many this proved impossible. Society regarded them as *"wild, wild women"*,[29] ex-prisoners who had been excommunicated by their Church. People, it appeared, were not yet ready to accommodate such confident and self-reliant women. Even during the conflict itself, their male counterparts were often shocked by the determination of these women. Eithne Coyle described one occasion when Austin Stack, Joe Blake and Florence McCarthy were arrested by CID and put in a police car. Florence took off her shoe and smashed the window. *"Her unladylike behaviour did not seem to appeal to Austin judging by the frozen expression on his face. That*

25. Civil War prisoner list – Kilmainham Gaol Collection
26. Margaret Buckley – The jangle of the keys. 1938. p.82
27. ibid p.102
28. Autograph Book – Kilmainham Gaol Collection
29. Margaret Buckley – The jangle of the keys. 1938. p.104

was fair enough, poor Austin was entitled to his opinion and Cumann na mBan were entitled to theirs, especially during this period ...".[30]

After the Civil War, Cumann na mBan continued to hold meetings and run campaigns. However its membership was severely depleted. The foundation of Fianna Fail further split the organisation. De Valera's decision to take the oath of allegiance alienated many of the hard-line republicans. The departure of their President, Countess Markievicz, to become a Fianna Fail T.D. was also a severe blow. As one of the organisation's main branches, Fairview survived, but others had to amalgamate. One of their campaigns involved influencing jurors in political trials. Anonymous letters urging acquittal were sent, signed only with the word *"Ghosts"*. Following a raid on Cumann na mBan headquarters in the late 1920s, a list of jurors was discovered, and Florence McCarthy was among those arrested and sentenced to six months in prison. Although it managed to continue into the 1940s, Cumann na mBan soon faded from existence.

The importance of Cumann na mBan cannot be underestimated in terms of Irish history or indeed the history of women. 1916, according to Hannah Sheehy Skeffington, was unique, *"the only instance ... in history where men fighting for freedom voluntarily included women"*.[31] For those women, it offered a chance to expand and challenge the role their society envisaged for them. While the Ireland which emerged did not always accept this new vision of womanhood, the role played by them in achieving Irish independence gave it a practical manifestation which can never be ignored.

Despite the fact that it was of comparatively short duration, the Civil War of 1922-1923 is one of the greatest watersheds in recent Irish history. It was primarily a war fought between two different groups accusing the other of sabotaging Ireland and her independence. *"It was not fought about partition since both sides ardently desired national unity, nor was it a struggle about social and economic issues."*[32] It could be said that in their different ways de Valera and Collins were, to a large extent, in fact responsible for the outbreak of Civil War *"Collins tried to do too much, de Valera too little."*[33] Both men had an unimaginable amount of support, their followers putting their leaders and their beliefs above all else, including family and friends. This war had devastating effects upon the country. Families fought with each other, and bitter feuds developed between friends. The damage caused was not to be easily repaired. (see Appendix 6)

30. Eithne Coyle's unpublished account of Florence McCarthy – UCD Archives
31. Margaret Ward (1996) – 'The league of women and Sinn Fein', History Ireland
32. John A. Murphy – Ireland in the twentieth century. 1975. p.54
33. Desmond Williams – The Irish struggle: 1916-1926. 1966. p.124

WORLD WAR II

Prior to the outbreak of World War II, de Valera was at the height of his powers. He had negotiated an end to the Economic War and had regained control of the controversial Treaty Ports.[34] His party had been in power for seven years and was pursuing a largely protectionist policy in its bid for self-sufficiency. After Germany invaded Poland, de Valera called a special meeting of the Dail on 2 September and introduced two bills: the First Amendment to the Constitution Bill and the Emergency Powers Bill. Article 28.3.3 of the constitution was amended to read *"that arising out of the armed conflict now taking place in Europe that a national emergency exists affecting the interests of the State"*. The Emergency Powers Bill gave the government almost unlimited powers to ensure the preservation of the State, public safety and the regulation of supplies. Ireland was to remain neutral.[35]

On 4 September it was announced that trade would continue with England.[36] In January 1941 a Tea Registration Card was introduced whereby a ration of two oz. per week was allowed and retailers had to pay a 10 shilling licence fee.[37] This allowance was halved at the beginning of April and a few days later it was halved again. When wheat imports were cut off the Irish had to make do with a 90% wheat extraction loaf which they found extremely unpalatable. Finally, in order to end the obvious injustices associated with severe shortages and rising prices, ration books were introduced in June 1942. Already 3 million books had been printed and the government was to fix the price of all rationed commodities. While the Lord Mayor, Alfie Byrne T.D. was cycling around his constituency, he was called over by a Mrs. Gleeson of 154 Summerhill. Showing him the loaf of bread in her arms, she said *"That one loaf of bread is for myself, and my husband and my eleven children"*.[38]

In 1942 to help ease the situation Dubliners were allocated plots throughout the city and in the Phoenix Park. When deer threatened to eat the vegetables they were culled (allowing many Irish people to taste venison for the first time).[39] In October, 1941 fuel boilers were installed in the Mansion House capable of supplying 40,000 hot meals a day. Four other similar centres were planned.[40] In 1945 rationing was still in force. The butter ration was reduced from 8 to 6 ounces per week and from February onwards Dublin's fish and chip shops were closed for four days a week due to a shortage of edible fat.[41]

34. Dermot Keogh –Twentieth century Ireland: nation and state. 1994. p.107
35. Dail Debates no. 77
36. Irish Times 4-9-1939
37. Dail Debates no. 82
38. Bernard Share – The emergency: neutral Ireland 1939-1945. 1978. p.38
39. Tony Gray – Ireland this century. 1994. p.156
40. ibid p.153
41. ibid p.162

As soon as the Emergency Powers Bill was passed, censorship came into force immediately. There was a thunderstorm during the All Ireland Hurling Final on Sunday, 3 September at Croke Park but no mention of this critical storm was reported in case the information might be used by the belligerents. There were 55 named categories, including weather forecasts, which newspapers had to submit for censorship to the Press Censorship Office in Dublin Castle.

When de Valera declared a neutral policy he received almost unanimous support in the Dail. On St. Patrick's Day 1943 de Valera set forward his notion of the ideal Ireland.[42] He realised, however, that despite the emigration of the disaffected and the screen of censorship, the electorate was not well disposed towards him. He tried to delay the election by a year but failed and it was finally held on 22 June 1943. Although Fianna Fail suffered great losses (their seats were reduced from 77 to 67), de Valera formed a government and continued in power for another year.[43] The Taoiseach did not enjoy the same control as previously and the following year, after the defeat of the second reading of the Transport Bill (9 May 1944), de Valera called for a general election. This time the opposition were not so well prepared. Richard Mulcahy, the new leader of Fine Gael, suggested a coalition of Fine Gael, Labour (which had split in the meantime) and Clann na Talmhain as an alternative to Fianna Fail. On 9 June 1944, however, the electorate returned Fianna Fail with a comfortable majority. De Valera's cabinet remained unchanged for the remainder of the war.[44]

NORTH STRAND BOMBINGS 1941

On the night of 31 May 1941, Ballybough experienced one of the most destructive events in its history. A German plane dropped bombs between Newcomen Bridge and the North Circular Road, levelling homes, destroying businesses, and leaving 39 people dead and hundreds more injured. Within the context of a World War the figures are small, but within the history of Dublin it was a major tragedy, and one which would be remembered for many years.

At 22:40 hours on 30 May, a large number of aircraft were reported to be proceeding north and south along the east coast. The searchlights in Dublin were first exposed at 00:04 a.m. and continued to be exposed and doused intermittently until 02:13 hours. Ground defences first came into action at 00:35 a.m. when Clontarf fired four rounds.[45]

Four bombs were dropped between 1:30 a.m. and 2:05 a.m. on a Saturday morning. The first landed outside the O'Connell Schools at the junction of

42. Joseph Carroll – Ireland in the war years, 1939-1945. p.117
43. ibid p.118
44. Bernard Share – The emergency – neutral Ireland, 1939-1945. 1978. p.74
45. Military Archives

North Richmond Street and the North Circular Road. Less than a minute later Summerhill Parade was struck. Both bombs exploded, although some witnesses claimed that a short time elapsed between contact and actual eruption. What followed seems almost bizarre. What is believed to have been the same plane crossed Dublin as far as Aras an Uachtarán in the Phoenix Park and deposited a third bomb beside the Dog Pound, before circling around once again to the North Strand. At 2.05 a.m. it released the fourth and most destructive bomb, a 500 pound land mine between the tram tracks running down the centre of the North Strand Road.

Ballybough was thrown into chaos. Censorship laws were being stringently enforced, so speculation as to the source of the bombs was not open to public debate, through the medium of the newspapers at any rate. The newspapers were therefore filled with minute details of the bombings, casualties, procedures in place to deal with the crisis and funeral arrangements, leaving behind a wealth of social history.

The first bomb which detonated outside the O'Connell Schools destroyed Mrs. Grice's shop at 582 North Circular Road, and severely damaged water, gas and electricity mains. Less than a minute later the second bomb landing on Summerhill Parade destroyed two houses, numbers 43 and 44. Three women were trapped under the rubble, one later died due to the seriousness of her

Large section of fin ring with words "HIER NICHT ANHEBEN", found in North Clarence Street.

Courtesy of the Military Archives

injuries, and the remaining two were trapped for nearly 50 minutes as the emergency services rushed to the scene.

The Emergency Forces were assisted by a large body of volunteers. People gathered in the streets in shock and disarray. The third 500 pound bomb fell between Newcomen Bridge and the Five Lamps, and crashed between the tram lines in the centre of the road causing a massive explosion, gorging a gaping crater from the centre of the road, and wiping out a stretch of houses along Charleville Mall. Over 20 houses were completely destroyed and a further 45 were so badly damaged that they had to be levelled by the Corporation in the days that followed. Another 300 were severely damaged and over 1000 suffered roof damage. Shattered glass lay everywhere and electricity cables sparked among the ruins. Two families were killed outright there; the Brownes and the Fitzpatricks. The Fitzpatricks owned a butcher shop and lived above the premises. Noel Fitzpatrick was a well known Dublin variety artiste. Numbers 23 to 35 on one side of the road, and numbers 153 to 164 on the other, lay in ruins. The Ambulance Service and Gardai provided official vehicles to move the injured and dying to the City hospitals, while taxis and private cars also rushed to the scene.

Excavations were difficult due to the nature of the buildings, tenements for the most part, and the work was long and slow as the frames of houses were held aloft while their inhabitants were pulled from the wreckage. Gas mains had also been hit and they were set alight in order to disperse the fumes. The bombs had also damaged the electricity supply and a few scattered houses became nursing stations, their remaining lights attracting the injured.

The number of dead was unclear at first. Sunday reports vary in their estimates, between 7 and 12. The city hospitals were crammed with hundreds of injured people and families searching for loved ones. The Rotunda, Drumcondra, Mater and Richmond hospitals had a steady stream of ambulances and private cars conveying the injured and dead. The Sunday papers issued requests to all those living in the area to report to the authorities, as a list of missing persons was growing. The Art Gallery on Parnell Square and Charleville Library became emergency administrative centres for the crisis.

Not alone had the bombs cost lives, they had also left over 800 people without homes. The first nights after the bombing saw the homeless pouring into the hostels on Baggot Street, Middle Abbey Street and the Convent of the Sisters of Charity on North William Street. Mrs. Thomas Clarke, the Lord Mayor of Dublin, housed 20 people in the Mansion House while appealing to the public for aid, especially in the form of clothing as some families had been left with literally nothing. The days that followed saw the Corporation inspecting the bombed areas, carrying out make-shift jobs on damaged properties and condemning others as uninhabitable. Cabra West, a new suburban housing development, tipped as one of the most ambitious in Western Europe at the time, was almost ready for habitation. It had been built in an attempt to alleviate the growing tenement problem in Dublin. The first tenant moved in to the *"Parish of the Most Precious Blood"* on the 1 June 1941, and in the following weeks the *"Northstranders"* moved to their new homes. Although the houses were ready, no schools, shops or a church were yet constructed, and the first years in this suburb of Dublin were far from easy.

The eventual number of dead was fixed at 39. Some were so badly injured that identification was impossible. Dublin Corporation offered to arrange and pay for the funerals of the victims of the bombs. Thursday 5 June was chosen as the date for the public funeral. Tuesday 3 June had seen the State Inquest into the cause of death of the victims. Dr. D.A. MacErlean, the City Coroner, declared asphyxiation and actual blast trauma as the main causes of death, although many had simply died of shock. The funerals were seen as a national event, with de Valera, Sean T. O'Kelly, Oscar Traynor and many other politicians and dignitaries attending. Many had made their way down to view the bomb areas. The Most Rev. Dr. McQuaid, Archbishop of Dublin, presided over the ceremony at the Church of Laurence O'Toole, while the Very Rev. M.A. O'Daly was the celebrant. Public representatives from every sphere attended, as did a huge crowd of ordinary Dublin people. Twelve of the victims were buried that day, two of them so badly mutilated that they were unidentified. The entourage of hearses drove through the city while the public paid their last respects before the burial in Glasnevin Cemetery.

A white enamel plate bearing the inscription *"Notbremshahn"* was found in a yard at South Cumberland Street by Denis Dunne. He said it was not there prior to the bombings as he had swept the yard and would have noticed it. The word translates as *"emergency brake stop"*. This may have been on one of the planes but was more usually used in trains in Germany. It was considered to be too heavy to be used as a normal plane fitting and evidence from most crashed planes showed that notices like this were painted on fabric or directly on to the cabin structure.[46] A large section of a fin ring with the words *"Hiernicht anheben"* was found in North Clarence Street. This translates as *"do not pull this"*.

The whole question of why the bombings occurred is still debatable. Ireland was officially a neutral state during World War II. Were the bombings of an accidental nature or the policy of a closet belligerent? The identity of the plane crossing Dublin on the night of the bombings was unknown. A number of bombs had been dropped in the eastern part of the country in the first half of the year, although none caused damage comparable to that suffered at

46. Bombing Incident ref. No. G2/X/0619, Military Archives

Ballybough. Interestingly, on 7 January 1941, following the dropping of a bomb in Carlow, Chris Doyle with an address at 30 Sackville Avenue, Ballybough, gave evidence to the Defence Forces about his sighting of a German Bomber flying over Dublin the night of that bombing.[47] There were doubts as to whether his testimony could be considered, as the altitude at which such an aircraft would be flying placed question marks over his ability to read any markings carried on its body, and he himself was not certain about the accuracy of the sighting. Nevertheless, his testimony was recorded as secret within the file of the Defence Forces. Three similar sightings were not recorded in the Defence Force's files in relation to the Ballybough bombings. However, parts of shrapnel salvaged from the wreckage of the bombings bearing the German Eagle and German lettering left little doubt as to the origin of the bombs. The Irish Minister in Berlin was ordered to protest to the German administration about the bombing and to demand that a guarantee be given that Germany would never again breach Irish air space. Germany reacted ambiguously stating they were unaware of any attack on Dublin, save from some reports on International Radio. Finally, after discussions and an investigation to establish the course of events, it offered to pay compensation to the Irish people, over £100,000 less, in fact, than that requested by the Irish Government. By doing so, it denied the purposeful bombing of Dublin by any of its personnel.

In 1998 a U.N. researcher discovered documentation to "Operation Roman Helmet" in a World War II archives at a Munich Air Force base. These refer to Hitler's orders for retaliation against Ireland for helping the British after the

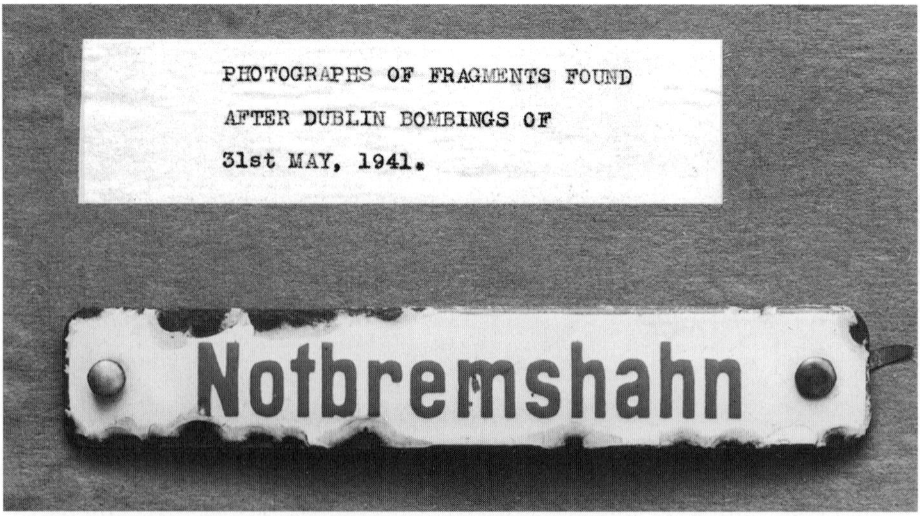

Courtesy of the Military Archives

47. ibid

Belfast Bombings. Fire stations and the Presidential residence were seen as legitimate targets.

Many have blamed Britain's radar device which fuzzed, as opposed to misdirected German air signals, perhaps causing a German pilot to believe that he was in fact over Britain instead of Ireland. Others believe that Germany intended to bomb Ireland as a quasi warning or punishment for her friendly neutrality towards Britain, which manifested itself not least in de Valera's sending of emergency aid to the victims of the Belfast bombings. What is clear is the fact that Ireland's declaration of neutrality was not simply a statement of non-involvement in an international war which all, or any, of the belligerent forces were willing to accept at face value. De Valera's role as Head of State was that of the juggling master while simultaneously keeping his Irish audience in ignorance of the reality of the situation.

In real terms in the eyes of de Valera and perhaps the public at large, the bombing of Ballybough was a political and defence issue, as opposed to the destruction of a community. Hardships were felt and yet there is a sense that perhaps simply due to Ireland's stance of neutrality, the body of the Irish people, coaxed by their leaders, did not believe in the reality of the war. Indeed

Courtesy of the Military Archives

some Irish officials such as Joe Walshe, Secretary of External Affairs, seemed to carry this naivete with them, believing that a German victory in the war would be good for Ireland, ignoring the fate of the other small nations which had been swallowed up by the war.[48] In fact Hitler had already pinpointed Dublin as one of the economic centres of the new regime if Germany won.

The *Irish Times* on the day after the bombing carried pictures of the destruction caused, but on the same page also reported how thousands of people travelled to Baldoyle for the Bank Holiday races. This sense of the war not really being true despite its arrival, however brief, on one's doorstep, owed a lot to the censorship laws. The editor of *The Times*, Bertie Smyllie, held a running battle with Frank Aiken throughout the War for this very reason. Indeed, in the first Dail Debate after the bombings, no significant mention of the bombings was recorded.[49] Instead T.D.s discussed whether or not they should hire a news reader for Sundays, and complaints received that the present news readers spoke too quickly. Professor Joe Lee comments incisively on Ireland's attitude to the war, claiming that Ireland was the only country in Europe which survived economically simply because it budgeted on defence.[50] The North Strand was lucky because the much praised emergency forces had enacted a mirror-image attack of Dublin the previous week, and because the scale of the bombings was relatively small. It is interesting to note that petrol rations for ambulances throughout the war remained the same as those for commercial vehicles. In real terms, Ireland was unprepared for an attack. The fall of France and de Valera's nervous suspicion that there were in fact German spies in Ireland, propelled him to increase the number of army personnel, the majority of whom remained ill-equipped and badly trained.[51] In comparison with other European countries and with the threat of invasion by three possibly interested parties (the US, the UK, Germany), the North Strand Bombings, while horrific in themselves, and on a local level far-reaching, can also be seen simply as the fate Ireland as a whole side-stepped.

Ballybough itself was not so lucky. Many families were left to grieve, homes were destroyed, businesses damaged and tracts of land left as wasteland. Modern flat complexes and buildings now fill some of the gaps. In 1991 a memorial was erected to the memory of the dead of the bombings by the local community and officials. (see Appendix 7)

48. J.J. Lee – Ireland 1912-1985: politics and society.1989. p.247
49. Dail Debates 4 June 1941
50. J.J. Lee – Ireland 1912-1985: politics and society.1989. p.234
51. R. Fisk – In time of war. 1983. p.66

CONCLUSION

Ballybough has always been regarded as a working class area. During the late nineteenth and early twentieth centuries the area had begun to change physically but this was short lived due to an emerging economic crisis which was endemic to Dublin and lasted until 1914. During this time there were high levels of unemployment, with the North Wall being the only place which continued to prosper.

Ballybough did manage to avoid the worst of the tenement conditions due to a lack of older style residences. Mortality levels were high but not as much as those in older parts of the city. It also had a limited social structure. Semi skilled labourers made up 21.5% of the local population in the 1901 Census (18.5% in the 1911 Census). Public Service employees represented 19% of the population in 1901 (16% in 1911). The majority of people could read and write and were predominantly Catholic. Over 25% of Ballybough residents in 1901 were employed in trades (27.5% in 1911).

With the advent of self-government in the 1920s, the situation did not change dramatically. If anything, housing conditions actually deteriorated. In the Dublin Civic Survey of 1925, housing was described as being *"a tragedy"*. Ballybough was mentioned as an unhealthy area, in particular the small streets behind the main. Mortality rates fell from 20.9 in 1914 to 14.36 per 1000 in 1940. If the city's mortality rate had fallen by 1922 to an average of 17.6, the North City No. 1 East District now had a rate of 19.6 per 1000, the 2nd highest in the city. Infant mortality rate, 4.9 per 1000, was the highest in the city. Tubercular mortality fell from 3.788 to 1.63 a situation linked with the development of the Welfare State in the 1930s.

The Civic Survey acknowledged Fairview Park and Croke Park but said the area had few recreational facilities and noted that much of the land was given over to poor allotment gardening. It stated that plans had been drawn up for the development of five acres at Friend's Fields and 89 acres at Croydon.

During the 1930s the city did not extend much beyond Ballybough, the exception being along the coast. Towards the end of this decade housing demands began to rise. Marino was developing and by 1950, Corporation policy shifted from a long-standing commitment to *"fringe areas"* more towards substantial blocks of flats in the city centre. Ballybough was included in this policy.

One of the most memorable events in Ballybough history took place during this era. The "big floods" occurred on the night of 8 Dec. 1954. By 9:30 p.m. there was a great fear among local people that Ballybough Bridge would not hold due to the amount of water in the Tolka. Later that evening the police arrived to evacuate people from their homes. Waves were said to be coming down Poplar Row. Masons' shop at the corner of Clonliffe Road had an upstairs and thus became home for many of the flood victims. The following day sea boats could be seen at Higginbottom's at Fairview Strand. The train bridge at the East Wall collapsed and the bottom part of Ballybough flats had flooded. Fortunately no natural disaster to this scale has happened in the area since.

The Inland Waterway association was formed in 1953 with the aim of advancing tourist amenities. In 1974 the Royal Canal Amenity Group (R.C.A.G.) was formed by Ian Bath and with the help of C.I.E. it cleared and restored areas of the canal. The government transferred ownership of the canals from C.I.E. to the O.P.W. (now Duchas) in 1978. The arrival of the latter has relieved some of the financial pressures associated with this type of restoration work. Much has been achieved with R.C.A.G and Duchas working together. Locks have been repaired and reopened and in June 1990 the canal was restored for navigation between Blanchardstown and Mullingar. The towpaths, which run alongside the canal, are a popular amenity for walkers.

Many of the churches and schools have undergone renovations and extensions added over the years. The Daughters of Charity continue to have a boys and girls school at North William Street. They are involved in pastoral work with the community and help operate a parish centre, a family resource centre, St. Anthony's Social centre and meals on wheels. They also provide accommodation for the homeless.

The Christian Brothers are still present at North Richmond Street. In 1990 the house was extensively renovated. One wing was turned into classrooms as an extension to the O'Connell Schools. The lower ground level was deigned to be the new home of the Allen Library, which is named after Br. W.P. Allen, who joined the Christian Brothers in 1907. He was both a teacher and historian. Following his return from Cashel in 1947 he divided his time between teaching and looking after the museum and library which now bears his name. The museum was originally started by Br. Louis Swan in 1886 and contained artefacts of industrial, agricultural, historic and natural significance.

Many past pupils of the school were involved in the 1916 Rising and subsequent political turmoil. Br. Allen knew many of them and therefore enlisted their help in finding objects of historical interest for the museum. Among the prized possessions is a half of the original Proclamation of Independence from 1916, the Ordnance Survey map of the Kerry coast used by Roger Casement as well as many other letters, photographs and memorabilia. In 1948 he was bequeathed the substantial library of a former past pupil, Canon J. McGuirk. In 1984, Br. Allen passed away but his legacy continues to grow today with researchers and visitors from all over the world frequenting the library. In 1991 the hard artefacts of the Allen Library were handed over to the State to mark the 75th anniversary of the 1916 Rising and in March 2000, the Allen Library was officially opened by An Taoiseach, Bertie Ahern T.D. The school continues to play an important role in the education of young people.

On 20 July 2000, the £600 million integrated area plan for the regeneration of Dublin's north east inner city was announced. Over 500 flats are to be demolished within five years and replaced with an equal number of high quality duplex housing, each with its own front door. The redevelopment also includes proposals for the construction of two new schools. Private investment has already been generated with the new £9 million Bord Gas office being located at Foley St. There are significant plans relating to the development of cultural facilities as well as improvements in the overall infrastructure of the area.

The changes locally and in neighbouring areas will radically alter old

Fairview floods, 1954. Courtesy of Br. Martin Byrne

Ballybough. New housing, new businesses, new community facilities and investments are long over due. The development of the north inner city will provide employment and many of the present plans have a 20% labour clause included. This means that local people must be employed on the projects. There is a fear by many that local needs and issues will not be addressed. As a result I.C.O.N. was established on 5 March 1998 as an umbrella organisation for all voluntary and community groups in the area. They are part of the Dublin Inner City Partnership founded in 1991 to look at long-term unemployment. I.C.O.N. provide a source of information, forum for debate and local policymaking and a means of lobbying issues within the community. They bring groups together and promote partnership between statutory agencies and business organisations in the area. The main issues they deal with are in relation to economic development, education and training, youth, childcare and family support, women, residents and tenants, sports and leisure, elderly, art and culture and drugs.

The area covered by I.C.O.N. is bounded to the south by the Liffey, to the east by the sea, to the north by the Tolka and Clonliffe Road and to the west by Dorset St. and East Arran St. During the 20th century the area saw a decline in population levels and economic growth. It now has high levels of unemployment, social disadvantage and environmental decay. The population in 1996 was 24,406, which was 15% higher than in 1991. This was mainly due to the development of apartment complexes in the overall area. It also has one distinguishing feature, relatively small average household sizes but with a high proportion of one parent families and their children.

And so concludes this story of Ballybough, of it people in time and place, of changes and developments, of conflicts and resolutions. Let's hope that all the current changes do not obliterate all that remains of the past but incorporate it into something to be cherished and proud of for this and future generations.

Appendix 1

LIST OF O.C.S. BOYS WHO FOUGHT IN 1916

Ashton, William
Begley, Joseph
Bermingham, Sean
Bermingham, Andrew
Billings, Joesph
Blanchfield, Peadar
Bracken, William
Byrne, Ambrose
Byrne, James C
Byrne, John
Byrne, Joesph
Byrne, Patrick
Byrne, Peter

Carton, Owen
Ceannt, Eamonn
Cody, Sean
Colbert, Cornelius
Coleman, Richard
Condron, Luke
Costello, Michael
Cotter, Thomas
Cotter, Joseph
Cotter, Richard
Cripps, Joseph
Cullen, Joseph

Daly, Liam
Delahide, Joseph
Derham, Michael
Devoy, John
Dolan, Joseph
Dowling, Thomas
Dunne, Thomas
Dwan, John

Flood, Sean
Furlong, John T

Gahan, Timothy
Geraghty, John
Giffney, Michael
Gogan, Richard
Gogan, Vincent
Griffin, Gerald J

Heuston, Sean
Holohan, Hugh
Holohan, Patrick
Hughes, Seamas

Jackson, Francis
Jackson, Joseph

Keating, Con
Keegan, John
Kelly, Fergus
Kenny, Henry V
Kenny, John
Kenny, Joseph
Kenny, Michael
King, John

Lawless, Michael
Lemass, Sean
Lemass, Noel
Lyons, Charles
Lyons, John E

McCarthy, Bernard
McDonald, John

McDonald, Patrick
McNestry, Patrick
McGarry, Sean
Mahon, Patrick J
Mahon, Thomas C
Mallon, James
Manning, Henry
Marie, Louis
Molphy, Charles
Monaghan, Philip
Morkan, Eamonn
Murphy, Michael
Murphy, Owen

Noonan, Christopher

O'Brien, Liam
O'Brien, Liam
O'Brien, Michael
O'Donnell, Micheal
Ó'hUallacháin, Gearóid
O'Leary, Patrick
O'Mahony, Eamonn
O'Neill, Sean
O'Kelly, Sean T
O'Reilly, Francis T
O'Rorke, Joseph
O'Rourke, Sean

Price, Eamonn
Price, John
Pugh, Thomas

Reardon, Daniel
Redmond, James
Reid, John
Reynolds, A P
Reynolds, John
Richmond, John
Ridgeway, Henry
Russell, Sean
Ryan, Martin

Scullen, Patrick
Sexton, James
Shelly, Denis
Shelly, Thomas
Sheppard, Michael S
Slater, Michael
Slater, Thomas
Slater, William
Stanley, Joseph
Stephenson, Patrick
Staines, William
Swan, Patrick
Sweeny, Alphonsus

Tallon, Joseph
Taylor, Thomas
Toomey, John
Toomey, Joseph
Thunder, Joseph

Walker, John
Walker, Michael
White, Michael
Wren, James

Appendix 2

LIST OF LOCAL DMP OFFICERS FROM 1901 & 1911

1901 Census

1. L. O'Reilly	Superintend. DMP	5 Nth. Richmond St.
2. P. Leahy	Const. DMP	12 Portland Row
3. D. Cantlon	Constable DMP	12 Richmond Cotts.
4. P. Ring	DMP pensioner	4 Sackville Gardens
5. P. Barrow	Retired Const'/Sgt	18 B. Newcomen Ave.
6. P. Byrne	Police pensioner	7 Annesley Place
7. E. McKeogh	Constable	2 Ballybough Rd.
8. Th. Thompson	ex Sgt. Police	61 Ballybough Rd.
9. J. Taylor	Police Constable	6 Bayview Ave.
10. J. Quinn	Police Sgt.	17 Bayview Ave.
11. P. Wall	Police Sgt.	111 Clonliffe Rd.
12. J. Fitzpatrick	ex Const.	5 Clonliffe Ave.
13. P. Saunders	Police Sgt.	5 Foster Terrace
14. J. Lawless	Police pensioner	14 Foster Terrace
15. W. Richardson	Police Const.	22 Foster Terrace
16. P. Sheehan	Police Const.	23 Foster Terrace
17. J. Dowd	Police pensioner	29 Foster Terrace
18. P. Tidd	Police Const.	19 Nth Richmond St.
19. J. Shanaghan	Police Const.	7 Nottingham St.
20. J. Harris	Police Const.	23 Nottingham St.
21. G. McLoughlin	Police Const.	5 Nth William St.
22. P. Heffernan	Police Const.	176 Nth Strand Rd.
23. W. Fox	Police Const.	39 Nth Strand Rd.
24. W. Grattan	ex Const.	2 Richmond Ctts.
25. P. Devoy	Police Sgt.	30 Spring Garden St.
26. G. Cartwright	Police Sgt.	4 Richmond Parade
27. M. Hanlon	Police Sgt.	5 Richmond Parade
28. P. Beirne	Police Sgt.	3 Summerhill Parade
29. J. McNabola	Police Sgt.	5 Summerhill Parade
30. M. Molphy	Policeman	22 Summerhill Parade

RIC

31. W. Kelly	ex head Const. RIC	50 Charleville Ave.
32. L. Halpin	RIC pensioner	10 Charleville Mall
33. R. McCutcheon	RIC pensioner	42 Fairview St.
34. P. Nolan	RIC Sgt	39 Bayview Ave.
35. M. Quinn	RIC pensioner	17 Clonliffe Rd.
36. P. Kennedy	ex RIC head Const.	36 Foster Terrace
37. J. Kelly	RIC pensioner	7 Mountjoy Parade
38. J. Mullholland	RIC pensioner	
39. W. Treacy	ex head Const. RIC	117 Nth Strand St.
40. Th. Morrissey	RIC pensioner	127 Nth Strand Rd.
41. J. Doherty	RIC pensioner	61 Nth Strand Rd.
42. M. McGarry	RIC pensioner	28 Portland Row
43. Thomas McHugh	RIC Const.	10 Richmond Ctts.
44. J. Beatty	RIC	5 Russell St.

1911 Census

1. M. Kelly	pensioner	3 Charlemount Parade
2. E. Traly	Constable	20A Cowteray Place
3. J. Sheahan	Constable	1 Foster Place Nth
4. W. Dwyer	Constable	11 Foster Terrace
5. T. O'Meara	Constable	14 Foster Terrace
6. T. Foster	pensioner	31 Foster Terrace
7. J. Larkin	Inspector	29 Foster Terrace
8. E. O'Reilly	Sergeant	34 Foster Terrace
9. M. Dollard	pensioner	83 Ballybough Rd.
10. M. Lowry	Sergeant	30 Clonliffe Rd.
11. P. Morkey	Sergeant	36 Clonliffe Rd.
12. W. Johnston	Constable	46 Clonliffe Rd.
13. M. Kirby	Constable	27 Clonliffe Rd.
14. T. McHale	Constable	33 Clonliffe Rd.
15. P. Tidd	pensioner	19 Nth Richmond St.
16. J. Curry	Constable	26 Annesley Place
17. J. Carroll	pensioner	34 Annesley Ave.
18. R. Adamson	Sergeant	20 Nottingham St.
19. J. Harris	Constable	23 Nottingham St.

20. J. Lynch	Sergeant	82 Nth Strand
22. J. Long	Constable	82 Nth Strand
23. T. O'Loughlin	pensioner	101 Nth Strand
24. E. Timlin	Sergeant	109 Nth Strand
25. J. Cunningham	Constable	11 Nth William St.
26. S. Galbraith	Inspector	13A Nth William St.
27. D. Cantlon	pensioner	2 Richmond Ctts.
28. T. Lenahan	pensioner	2 Russell Place
29. T. Lally	pensioner	14 Russell Place
30. J. Brady	Sergeant	11 St. James Ave.
31. P. Beirne	Sergeant	3 Summerhill Parade
32. T. McNabola	Constable	5 Summerhill Parade
33. C. Bailey	pensioner	19 Summerhill Parade
34. R. Storey	Sergeant	2 Ulster Terrace
35. J. O'Sullivan	Constable	1 Waterloo Ave.
36. J. Flemming	Constable	8 Waterloo Ave.

Appendix 3

I.R.A DUBLIN BRIGADE*

O/C Oscar Traynor	G.H.Q.
Sean Russell	G.H.Q.
Capt. Frank Henderson	F coy 2nd Batt.
Capt. Leo Henderson	B coy 2nd Batt.
VOL. William Walsh	F coy 2nd Batt.
VOL. Joseph Billings	B coy 2nd Batt.
VOL. Liam McGinley	F coy 2nd Batt.
VOL. P.J O'Reilly	E coy 2nd Batt.
VOL. Peter Carpenter	
VOL. Matthew Parnell	

IRISH CITIZEN ARMY*

Vol. Joseph Whelan	I.C.A.	fought Annesley Bridge & Metropole Hotel
Vol. Daniel Courtney	I.C.A	fought Annesley Bridge & GPO
Vol. John Boylan	I.C.A.	fought Annesley Bridge
Vol. Vincent Poole	I.C.A	fought Annesley Bridge & GPO
Vol. Andrew Redmond	I.C.A.	fought Annesley Bridge & Imperial Hotel
Vol. Peter Carpenter	I.C.A.	fought Annesley Bridge & Metropole Hotel[1]

*Allen Library Archive & ICA Roll of Honour – incomplete – men from Ballybough who fought.

E COMPANY 2nd BATTALION GHQ

Capt. Thomas Weafer (KIA)
Lt. Michael Brady
Joe Callan
James Carrigan
T. Crimmins
Michael Croke
F. Dunne
T. Ennis
J. Fitzharris
Ignatius Flynn
A. Furlong
Joe Furlong
James Hunter
T. Leahy
L. Mackey
P. Mitchell (Red Cross)
T. Murray
Matthew O'Mahony
P. O'Moore
T. Roche
S. Russell
P. Weafer
J. White[2]

1. R.M. Fox – The Irish Citizen Army. p.227-232
2. J.M. Heuston – H.Q. Battalion, Easter Week. 1916. Printed by Nationalist Printers, Carlow – Allen Library

Appendix 4

LOCALS WHO FOUGHT IN 1916

SURNAME	FORENAME	ADDRESS	BATTALION	FOUGHT	INTERNED
Billings*	Joseph	24 Bayview Ave.	B Coy 2nd Batt	GPO, Moore St.	Knutsford
Breen	William	Fairview Strand	BGE Engs	GPO	Frongoch
Breslin	Toby	2 Fairview Corner	E Coy 3rd Batt	Boland's	Frongoch, Wakefield
Byrne*	Patrick	17 N. Richmond St.	C Coy 1st Batt	GPO	Frongoch
Callan*	Joseph	15 Clonliffe Ave.	E Coy 2nd Batt	GPO	Knutsford, Frongoch
Canny		70 N. Strand Rd.		GPO	Knutsford
Carney	Francis	24 Cadogen Rd.	B Coy 2nd Batt	Jacob's	Stafford
Carrigan	James	18 N. Strand Rd.	Coy 2nd Batt	GPO	
Casey	Hugh	13 Clonliffe Rd.		Four Courts	
Coghlan	Thomas	55 N. Strand Rd.			
Colley	Harry	69 Clonliffe Rd.		GPO	
Connolly	Mary	4 N. Richmond St.			
Conroy	James	4 N. Richmond St.	F Coy 2nd Batt	Four Courts	
Daly*	Liam	188 Clonliffe Rd.	Coy 2nd Batt	GPO, O'Connell St.	
Darney	Johnny	9 Clonliffe Ave.			Wakefield
Darritt	D.	4 Russell St.			Stafford
Devoy	James	Fairview Strand	B Coy 2nd Batt	GPO	Frongoch
Doherty	J.	7 Ballybough Rd.			Knutsford
Dunne	Frank	1 Clonmore Rd.	E Coy 2nd Batt	GPO	Wakefield, Frongoch
Early	John	Richmond Pl.	B Coy 2nd Batt	GPO, Four Courts	Frongoch
Flood*	J.	19 Summerhill Pde.	C Coy 1st Batt	GPO	Stafford
Flood*	Sean	19 Summerhill Pde.		Four Courts	Frongoch
Friel	P.	17 St. Joseph's Villas			
Geoghegan	J.J.	134 N. Strand Rd.			Stafford
Gilligan	Patrick	27 Bayview Ave.	F Coy 2nd Batt	Four Courts	
Gregory	John	28 Cadogan Rd.	E Coy 2nd Batt	Jacob's	Knutsford
Hannan	James	1 Bayview Ave.			
Hanrahan	Edward	N. Strand Rd.	F Coy 2nd Batt	Jacob's	
Hogan	Patrick	53 Clonliffe Rd.			
Hunter	James	13 Sackville Ave.	E Coy 2nd Batt	GPO	

SURNAME	FORENAME	ADDRESS	BATTALION	FOUGHT	INTERNED
Hutchinson	Joseph	12 Summerhill Pde.	E Coy 2nd Batt	GPO	Knutsford, Frongoch
Kearney	Thomas	N. Strand	E Coy 4th Batt	GPO	
Kenny*	John	22 O'Sullivan Ave.	C Coy	Four Courts	
Keogh	Cyril	Richmond Pl.	Frongoch		
King	Leo	4 Sackville Gdns.	Frongoch		
Lynch*	John	N. Strand	C Coy 1st Batt	GPO	Frongoch
Lyons	E.	15 Factory Tce.		Four Courts	Knutsford
Lyons	Edward	Foster Pl.	B Coy 2nd Batt	Jacob's	Frongoch
McCabe	Kevin	559 NCR	E Coy 1st Batt	GPO	Frongoch
MacDonagh	Michael	N. Strand Rd.			Frongoch
McDonald	Michael	84 N. Strand Rd.			Knutsford
McDonnell	Thomas	N. Strand			Frongoch
Mackey	Laurence	23 N. William St.	E Coy 2nd Batt	GPO	
Mackey	Michael	23 N. William St.	C Coy 2nd Batt	GPO	Knutsford
Madden	J.	27 Clonliffe Ave.	C Coy 1st Batt	GPO	Frongoch, Stafford
Melinn	Seamus	107 Summerhill	B Coy 2nd Batt	Jacobs	Lewes
Meehan	William	50 Foster Tce.	D Coy	Four Courts	
Mitchell	Patrick	Sackville Gdns.	E Coy 2nd Batt/ Red Cross		Frongoch
Moore	William	21 Cadogan Rd.			Knutsford
Moran	William	Cadogan Rd.			Frongoch
Murphy	John	N. Strand	E Coy 2nd Batt	Four Courts	
Murphy*	Michael	9 Aldborough Pde.	F Coy 2nd Batt	GPO	Frongoch
Murtagh	Joseph	83 N. Strand Rd.	Fianna Eireann	GPO	
Nugent	Patrick	8 Charleville Ave.	C Coy 2nd Batt	GPO	Knutsford
O'Connor	James	101 Clonliffe Rd.	B Coy 1st Batt	GPO	
O'Connor	Patrick	1 Charleville Mall	E Coy 4th Batt	GPO	
O'Hanrahan	Mary	149 N. Strand Rd.	C na mBan	GPO	
O'Neill*	John	61 Ballybough Rd.	ICA	GPO	Wandsworth
O'Reilly	John	3 Ballybough Lane	ICA	Stephen's Green	Stafford
O'Reilly	S.P.	3 Ballybough Lane		GPO	Frongoch
Pugh*	Thomas	9 Charleville Mall	B Coy 2nd Batt	Jacob's	Knutsford, Frongoch
Purcell	C.	35 James's Ave.		GPO	Knutsford
Reid*	J.	41 St. Mary's Tce.	B Coy 3rd Batt	GPO	Knutsford, Frongoch
Reilly	P.	5 Charleville Rd.	E Coy 2nd Batt	Jacob's	Knutsford
Reynolds*	P.	16 Clonmore Rd.	A Coy 1st Batt	GPO	Stafford
Ring	Chris	5 Sackville Gdns.	C Coy 2nd Batt	GPO	Stafford, Frongoch

SURNAME	FORENAME	ADDRESS	BATTALION	FOUGHT	INTERNED
Ring	Joseph	17 Clonmore Tce.	C Coy 2nd Batt	GPO	Frongoch, Stafford
Ring	Liam	5 Sackville Gdns.	C Coy 2nd Batt	GPO	
Ring	Patrick	6 Sackville Gdns.		GPO	Stafford, Frongoch
Ring	W.	4 Sackville Gdns.	C Coy 2nd Batt		Stafford
Robbins	F.	39 N. William St.	ICA	Stephen's Green	Knutsford, Frongoch
Rooney*	J.	36 Fairview Strand	Fingal Brig.	Ashbourne	Knutsford
Rossiter	Charles	32a Sackville Gdns.	F Coy 2nd batt	GPO	
Russell	J.	68 N. Strand Rd.			Knutsford, Frongoch
Russell*	Sean	66 N. Strand Rd.	E Coy 2nd Batt		
Ryan	W.	70 N. Strand	Kimmage Garr.	Four Courts	Knutsford
Scallan	J.J.	St. Joseph's Ave.	Hib. Rifles	GPO	Wandsworth, Frongoch
Scully	William	49 Clonliffe Ave.		Four Courts	
Smith	Michael	2 Bayview Ave.	E Coy 2nd Batt	Jacob's	Knutsford
Scanlon	C.	2 N. Richmond St.	C Coy 2nd Batt	GPO	Knutsford
Tallon*	James	2 N. Richmond St.	B Coy 1st Batt	GPO	Wakefield
Toomey*	J.	10 Clonmore Tce.	B Coy 2nd Batt	GPO	
Toomey	T.	30 Clonliffe Ave.			Knutsford
Traynor	C.	55 Jones's Rd.			Knutsford
Walker*	J.	37 Addison Rd.	G Coy 2nd Batt	Jacob's	Stafford
Walker*	M.	37 Addison Rd.	G Coy 2nd Batt	Jacob's	Stafford
Wheatley	Thomas	8 N. William St.	B Coy 2nd Batt		
Whelan	W.	31 Ballybough Rd.			Stafford, Frongoch
Williams	H.	72 Cadogan Rd.	D Coy 2nd Batt	Jacob's	Stafford

Glossary

coy = company
batt = battalion
Bdge Engs. = Brigade Engineers
C na mBan = Cumann na mBan
ICA = Irish Citizen Army
Fingal Brig. = Fingal Brigade
Hib. Rifles = Hibernian Rifles

* Attended O'Connell Schools

Appendix 5

E COMPANY 1920 – SELECTED MEMBERS

NAME	ADDRESS	OCCUPATION	EMPLOYER	ENLISTED
Begley, D	15 Newcomen Court	Boiler maker	Port & Docks	1918
Cahill, H	623 NCR	Mechanic	self employed	1917
Cahill, R	623 NCR	Mechanic	self employed	1917
Callan, J	15 Clonliffe Ave	Motor Driver		1914
Dalton, P	4 Fairview Strand	Carpenter		1918
Daly, J	35 Nth Strand Rd	Electrician	Dockrell & Co	1915
Daly, Wm	35 Nth Strand Rd	Electrician	Dockrell & Co	1915
Dixon, Wm	14 St Josephs Ave	Tin Smith	Anglo American Oil Co	1916
Doyle, A	1 Portland Row	Library Assistant	National Library	1917
Dunne, F	1 Clonmore Rd	Bookbinder		1915
Ennis, T	3 Richmond Crescent	Checker	MGWR	1914
Fleming, Wm	22 Charleville Ave	Casual		1919
Flynn, P	19 Charleville Mall	Checker	MGWR	1919
Freyne, J	24 Charleville Ave			1920
Freyne, P	24 Charleville Ave			1920
Hunter, J	15 Sackville Ave	Carpenter	Russ & Walpoles	1915
Kehoe, T	5 Richmond Crescent	Quay Labourer	LNWR	1915
Kenny, J	287 Richmond Rd	Plasterer	Self Employed	1914
Lynch, M	11 Portland Row	Office Boy	Agricultural Wages Board	1919
Macken, J	17 Richmond Cotts	Lawyer		1917
McClean, Wm	159 Nth Strand Rd	Compositor	Thoms	1918
Mitchell, P	1 Sackville Gardens	Brick Layer		1915
Murphy, J	35 Jones's Rd			1918
Parsoons, P	Newcomen Cotts	Checker	MGWR	1917
Reilly, P	14 Nth Strand Rd	Labourer	Quays	1915
Russell, J	68 Nth Strand Rd	Carpenter		
Scanlan, Wm	7 Addison Rd	Draper's Assistant	Hickey & Co	1918
Smyth, M	Nth William St	Coach Painter		1915
Walker, J	37 Addison Rd	Fitter	Self Employed	1914
Walker, M	37 Addison Rd	Compositor	Lalors	1914

Appendix 6

PRISONERS LISTS: 1922 TO 1923

NAME	ADDRESS	PLACE INTERNED	DATE
John Barry	48 North Strand Road	Mullingar	15/9/22
Leo Billings	24 Bayview Avenue	Maryboro	07/8/22
W.E. Brown	11 North Richmond Street	Gormanstown	12/9/22
Thomas Brooks	55 Foster Terrace	Newbridge	30/08/22 Released 11/12/22
Maurice Carr	38 St. Mary's Road North Strand	Mountjoy Newbridge	21/10/22 31/12/23 Released 19/01/23
John D. Cashlin	1 Cadogan Road	Curragh	27/11/22
Henry Carr	3 Ballybough Road	Curragh	27/11/22
C. Clarke	Charlemont Mall	Mountjoy	15/09/22
Frank Concannon	4 Charlemont Parade	Mountjoy	11/08/22
John Coonihan	15 Sackville Avenue	Mountjoy	15/09/22
Eugene Corcoran	63 Ballybough Road	Mountjoy	15/09/22
Sean Conlon	Bayview House	Mountjoy	15/09/22
Miss Eileen Colgan	1 North Strand	Kilmainham	20/03/23
Joe Cunningham	18 Upper Jones Terrace	Mountjoy	15/09/22
James Davidson	46 North Strand Road	Newbridge	20/12/22
Owen Donn	4 Shamrock Place North Strand	Wellington Gormanstown	02/09/22 14/09/22
A. Doyle	St. Joseph's	Mountjoy	15/09/22
Paddy Doyle	20 Bayview Avenue	Mountjoy Newbridge	21/10/22 31/12/22
John Dowdal	14 Sackville Avenue	Mountjoy	05/03/23
Tom Duke	St. Margaret's	Tin Town II	Released 17/12/25
Edward Duke	St. Margaret's	Mountjoy	15/09/22
Ellis Ellans	17 Northbrook Avenue	Wellington Gormanstown	12/09/22 14/09/22
James Ellis	31 Foster Terrace	Curragh	27/11/22 Released 12/02/23
James Gibson	O'Sullivan Avenue	Maryboro Tin Town II	07/08/22 22/02/23
John Gannon	Georgina Cottages	Gormanstown	14/09/22
Josh Gillich	14 Ardmore Avenue North Circular Road	Newbridge	20/12/22 Released 12/02/23
Vincent Gogan	371 North Circular Road	Mountjoy	04/02/23
Richard Gogan	371 North Circular Road	Mountjoy	04/02/23
Jer Hargrove	10 Mable Street	Mountjoy Newbridge	15/09/22 31/12/22

P. Halpin	24 Summerhill Parade	Mountjoy	15/09/22
Harry Hazlewood	11 Clonliffe Avenue	Mountjoy	15/09/22
John Harrison	45 North Strand Road	Mountjoy Newbridge	21/10/22 31/12/22
Frank Henderson	75 North Circular Road	Mountjoy	10/03/23
Alex Kerr	58 North Strand Road	Maryboro	07/08/22
Thomas Keenan	14 St. David's Terrace	Newbridge	20/12/22
Lee Kellingham	403 North Circular Road	Mountjoy	03/02/22 Released 03/03/23
Denis Kerrigan	15 Carnew Street	Mountjoy	30/01/23
William Hegarty	17 Emmet Street	Curragh	28/11/22
John Kinlan	83 Summerhill	Curragh	27/11/22
Patrick Leonard	27 Annesley Avenue	Mountjoy Newbridge	15/09/22 31/12/22
Liam Lucas	89 Summerhill	Gormanstown	12/09/22
Val MacEntee	24 North William Street	Gormanstown	12/09/22 Released 12/01/23
James Morrissey	21 Belvedere Place North Circular Road	Wellington Gormanstown	12/09/22 14/09/22
Liam Moore	422 North Circular Road	Gormanstown	12/09/22
Michael Mohan	12 James Avenue	Maryboro	07/08/22
Mary Moore	422 North Circular Road	Kilmainham	06/04/23
Miss R. Mooney	17 Rutland Cottages	Kilmainham	27/04/23
Michael Murphy	1 Leinster Avenue	Maryboro	04/08/22
Patrick McArdle	10 Portland Row	Mountjoy	07/03/23
Edward McArdle	10 Portland Row	Mountjoy	24/04/23
Thomas McCarthy	13 Portland Row	Wellington	12/09/22
Thomas McDermott	25 Summerhill	Wellington	12/09/22
Sean McEvoy	10 Clonmore Road	Mountjoy Newbridge	15/09/22 31/12/22 Released 03/01/23
Patrick McGuirk	2 Cottage Place	Newbridge	31/08/22
John Maguire	570 North Circular Road	Newbridge	20/12/22
Andrew McKenna	35 Ballybough Road	Mountjoy	05/03/23
Michael Mahon	North Strand	Beggars Bush	15/09/22
B. McQuillen	96 North Circular Road	Mountjoy	15/09/22
John Neary	3 Donard Terrace	Newbridge	20/12/22 Released 11/01/23
John Nicholson	2 Ulster Terrace North Strand	Wellington Newbridge	12/08/22 21/08/22 Released 11/04/23
Thomas Nolan	11 Spring Garden Street	Mountjoy Newbridge	15/09/22 31/12/22
L. O'Brien	18 North Circular Road	Portobello	12/08/22
Eamonn O'Dwyer	43 Cadogan Road	Mountjoy Arbour Hill	07/03/23 11/04/23
John O'Flanagan	56 Ballybough Road	Maryboro	07/08/22
Patrick O'Hanrahan	442 North Circular Road	Mountjoy	15/09/22

Appendix 7

2 JUNE 1941 – *THE IRISH TIMES*

Casualties:

Mary Browne (75)	24 North Strand Road
Harry Browne, son	
Mary Browne (33), wife	
Maureen Browne (7)	
Nan Browne (5)	
Edward Browne (3.5)	
Angela Browne (2)	
Richard Fitzpatrick	28 North Strand Road
Ellen Fitzpatrick, wife	
Madge Fitzpatrick	
Noel Fitzpatrick	
Mrs McNally	155 North Strand Road
J. Murray	156 North Strand Road
Mrs. Ellen Boyle	157 North Strand Road
Patrick Callely	162 North Strand Road
Elizabeth Daly	162 North Strand Road
Charles Sweeney	11 North Strand Road
Marion Holton	156 North Strand Road
Mr. & Mrs. John Foran	155 North Strand Road
Alice Desmond	156 North Strand Road
James Fitzpatrick	156 North Strand Road
Josephine Fagan	157 North Strand Road
Thomas Carroll	157 North Strand Road
William McLoughlin	41 Summerhill Parade
Patrick McLoughlin	41 Summerhill Parade
X unidentified bodies	

SATURDAY 1 JUNE 1941 – *IRISH INDEPENDENT*

Shops and other premises destroyed or damaged on the west side of the North Strand:

23-24	M. Fagan, family grocer
25	M. Dempsey, draper
26	G. Jordan, butcher
27	R. Fitzpatrick, victualler

28	P. Fitzpatrick, jeweller
29	W. Granville, general stores
30	North Strand Mission Hall
31	W. Lynch, grocer
32	J.A. Pattison, chemist
33	T. Roche, hairdresser
34	M.J. Roddy, confectioners
35	North Strand Post Office

On the opposite side the following houses were badly damage and at least 10 were completely destroyed

153	Denis Newcomen
154	T. Peakin
155	Mrs. Mary McFall
156	J. Bermingham
157	flats
158	Norah Grafton
159	Mrs. Quinn
160	Mrs. M. Hastings
161	T. Donery
162	Mrs. Mary Montgomery
163	Miss Mary Behan
164	J. M. McCarthy, undertaker

Also destroyed were:

582 North Circular Road, Mrs Grice's Shop
43 & 44 Summerhill Parade

Bibliography

SECONDARY SOURCES

Aalan, F.H.A.	*Approaches to the working-class housing problem in late Victorian Dublin*. Rainer Joha Bender (ed.)
	'The working-class housing movement in Dublin, 1850-1920' in Michael J. Bannon (ed) "*The emergence of Irish planning 1880-1920*". Dublin (1985)
	M. Daly's *Housing conditions and the genesis of housing reform in Dublin, 1880 - 1920*
Andrews, C.S.	*Dublin made me: an autobiography*. (1979)
Anon	*New city pictorial directory*. (1850)
Anon	*The industries of Dublin*. (1786)
Anon	*Dublin's fighting story*
Archdall, M.	*Monasticon Hibernicum Vol. 1*. (1873)
Atkinson, N.	*Irish education: a history of educational institutions*. (1969)
Atkinson, Sarah	*Old houses restored*
Ball, F. Elrington	*A history of County Dublin*. (1920)
	Southern Fingal, being the sixth part of a history of County Dublin. (1920)
Ballagh, Robert	*Dublin*. (1981)
Bannon, M.J.	*A hundred years of Irish planning. Vol. 1. The emergence of Irish planning* 1880-1920
Barry, T.B.	*The archaeology of medieval Dublin*. (1987)
Bazalgette, J.W.	*Report on the Dublin Sewage Utilization Bill*. (1868)
Beckett, J.C.	*The making of modern Ireland 1603-1923*. (1966)
Bennett, Douglas	*Encyclopaedia of Dublin*
Boylan, Henry	*This arrogant city: a readers' & collectors' guide to books about Dublin*. (1983)
Bradley, John (ed)	*Viking Dublin exposed*. (1984)
Brazil, Thomas	Report to the Corporation of Dublin on the proposed supply of the city and suburbs with pure water at high pressure. (1854)
British Association	*Handbook to the Dublin district*. (1908)
Broad, Ian	*Mediaeval Dublin: two historic walks*. (1982)
Bronsted, J.	*The Vikings* (trans. by Estrid Bannister-Good). (1960)
Broughton R.	Accounts etc. presented to the House of Commons relating to et al inland navigation of Ireland and the port of Dublin. (1806)
Buckley, M.	*The jangle of the keys* Dublin. (1938)
Burke, Helen	*The people and the Poor Law in 19th century Ireland*. (1987)

Butel P. & Cullen L.M.(eds.) *Cities and merchants: French and Irish perspectives on urban development, 1500 - 1900.* (1986)

Byrne, Edward *Crown and Castle: British rule in Ireland 1800-1830.* (1978)

Byrne, Matthew *Dublin and her people.* (1987)

Canny, Nicholas *The formation of the old English elite in Ireland.* (1975)

Carey, Tim *Hanged for Ireland: the forgotten ten.* (2001)

Carroll, Joseph T. *Ireland in the war years 1939-1945.* (1975)

Carter, E. *An historical geography of the railways of the British Isles.* (1959)

Chart, D.A. *Dublin.* (1907)

Chart, G.D.A. *Unskilled labour in Dublin.* (1914)

Clarke, Desmond *Dublin.* (1977)

Clarke, Howard *Dublin c.840 - c.1540: the mediaeval town in the modern city.* (1978)

Clarke, P. *The Royal Canal: the complete story.* (1992)

Coffey, Andrew *A view &c.* (1829)

Collins, James *Life in old Dublin.* (1913)

Condon, K. (Rev) *The missionary college of All Hallows* (1986)

Conlin, Stephen & De Courcy, John *Anna Liffey: the river of Dublin.* (1988)

Coogan, Tim Pat *Michael Collins: a biography.* (1991)

Cooke, J. *Ireland's premier coachbuilders*

Cosgrave, Dillon *North Dublin: city and environs.* (1909)

Cosgrave, E. MacDowel & Strangeways, Leonard R. *The illustrated dictionary of Dublin.* (1895)

Coughlan, John *Memories: a pictorial celebration for Dublin's Millennium.* (1988)

Craig, Maurice *Dublin 1660-1860.* (1980)

The architecture of Ireland from the earliest times to 1880. (1982)

Crossman, V. *Local government in 19th century Ireland.* (1995)

Cullen, L.M. *Princes and pirates: the Dublin Chamber of Commerce 1783-1983.* (1983)

Culliton, James *The City Hall.* (1982)

Curtin, Nancy *United Irishmen: popular politics in Ulster & Dublin 1771-1798.* (1994)

Daiken, Leslie *Out goes she: Dublin street rhymes with a commentary.* (1963)

Dalton, Charles *With the Dublin Brigade (1917-1921).* (1929)

D'Alton, John *The history of the County Dublin.* (1976)

Daly, Mary E. *Dublin, the deposed capital: a social and economic history 1860-1914.* (1985)

'Late 19th and early 20th century Dublin' in "*The town in Ireland*".Harkness & O'Dowd (eds).

De Burca, M. *The G.A.A.: a history.* (1980)

De Courcy, J.W. *The Liffey in Dublin.* (1996)

Delaney, Ruth	*Ireland's Royal Canal 1789-1992.* (1992)
Dickinson, P.L.	*The Dublin of yesterday.* (1929)
Dickson, D. (ed)	*The gorgeous mask: Dublin 1700-1850.* (1987)
Donnelly, N.	*A short history of Dublin parishes.* 1910-1915
Dowling, P.J.	*A history of Irish education: a study in conflicting loyalties*
Dublin Corporation	*Official Guide to the City of Dublin.* (1965)
Dublin Marine	*The port of Dublin: 100 years of Dublin port, a century of Research change.* (1967)
Duggan, John P.	*A history of the Irish army.* (1991)
Edwards, R.D. &Williams, D.T.	*The great famine: studies in Irish history 1845-1852.* (1956)
Ellis, S.G.	*Reform & revival: English government in Ireland 1470-1534*
Fagan, Patrick	*The second city: portrait of Dublin 1700-1760.* (1986)
Fisk, Robert	*In time of war.* (1983)
Fitzpatrick, D.	*Politics and Irish life 1913-1921: provincial experience of war and revolution.* (1977)
Fitzpatrick, S.	*Dublin: a historical and topographical account of the city.* (1907)
Fitzpatrick, W.J.	*History of the Dublin Catholic cemeteries.* (1900)
Flinn, D. Edgar	Official report on the sanitary circumstances and administration of the city of Dublin with special reference to the causes of high death rate (1906)
Flood, Donald T.	*Historical evidence for the growth of North Bull Island*
Fox, R.M.	*History of the Irish Citizen Army.* (1943)
Garrett, Arthur	*In ages past: the story of North Strand Church and Day Schools.* (1985)
Georgian Society	Records (5 vols). 1909-1913
Gilbert, John T.	*The Chartularies of St. Mary's Abbey* (2 vols) 1884
	A history of the City of Dublin (3 vols). (1978)
Gill, M.H. & Son (ed)	*Guide to Catholic Dublin.* (1932)
Gilligan, Henry A.	*A history of the port of Dublin.* (1989)
Gleeson, James	*Bloody Sunday.* (1962)
Gorham, Maurice	*Ireland yesterday.* (1971)
	Dublin from old photographs. (1972)
	Dublin old and new. (1975)
Granville, Gary	*Divided City: portrait of Dublin 1913.* (1978)
Guinness, Desmond	*Portrait of Dublin.* (1967)
	Georgian Dublin. (1979)
Gwynn, Stephen	*Dublin old and new.* (1940)
Hall, S. & Mrs. S.C.	*Ireland: its scenery, character etc.* (3 vols). (1842)
Harris, Walter	*The history and antiquities of the city of Dublin from earliest accounts.* (1766)
Harvey, John	*Dublin: a study in environment.* (1949)

Hayward, Richard	*Leinster and the City of Dublin.* (1949)
Herlihy, Jim	*The Royal Irish Constabulary.* (1997)
Hill, J.R.	*The politics of privilege: Dublin Corporation and the Catholic Question, 1792 - 1823*
Hobson, Bulmer	*A short history of the Irish Volunteers.* (1918)
Hopkinson, Michael	*Green against green: the Irish Civil War.* (1988)
Hughes, Kathleen	*The Church in early Irish society.* (1972)
Jeffrey, D.W. *et al* (ed.)	*North Bull Island, Dublin Bay: a modern coastal natural history.* (1977)
Johnson, J.	*A tour in Ireland.* (1844)
Johnson, Nevil	*Dublin: the people's city.* (1981)
Joyce, James	*Dubliners.* (1981 reprint)
Joyce, P.W.	A *social history of ancient Ireland.* Vol. 1. 1913 (2nd ed)
Joyce, Weston St. J.	*The neighbourhood of Dublin.* (1939)
Kearns, Kevin Corrigan	*Georgian Dublin: Ireland's imperilled architectural heritage.* (1983)
	Dublin tenement life. (1996)
Kain, Richard M.	*Dublin in the age of William Butler Yeats and James Joyce.* (1972)
Kelleher, Terry	*The essential Dublin.* (1979)
Kelly, Patrick	*Drumcondra, Clonliffe and Glasnevin township, 1878-1900*
Kennedy, P.G.	*An Irish sanctuary: North Bull Island.* (1953)
Kennedy, Tom (ed.)	*Dublin handbook*
	Victorian Dublin
Keogh, Dermot	*Twentieth century Ireland: nation and state.* (1994)
Kilroy, Jim	*Howth and her trams.* (1986)
Kinealy, Christine	'The Poor Law during the great Famine: an administration in crisis' in E.M.Crawford, *Famine: The Irish Experience 900-1900.* (1989)
Kingston, John (Rev)	*The parish of Fairview.* (1953)
Kissane, Noel	*The Irish famine: a documentary history.* (1996)
Kohl, J.H.	*Travels in Ireland* (1842)
Kotsonouris, Mary	*Retreat from revolution: the Dail Courts 1920-24.* (1994)
Lalor, Brian	*Dublin.* (1981)
Lee, J.J.	*Ireland 1912-1985: politics & society.* (1989)
Lewis, Samuel	*A history and topography of the city of Dublin.* (1980)
Little, George A.	*Dublin before the Vikings: an adventure in discovery*
Litton, Helen	*The Irish famine: an illustrated history.* (1994)
Loeber, Rolf	*The geography & practice of English colonisation in Ireland*
Luddy, Ailbe (Rev)	*St. Mary's Abbey, Dublin.* (1935)
	Remains of old St. Mary's Abbey Dublin and researches AD (1886)

Lyons, F.L.S.	*Ireland since the famine.* (1973)
Lynch, D. & O'Donoghue, F.	*The I.R.B. and the 1916 Rising.* (1957)
Macardle, Dorothy	*The Irish republic.* (1951)
Mapother, E.D.	*The sanitary state of Dublin: in papers concerning public health.* (1864)
Martin, F.X. (Rev)	*The Howth Gun-Running.* (1964)
	'The 1916 Rising – a coup d'etat or a 'Bloody Protest" (1968) in *Studia Hibernia Vol. 8*
M.G.	*The love story of Thomas Davis, told in the letters of Annie Hutton.* Joseph Hone (ed)
McCoole, Sinead	*Guns & chiffon Dublin* (1997)
Harper-McCoy, G.A.	'A military history of the 1916 Rising' & 'The conduct of the Anglo-Irish war' in Desmond Williams (ed) *"The Irish struggle 1916-1926".* (1966)
McCready, C.T.	*Dublin Street names, dated and explained.* (1892)
McCullough, Niall	*Dublin: an urban history.* (1989)
McDermott, M.	*Dublin's architectural development 1800-1925.* (1988)
McDowell, R.B.	*Ireland in the age of imperialism and revolution 1760-1801.* (1979)
MacEoin, Uinseann	*Survivors Dublin.* (1980)
McGuinness, Donal	From the Dublin Millennium Book: Baile Atha Cliath 1000 years. *Proposals and overview for future development.* (1988)
McIntyre, Dennis	*The meadow of the bull: a history of Clontarf.* (1976)
McIvor, Muriel	*Clontarf, past and present.* (1976)
MacLoughlin, Adrian	*Guide to historic Dublin.* (1979)
MacNeill, John	*History of the G.N.R. extension*
McParland, E.	*Strategy in the planning of Dublin, 1750 - 1800 (see Butel & Cullen)*
MacThomais, Eamonn	*Me jewel and darlin' Dublin Dublin.* (1980)
McQuillan, Jack	*The railway town: Drogheda*
Maxwell, Constantia	*Dublin under the George.* (1937 & 1946)
Maxwell, W.H.	*History of the Irish Rebellion in 1798.* (1845 & 1864)
Mitchell, A.	*Labour and Irish politics 1890-1930.* (1974)
Mokyr, Joel & O'Grada Cormac	Poor and getting poorer? Living standards in Ireland before the Famine.pp.209-35. in *Economic History Review*
Moody, T.W. & Martin, F.X. (Rev)	*The course of Irish history.* (1967)
Munster, Robert	*The history of the Irish newspaper.* (1967)
Murnan, Brian	*On common ground.* (1988)
Murphy, John A.	*Ireland in the twentieth century.* (1975)

Murphy, Denis (Rev)	Triumphalia chronologia monasterii sanctae crucis in (ed) *Hibernia de Cisterciensium Hibernorum viris illustribus* Dublin. (1895) Cistercian monasteries in the Kingdom of Ireland
Murray, K. A.	*Ireland's first railway.* (1981)
Murray, Peter	'Electoral politics and the Dublin working class before the first World War' 1980 in *Saothar 6*
NCEA	*Gardiner's Dublin: a history and topography of Mountjoy Square and environs.* (1991)
Neary, Bernard	*North of the Liffey: a character sketch book.* (1984)
Neary, Bernard	*Waiting for the 22: celebrating 50 years of Cabra West*
Nelligan, David	*The spy in the Castle.* (1968)
Neville, Parke	*Report on the unhealthy districts of the borough of Dublin* (1864) *Report to the Lord Mayor etc. of the City of Dublin on the sewerage of the city and proposed plans for improving the same.* (1853)
Norris, David	*Joyce's Dublin.* (1982)
Nowlan, Kevin B.	*The making of 1916: studies in the history of the Rising.* (ed) (1969)
O'Brien, G.	*The economic history of Ireland from the Union to the Famine.* (1921)
O'Brien, Joseph V.	*Dear dirty Dublin: a city in distress 1899-1616.* (1982)
O Broin, Art	*Faces of old Leinster.* (1978)
O Broin, Sean	*The Book of Finglas.* (1980)
O'Connell, D.	*The antique pavement.* (1975)
O'Carroll, Derval & Fitzpatrick, S.	*Hoggers, Lords and railwaymen: a history of the Custom House Docks.* (1996)
O'Connor, John	*The workhouses of Ireland's poor.* (1995)
O'Donnell, E.E.	*The annals of Dublin's fair city.* (1987)
O'Dwyer, Frederick	*Lost Dublin.* (1981)
O'Farrell, P.	*Who's who.* (1997)
O'Keeffe, John	*Recollections of the life of John O'Keeffe.* Vol.1. (1826)
Osborough, W.N.	*Law and the emergence of modern Dublin: a litigation topography for a capital city.* (1996)
Otway-Ruthven, J.	*The medieval church lands of Co. Dublin.* (1961)
Packenham, T.	*The year of liberty: the bloody story of the great Irish Rebellion of 1798.* (1969 & 1972)
Patterson, E.	*The great G.N.R. of Ireland*
Pearl, Cyril	*Dublin in bloomtime: the city James Joyce knew.* (1969)
Postgate, R.	*Story of the year of 1798.* (1969)
Pritchett, V.S.	*Dublin: a portrait.* (1967)
Quinn, Edward	*James Joyce's Dublin.* (1974)
Ronan, Myles V. (Rev)	*The Reformation in Dublin 1536-1558.* (1923)

Ryan, Meda	*Michael Collins and the women in his life.*
Ryan, W.P.	*The Irish labour movement.* (1919)
Sadleir, Thomas & Dickinson, Page L.	*Georgian mansions in Ireland.* (1915)
Share, Bernard	*The emergency: neutral Ireland 1939-1945.* (1978)
Sharp, Edmund	*Cistercian architecture from remains of old St. Mary's Abbey*
Sherry, Richard	*Holy Cross College, Clonliffe, Dublin: college history and centenary record Dublin.* (1962)
Shillman, Bernard	*A short history of the Jews of Ireland.* (1945)
Skinnider, M.	*Doing my bit for Ireland.* (1917)
Smith, Cecil W.	*The great hunger.* (1962)
Sweeney, Clair R.	*The rivers of Dublin*
The Lords Justices & Council of Ireland	*A proclamation.* (1821)
Tallion, Ruth	*When history was made: the women of 1916 Belfast.* (1996)
Thackeray, W.M.	*The Irish sketch book.* (1887)
Thomson, F.M.L.	*The rise of respectable society: a social history of Victorian Britain 1830-1900.* (1988)
Tinsley, M.K.	*The bridges over the Liffey.* (1973)
Townshend, C.	*The British campaign in Ireland 1919-1921: the development of political and military policies.* (1975)
	Political violence in Ireland: government and resistance since 1848 (1983)
	An account of the rise and progress of the Royal Canal in Ireland and also of the opposition thereto (1797)
	Dublin main drainage scheme: souvenir handbook, Dublin. (1906)
	A friend to national industry: facts and arguments respecting the great utility of an extensive plan of inland navigation in Ireland. 1800
Valiulus, Maryann	*Portrait of a revolutionary: General Richard Mulcahy and the founding of the Irish Free State.* (1992)
Vaughan, W.E.	A new history of Ireland: Ireland under the Union 1801-70
Wall, Maureen	*The background to the Rising from 1914 until the issue of the countermanding order on Easter Sunday 1916*
	The plans & the countermand: the country & Dublin". (1969)
	The making of 1916
Walsh, John	*Rakes and ruffians: the underworld of Georgian Dublin.* (1979)
Warburton, Whitelaw& Walsh	*History of the City of Dublin* (2 vols). (1818)
Ward, Margaret	*Unmanageable revolutionaries: women and Iriah nationalism.* (1983)

Webb, John J. *The guilds of Dublin.* (1929)
Industrial Dublin since 1698 & the silk industry in Dublin. (1913)

Westropp, M.S.D. *Irish glass: a history of glass-making in Ireland from the sixteenth century.* (revised ed. 1978)

Whelpton, Eric *The Book of Dublin.* (1948)

White, George P. *Investment of capital in railways*

White, Newport B. *Extent of Irish monastic possessions Co. Dublin. Cistercian Abbey of St. Mary, Dublin. Monastery of the Blessed Mary near Dublin.* (1943)

Whitehead, Trevor *Dublin firefighters.* (1970)

Williams, Desmond *The Irish struggle 1916-1926.* (1966)

Wilson, Philip *The beginnings of modern Ireland Dublin.* (1914)

Wrenn, Trevor *The villages of Dublin.* (1982)

Wright, Arnold *Disturbed Dublin: the story of the Great Strike 1913-14*

Wullarkey, T. *St. Mary's Abbey*, Vol. 4. 1960-1961

MAPS OF DUBLIN

John Speed 1610
Down Survey 1658
Sir Bernard de Gomme 1673
Thomas Phillipps 1685
Greenville Collins 1686
Captain Pratt 1708
Herman Moll 1714
Charles Brooking 1728
John Roque 1754, 1756 & 1757
S J Neele 1797
J Cooke 1822
M Heffernan 1861 & 1868
Ordnance Survey 1837 onwards
Dublin Civic Survey 1925
Howard B Clarke 1978

PERIODICALS AND JOURNALS

Almanak Registry Directory
Analectica Hibernica
An t-Óglach
Architectural History

Bonaventura

Calendar of Ancient Records of Dublin
Calendar of the Patent Rolls, Ireland
Calendar of State Papers, Ireland
Capuchin Annual
Collectanae Hibernica

Dublin Brigade Review
The Dublin Builder
Dublin Diocesan Historical Record
Dublin Historical Record
Dublin Journal of Medical Science
Dublin Opinion
The Dublin Penny Journal
Dublin Review

The Environmental Information Service, Dublin
The Evening Press

Finn's Leinster Journal
Freeman's Journal
Friendship

The Garda Review
The Gentleman's & Citizens's Almanak

Hibernian Journal
History Ireland

Irish Architectural Archive – material relating to Ballybough and Fairview
The Irish Builder
Irish Ecclesiastical Record
Irish Georgian Society Bulletin
The Irish Independent
Irish Historical Studies
The Irish Monthly,
The Irish Press
The Irish Independent
The Irish Times
The Irish Worker

Journal of the Geological Society of Ireland
Journal of the Irish House of Commons (1613 - 1800)
Journal of the Irish House of Lords (1634 - 1800)
Journal of the Royal Society of the Antiquaries of Ireland

Leahar na mBan (1918)

Mansion House Committee Reports
The Maynooth Review
Medical Charities of Ireland – Fourth report 1856

Neure Forschungen zur Socialgeographie von Irland Mannheim. (1984)
Northside People (11 June 1997)

Pipe Water Work
Post Office Dublin Directory & Calendar
Proceedings of the Royal Irish Academy

Register of Electors. in force from 15th February 1995 to 14th February 1996

Saunder's Newsletter
Statistical and Social Inquiry Society of Ireland Journal
Studies

Thom's Directory

Watson's Dublin Directory
Wilson's Dublin Directory

CONTEMPORANEOUS SOURCES

The Books of Survey and Distribution
Bureau of Military History

Calendar of State Papers – Ireland, Elizabeth, 1588-1592, Vol. CXLVI, pp. 243
Calendar of State Papers – Ireland, Vol. CCXLIX, pp. 470
Calendar of State Papers – Ireland, Vol. CCLI, pp. 300, 584
Calendar of State Papers – Ireland, James I, 1606-08, pp. 56, 301-302, 419
Calendar of State Papers – Ireland, Charles II, 1663-65, pp. 43-44
Calendar of the Carew manuscripts. Vol. 5 Book of Howth, miscellaneous Dublin 1871
Calendar of State Papers 1509-1573
Calendar of Patent Roll, James I
Calendar of Ancient Records of Dublin
The Census for: 1659, 1798, and throughout the 19th and 20th century
Civil Survey, Co. Dublin, 1655-6. Barony of Coolock, pp. 178-181
Fifth report of the Commissioners of Irish education enquire

Corporation Reports 1871, Report from John Norwood, Esq., LL.D., J.P. suggesting new scheme for more effective scavenging of the City and disposal of scavenging stuff. Dublin: Joseph Dollard, 1871

Corporation Reports 1871, In re: State of streets. Report from City Engineer to Committee of the Whole Council. Dublin, Joseph Dollard, 1871

Corporation Reports, Vol. 1, 1900, pp. 483-487 "Report of the Water Works Committee

Corporation Reports, Vol. 2, 1899, No. 94, pp. 635-536 "Report of the Paving Committee, Councillor J.J.O'Meara

Corporation Reports, Vol. 2, 1899, pp. 700-703 "Admission of Fever Patients to Hospital"

Corporation Reports, Vol. 2, 1899, pp. 716-748 "Notification of Infective Diseases"

Corporation Reports, Vol. 2, 1899, p. 760

Corporation Reports, Vol. 3, 1900, No. 149, pp. 303-305 "Report of the Paving Committee, Recommending that the Sanction of the Municipal Council Be Given to the Construction of Two New Roads, Forming Extensions of Clonliffe Avenue and Foster Terrace"

Corporation Reports, Vol. 1, 1901, No. 31, pp. 181-185 "Report of the Water Works Committee. Councillor James Hennessy, Chairman, Dublin, Cahill, 1901

Corporation Reports, 1902, Vol. 3, No. 196, p. 331 "Report of the Paving Committee. Re: Commending the Name of Addison Street, Fairview, To Be Changed to Addison Road.J. F. McCarthy, J.P., Chairman"

Corporation Reports, 1903, No. 95, pp. 1-2 "Report of the Improvements Committee with Reference to the Inclusion of the Clontarf Area in the Maw Drainage System"

Corporation Reports, Vol. 2, 1903, No. 64, pp. 197-198 "Report of the Public Libraries Committee, Recommending the Extension of the Charleville Mall Library to Accommodate the Gilbert Collection"

Corporation Reports, 1903, No. 96, p. 1 "Report of the Public Health Committee. Re: Retirement of Mr. John J. Murray, Their Book-keeper in the City Accountant's Office"

Corporation Reports, pp. 493-499 "Reports of the Lighting Committee on the Electric Lighting of Clontarf, John Irwin, Chairman"

Corporation Reports, Vol. 2, 1904, pp. 179-183 "Report of the Improvements Committee"

Corporation Reports, Vol. 2, 1904, No. 92, pp. 303-314 "Report of the Cleansing Committee, Alderman John Davin, Chairman". Dublin, Dollard, 1904

Corporation Reports, Vol. 2, 1904, No. 93, pp. 315-316 "Report of the Improvements Committee, Submitting a Report of the Eleventh Inspection of the Dublin Main Drainage Works, Thomas Kelly, Chairman"

Domes Day Book, Ireland, 1870

Dublin Assembly Roll. 1778: Card Vol. 13, pp. 2-5, 252-255, 426-427, 476-477

Dublin Assembly Roll. 1807: Card Vol. 16, pp. 22-25, 44-45

Dublin Assembly Roll. 1808: pp. 84-85, 94-95, 98-99

Dublin Assembly Roll, 1809: pp. 164-165
Dublin Assembly Roll, 1812: pp. 318-319
Dublin Assembly Roll, 1823: Card Vol. 18, pp. 40-41
Dublin Assembly Roll, 1824: pp. 90-91, 100-101
Dublin Assembly Roll, 1825: pp. 108-109, 122-125, 128-129
Dublin Assembly Roll, 1827: pp. 230-231
Dublin Assembly Roll, 1828: pp. 266-267, 294-295
Dublin Assembly Roll, 1830: pp. 388-389, 408-409
Dublin Assembly Roll, 1831
Dublin Assembly Roll, 1832-1841: Card Vol. 19, pp. 1-3, 54-55, 70-71, 140-141
Calendar of Rolls of the City of Dublin
Dail debates
The Down Survey Books of Reference
Dublin Sanitary Association reports 1873-1914

Fiants of Henry VIII, Edward VI & Elizabeth I

Griffith's Valuation

The Hearth Money Rolls (1660 - 1670)

Irish Municipal Acts

Molyneaux's Survey of Dublin 1682

Parish Registers
19th Century Government Commission
Parliamentary Papers – Dublin turnpikes enquiry: report of Abraham Haywood, H.M. Counsel 1854-55
Poor Law Commissioners reports

Registry of Deeds Memorial (1708 onwards ...)
Report of the inquiry into the housing of the working classes of the city of Dublin 1939/40

Sewers and drains: under the Towns Improvement Clauses Act 1847
Sources of Local History, Chapter 4. Maps and Surveys
Statutory Instruments, S.I. No. 12 of 1986, County Borough of Dublin (Wards), Regulations, 1986

POSTGRADUATE THESES

Burke, Nuala	Dublin 1600 - 1800: A study in urban morphogenesis Ph.D. thesis, University of Dublin 1972
Fitzpatrick, B.	The Municipal Corporation of Dublin, 1603 - 40 Ph.D. thesis, University of Dublin 1985
Murray, Peter	Citizenship, colonialism and self-determination: Dublin in the United Kingdom 1885-1918 Ph.D thesis, Trinity College Dublin 1987

O'Flanagan, Neil — Dublin City in an Age of War and Revolution 1914 - 24
M.A. thesis, National University of Ireland 1986

UNPUBLISHED WORKS

Gertie Colley Murphy's account of her role in 1916
Eithne O'Moore (daughter of Esther Wisely O'Moore)
Statement of Patrick O'Daly

INTERVIEWS

with Tony Roche (grandson of Nora O'Daly)
with Dr. Colin Stray, Wolfson College, Cambridge

ARCHIVES

Allen Library Collection

UCD – The Eithne Coyle O'Donnell papers
Sighle Humphries papers

National Library Pamphlets P463

National Archives – 1798 papers
Musgrave's memoirs 620/28/3
Nally letters 620/10/121

The Dublin Corporation Archives:
Wide Street Commission Maps
Corporation Reports

Military Archives: Bombing incident G2/X/0619 & Bombing Incident photo album.